Nationalism and National Identities

Nationalism and nationalist ideas are a major force in the contemporary world. This volume brings together original papers from a number of countries dealing both with theories and case studies of particular national contexts. Taken together, these papers shed light on the processes through which nationalist sentiments and ideas are articulated and given social and political meaning in specific situations. They cover a broad range of different kinds of nationalist movements and ideologies, using a variety of theoretical perspectives and based on varying empirical methodologies. The cases covered include a comparison of Bosnia-Herzegovina and the North Caucasus, the role of religion in nationalist sentiment in Spain, ethnicity and nationalism in Turkey, Basque nationalism, the Basque diaspora across the Atlantic, the patrimonial state and inter-ethnic conflict in Nigeria, and nationalist movements in Uzbekistan and Tajikistan. Though this is the empirical focus, all chapters raise relevant theoretical questions and challenge differing approaches to the phenomenon of nationalism in the social sciences.

This book was originally published as a special issue of *Ethnic and Racial Studies*.

Martin Bulmer is Emeritus Professor of Sociology at the University of Surrey, UK. He retired in 2008, prior to which he was also Director of the ESRC Question Bank. He has edited the journal *Ethnic and Racial Studies* since 1993.

John Solomos is Professor of Sociology at City University London, UK. He has carried out extensive research on race, politics and social change and on theories of race and ethnicity. He is co-editor of *Ethnic and Racial Studies*.

Ethnic and Racial Studies

Series editors: Martin Bulmer, *University of Surrey, UK*, and John Solomos, *City University London, UK*

The journal *Ethnic and Racial Studies* was founded in 1978 by John Stone to provide an international forum for high quality research on race, ethnicity, nationalism and ethnic conflict. At the time the study of race and ethnicity was still a relatively marginal sub-field of sociology, anthropology and political science. In the intervening period the journal has provided a space for the discussion of core theoretical issues, key developments and trends, and for the dissemination of the latest empirical research.

It is now the leading journal in its field and has helped to shape the development of scholarly research agendas. *Ethnic and Racial Studies* attracts submissions from scholars in a diverse range of countries, fields of scholarship and crosses disciplinary boundaries. It has moved from being a quarterly to being published monthly and it is now available in both printed and electronic form.

The Ethnic and Racial Studies book series contains a wide range of the journal's special issues. These special issues are an important contribution to the work of the journal, where leading social science academics bring together articles on specific themes and issues that are linked to the broad intellectual concerns of *Ethnic and Racial Studies*. The series editors work closely with the guest editors of the special issues to ensure that they meet the highest quality standards possible. Through publishing these special issues as a series of books, we hope to allow a wider audience of both scholars and students from across the social sciences to engage with the work of *Ethnic and Racial Studies*.

Other titles in the series include:

The Transnational Political Participation of Immigrants
Edited by Jean-Michel Lafleur and Marco Martiniello

Anthropology of Migration and Multiculturalism
Edited by Steven Vertovec

Migrant Politics and Mobilisation: Exclusion, Engagements, Incorporation
Edited by Davide Però and John Solomos

New Racial Missions of Policing: International Perspectives on Evolving Law-Enforcement Politics
Edited by Paul Amar

Young People, Ethnicity and Social Capital
Edited by Tracey Reynolds

Cosmopolitan Sociability
Edited by Tsypylma Darieva, Nina Glick Schiller and Sandra Gruner-Domic

Retheorizing Race and Whiteness in the 21st Century
Edited by Charles A. Gallagher and France Winddance Twine

Theorising Integration and Assimilation
Edited by Jens Schneider and Maurice Crul

Ethnic and Racial Minorities in Asia: Inclusion or Exclusion?
Edited by Michelle Ann Miller

Diasporas, Cultures and Identities
Edited by Martin Bulmer and John Solomos

Gender, Race and Religion: Intersections and Challenges
Edited by Martin Bulmer and John Solomos

Latino Identity in Contemporary America
Edited by Martin Bulmer and John Solomos

Migration: Policies, Practices, Activism
Edited by Martin Bulmer and John Solomos

Nationalism and National Identities
Edited by Martin Bulmer and John Solomos

Methods and Contexts in the Study of Muslim Minorities: Visible and Invisible Muslims
Edited by Nadia Jeldtoft and Jørgen S. Nielsen

Nationalism and National Identities

Edited by
Martin Bulmer and John Solomos

First published 2012
by Routledge
2 Park Square, Milton Park, Abingdon, Oxfordshire OX14 4RN

Simultaneously published in the USA and Canada
by Routledge
711 Third Avenue, New York, NY 10017

First issued in paperback 2014

Routledge is an imprint of the Taylor & Francis Group, an informa business

© 2012 Taylor & Francis

This book is a reproduction of *Ethnic and Racial Studies*, volume 32, issue 4. The Publisher requests to those authors who may be citing this book to state, also, the bibliographical details of the special issue on which the book was based.

All rights reserved. No part of this book may be reprinted or reproduced or utilised in any form or by any electronic, mechanical, or other means, now known or hereafter invented, including photocopying and recording, or in any information storage or retrieval system, without permission in writing from the publishers.

Trademark notice: Product or corporate names may be trademarks or registered trademarks, and are used only for identification and explanation without intent to infringe.

British Library Cataloguing in Publication Data
A catalogue record for this book is available from the British Library

ISBN 13: 978-0-415-68633-4 (hbk)
ISBN 13: 978-1-138-81740-1 (pbk)

Typeset in Times New Roman
by Taylor & Francis Books

Disclaimer
The publisher would like to make readers aware that the chapters in this book are referred to as articles as they had been in the special issue. The publisher accepts responsibility for any inconsistencies that may have arisen in the course of preparing this volume for print.

Contents

Notes on contributors viii

1. Introduction: Nationalism and national identities
   Martin Bulmer and John Solomos   1

2. Accounting for separatist sentiment in Bosnia-Herzegovina
   and the North Caucasus of Russia: a comparative analysis of
   survey responses
   John O'Loughlin and Gearóid Ó Tuathail (Gerard Toal)   5

3. From National-Catholicism to Democratic Patriotism?
   Democratization and reconstruction of national pride: the
   case of Spain (1981–2000)
   Jordi Muñoz   30

4. 'Exclusive recognition': the new dimensions of the question
   of ethnicity and nationalism in Turkey
   Cenk Saracoglu   54

5. The politics of war memory in radical Basque nationalism
   Diego Muro   73

6. The patrimonial state and inter-ethnic conflicts in Nigeria
   Ukana B. Ikpe   92

7. Basque-Atlantic shores: ethnicity, the nation-state and the
   diaspora in Europe and America (1808–98)
   Fernando Molina and Pedro J. Oiarzabal   111

8. How master frames mislead: the division and eclipse of
   nationalist movements in Uzbekistan and Tajikistan
   Lawrence P. Markowitz   129

Index   152

Notes on contributors

Ukana B. Ikpe is Senior Lecturer in the Department of Political Science and Public Administration at the University of Uyo, Nigeria.

Lawrence P. Markowitz is Visiting Professor of Politics at Oberlin College, USA.

Fernando Molina is currently a Ramón y Cajal Researcher at the University of the Basque Country, Leioa, Spain.

Jordi Muñoz is a PhD candidate in the Political and Social Sciences Department at the Universitat Pompeu Fabra (Barcelona), Spain. During the 2007_08 academic year he was also a Visiting Assistant in Research in the Political Science Department, Yale University, USA.

Diego Muro is Lecturer in European Studies at King's College London, UK. He is the author of various articles on Spanish politics and of *Ethnicity and Violence: the Case of Radical Basque Nationalism* (2008).

Pedro J. Oiarzabal is at the University of Deusto, Bilbao, Spain.

John O'Loughlin is Professor of Geography at the Institute of Behavioral Science, University of Colorado at Boulder, USA.

Cenk Saracoglu is Lecturer in Political Science and International Relations at Middle East Technical University, Northern Cyprus.

Gearóid Ó Tuathail (Gerard Toal) is Professor of Government and International Affairs, Virginia Polytechnic Institute & State University, USA.

Introduction: Nationalism and national identities

Martin Bulmer and John Solomos

This edited volume is composed of a number of chapters that are concerned broadly with questions of nationalism and constructions of national identities. This is a theme that we have covered in some depth in *Ethnic and Racial Studies* over the past four decades, both through the publication of key theoretical papers and through case studies of nationalism in specific nation-states and geopolitical environments. It is also a field of scholarship and research that has grown in importance over the past few decades, along with the revival of nationalist movements and ideologies in various parts of the globe (Brubaker et al., 2006; Calhoun, 2007a).

The various chapters in this volume represent a diverse range of perspectives and are not linked by a singular analytical or regional focus. Indeed, they are written from rather different theoretical perspectives and cover a wide range of countries and draw on a range of methodologies. Taken together, however, they shed light on the processes through which nationalist sentiments and ideas are articulated and given a social and political meaning in specific situations. They cover a broad range of different kinds of nationalist movements and ideologies, and they also draw on different theoretical perspectives and empirical methodologies.

Key themes and arguments

The first chapter by John O'Loughlin and Gearóid Ó Tuathail focuses on a comparison of forms of ethnic separatism in two important geopolitical environments, namely Bosnia-Herzegovina and the North Caucasus. The main focus of the chapter is a critical comparison of attitudes to ethnic separatism in the two geopolitical environments, and the authors draw on surveys in both locations. The authors emphasize the need to situate the commonalities and differences between the two regions within a wider social as well as political frame. They also highlight the importance of locality and levels of trust as important factors in explaining the role of separatist sentiment in both of their case study locations.

NATIONALISM AND NATIONAL IDENTITIES

The next chapter by Jordi Muñoz explores the evolution of ideas about the nation and national identity in the context of the democratic transition in Spain after the period of the Franco dictatorship. The emphasis in this chapter is on the role of ideology, religion and region of residence as factors in explaining national pride and its role in the process of political democratization and the evolution of new forms of democratic political identity. An important theme that underlies Muñoz analysis is that processes of democratization necessarily rely on a re-invention of ideas about the nation and the role of political identities within the broader collectivity.

This is followed by Cenk Saracoglu study of the construction of political identities in the context of contemporary Turkish society. Drawing on the growing role of internal migration from Eastern Anatolia to the major urban conurbations, Saracoglu suggests that the tendency to identify these migrants as Kurdish is in fact not the result of the actions of political and state institutions, but a process of ethnic identity formation that owes much to the everyday processes of social and cultural change that have shaped the urban spaces of contemporary Turkish society. In doing so Saracoglu suggests that the tendency to focus much discussion about the role of Kurdish identity in Turkey on the role of the state is in fact quite misleading, since it is perhaps equally important to look at city life as a space through which such political identities are both made and re-made.

Diego Muro shifts the focus somewhat by examining how the ideological and political discourses of radical forms of Basque nationalism engage with the question of war memory. Muro argues that within the political rhetoric of ETA the language of war memory is used as a way of justifying the contemporary role of political violence. The usage of historical memory takes the form partly of utilizing the collective memory of the Spanish Civil War and earlier conflicts as a way of justifying the violence of ETA's actions and to draw an ethnic boundary between Basques and Spaniards. The chapter illustrates the use of war memory as a political tool for fixing ethnic boundaries and as a tool for re-imagining the past as a series of heroic past wars that culminate in the on-going violent struggle between the Spanish state and Basque radicals.

A recurrent theme in the analysis of contemporary Africa is the linkage between conflicts and forms of ethnicity. This is highlighted in the chapter by Ukana Ikpe, which examines this issue from the perspective of how conflicts that have been pervasive in Nigerian society since independence have been seen through the lens of inter-ethnic conflict and communal clashes. Ikpe's analysis highlights the role of the state in shaping ethnic politics in postcolonial societies such as Nigeria. He argues that the structure of state institutions is heavily dependent on forms of clientelist politics, with state officers dispensing resources to clients in exchange for loyalty and services. This is a phenomenon of the postcolony that has been noted by other commentators on African state institutions (Mbembe; 2001).

The chapter by Pedro J. Oiarzabal returns to the Basque case, but explores it from a rather different angle from that of Muro. Drawing on both historical and contemporary sources Muro explores the mechanisms through which Basque ethnic identity helped to shape processes of national identification and state building on both sides of the Atlantic, including Spain and Latin America. In this sense Basque ethnicity is not merely a part of the formation of Basque ethno-nationalist politics but has played a role in wider discursive formations and political struggles.

This is followed by Lawrence Markowitz's comparison of the nationalist movements in Uzbekistan and Tajikistan. Markowitz is particularly interested in how low nationalist mobilization in Tajikistan and Uzbekistan has to be seen in the context of the ways in which nationalist movements and their leaderships either took or missed the opportunities offered to them by the changing political environments. In emphasizing the role of political leadership this chapter returns to a recurrent theme in this issue as a whole, namely the importance of political mobilization in shaping the boundaries of how the nation is defined and struggled over.

Two of the chapters in this volume, on Bosnia-Herzegovina and the North Caucasus and on Uzbekistan and Tajikistan, are explicitly comparative, and this enhances their interest, particularly when the comparison is between societies quite far removed from each other. In general, we think that there is currently insufficient comparative work in the field of ethnic and racial studies, both at a general theoretical level (Schemerhorn, 1970) and in comparative studies of specific societies or aspects of those societies (Akenson, 1992; Shafir, 1995).

The question of nationalism and nationalist politics seems likely to remain an important concern for scholars working in the field of ethnic and racial studies. This is not to say that we can imagine that nationalisms as they exist today represent the same discursive formation as earlier forms of nationalist politics. Craig Calhoun, among others, has pointed to the inherently political nature of national identity, and the pervasive role of political movements in shaping both nation-states and democratic institutions (Calhoun, 2007b). From this perspective it is important that research and scholarship on these issues address the question of what explains the continuing role of nationalism as a source of mobilization and political identity formation.

References

AKENSON, D. H. 1992 *God's Peoples: Covenant and Land in South Africa, Israel, and Ulster*. Ithaca: Cornell University Press.
BRUBAKER, R., FEISCHMIDT, M., FOX, J. & GRANCEA, L. 2006 *Nationalist Politics and Everyday Ethnicity in a Transylvanian Town*. Princeton: Princeton University Press.

CALHOUN, C. J. 2007a 'Nationalism and Cultures of Democracy', *Public Culture*, vol. 19, no. 1, pp. 151-73. 2007b *Nations Matter: Culture, History, and the Cosmopolitan Dream*. London: Routledge.

MBEMBE, A. 2001 *On the Postcolony*. Berkeley: University of California Press.

SCHEMERHORN, A. A. 1970 *Comparative Ethnic Relations: A Framework for Theory and Research*. Chicago: University of Chicago Press.

SHAFIR, G. 1995 *Immigrants and Nationalists: Ethnic Conflict and Accommodation in Catalonia, the Basque Country, Latvia, and Estonia*. Albany: State University of New York.

Accounting for separatist sentiment in Bosnia-Herzegovina and the North Caucasus of Russia: a comparative analysis of survey responses

John O'Loughlin and Gearóid Ó Tuathail (Gerard Toal)

Abstract

A tenet of modern studies of nationalism is that mobilized nations will want to live separately from members of other groups to achieve ethno-territorial goals. A comparison of attitudes to a question on preferences for ethnic separatism for two zones of conflict, Bosnia-Herzegovina and the North Caucasus of Russia, reveals large differences both between and within the regions. For the 2,000 respondents surveyed in each region in December 2005, more than half of those in Bosnia-Herzegovina believed that geographic separatism would improve the state of ethnic relations while the comparative figure for the North Caucasus was only 14 per cent. When examining sub-categories of the ethnic groups in each region, traditional social science factors, such as religiosity, material status and levels of ethnic pride, yielded significant differences but more so for Bosnia-Herzegovina than for the North Caucasus. Intuitive factors, such as experience with violence during the wars, were not consistently revealing and significant. The best explanations for separatist sentiment in both locations were geographical location (individual towns and counties) and respondents' levels of general trust.

'To live in a territory of one's own': since the advent of modern nationalism, this attitude has been a powerful force challenging the interstate system and re-making the borders of the world political map. Yet, it is far from obvious just what kind of territorial order the claim implies or how it is to be created. The ideological aspiration for the convergence of an imagined collective identity and a territorial region can be termed 'ethno-territorialism', and human history over the last century records a number of grandiose projects by state elites to draw and re-draw maps and re-engineer the spaces of human settlement to conform to the seductive simplicity of ethno-territorial visions (Mazower 1998). In regions of ethnic, cultural and religious diversity that are experiencing rapid modernization, urbanization and political transition, ethno-territorialism is presented as a 'solution' by some political forces to the anxieties, insecurities and fears that accompany these processes. 'To each group, its own space' is an accompanying seduction that proffers an apparently simple spatial solution to what is politically constructed as the 'unnaturalness' of cultural heterogeneity and ethnic or nationality mixing. In power and in control of the coercive and ideological apparatus of the modern state, such visions can lead to minority oppression, political instability and, if taken to extremes, ethnic cleansing and genocide (Brubaker 2004; Mann 2004).

This paper examines the contemporary strength of exclusivist ethno-territorial sentiment in two human geographic regions that are well known for their cultural and demographic diversity, Bosnia-Herzegovina and the North Caucasus region of the Russian Federation. Both Bosnia-Herzegovina (BiH) and the North Caucasus are regions with great ethnic diversity where the post-Communist transitions have given rise to political instability, the flaring of ethno-territorial ideologies in the face of official creeds of multi-ethnic coexistence, and the use of collective violence by outside and local parties to organize political space to conform to their authority. Both regions have distinctive histories of ethnonationalist identification and the institutionalization of 'national' identities in local governance structures. Both also have localized geographies of ethnic concentration and histories of competition over land, landscape icons and public space. Finally, both places are conditioned by their geopolitical setting which provides a structure of constraint and opportunity which can exacerbate or dampen ethno-territorial thinking.

Part of a larger project on 'civil war outcomes', this paper analyses the results of a 4,000-person social survey conducted in both regions (2,000 respondents in each) in November and December 2005. The paper analyses responses to the following general claim: 'Ethnic relations in my locality will improve when all nationalities/ethnicities are separated into territories that belong only to them.'[1] The question was deliberately designed to articulate, in simple common sense terms, what we characterize as the aspiration to 'ethno-territorial separatism' perceived and represented as an abatement mechanism and possible 'solution' to ethnic/nationality conflict and strife. Our analysis, involving extensive cross-tabulation of the ethnic preferences in the survey results, is divided into three parts. Part one briefly discusses the literature on nationalist ideologies in post-Communist states and prevailing explanations of ethno-territorial separatist attitudes. Part two comparatively discusses the results from BiH and those from the North Caucasus. Part three elaborates a comparison of our results from both regions to the broader literature on nationalism and concludes the paper.[2]

Five hypotheses about ethno-territorial separatist attitudes

Our paper is motivated by two central questions: (1) what is the character and intensity of ethno-territorial separatism in contemporary post-war Bosnia-Herzegovina (BiH) and the North Caucasus? and (2) what are the determining factors that explain its valuation across survey respondents? We examine here only the social, and not diplomatic and interstate, determinants of ethno-territorialism. Academic studies on nationalist ideologies in the post-Communist societies provide a plethora of accounts which can be used to organize and explain our research findings. We have taken this literature and generated five hypotheses about what accounts for support for ethno-territorial separatism, hypotheses which we then examine empirically. Our choice of these hypotheses reflects existing research evidence from the regions we are studying as well as larger theoretical literatures. We do not claim that this list is either comprehensive or exhaustive but argue that it reflects major prevailing assumptions about the social determinants of separatism. Nor are we implying any direct causal mechanism from these variables to separatism, which leads us to use the rather general non-specific 'connected to' in our hypotheses:

1. Support for ethno-territorial separatism is connected to high levels of ethnic/national pride and suspicion

Primordialist perspectives point to the transcendent bonds and durable 'givens' that are at the centre of the experience of nationalism for its adherents and believers. Nationalists themselves tend to be selectively historic and essentializing primordialists, and they are justly contrasted to social constructivists who emphasize the historic and socially produced nature of all feelings of identity and community. Recent theoretical thinking on nationalism has sought to accommodate the insights of primordialism (ethnic identities are a priori social facts) within social constructivism (Wieland 2001). Those scholars of nationalism who emphasize the social power of primordialism explore the way in which primordialism is socially constructed and emphasize the role of durable social institutions in the production and reproduction of ethnic identities and ethno-territorial attitudes. Through families and churches, schools and sports, music and dance, nationalist subjectivity is learnt as performance. Boundaries are created between groups and bonds of trust forged within groups in performative opposition to outside groups who are viewed with suspicion. Petersen (2002) emphasizes the importance of emotion, resentment and status reversal in the breakup of Yugoslavia. This perspective points us to the strength of feelings of ethnic identity and trust in explaining variations in attitudes towards ethno-territorial separatism. Our expectation is that within ethnic groups, those who have greater levels of collective group self-worth and who are suspicious of the interests and motivations of other groups will have a higher rate of preference for the ethno-territorial separation option.

2. Support for ethno-territorial separatism is connected to levels of religiosity

Social primordialism also points us to the importance of religion in the performative (re)production of ethnic/national identity. In addition, classic sociological modernization theories – including the Marxism that informed the Soviet and Titoist conceptualization of nationality – lead us to expect that religiosity, as an anchor of traditional identities and a force generally hostile to modernity, will be associated with ethnic particularism and social intolerance. Religiosity is worth foregrounding in the case of Yugoslavia because it is the social primordial basis – what Wieland (2001, p. 212) terms the 'epicentre' of ethnicity as a concept of action which singles out one primordial characteristic as the main point of contrast to another similar group – for the same south Slavic people to recognize, organize and constitute themselves as separate nations. Churches became the incubators of nationalism, and religiosity is a strong predictor of ethnic intolerance. In a survey conducted in the winter of 1989/90, Hodson, Sekulić and Massey (1994) found that religiosity had the largest standardized negative effect on tolerance. Ethnic hatred and intolerance themselves, however, are insufficient explanations for the dissolution of Yugoslavia (Sekulić, Massey and Hodson 2006). Further, Kunovich and Hodson (1999) argued, on the basis of survey data from Croatia, that religiosity does not cause ethnic intolerance. They found support for a 'salience hypothesis' – religion as the salient marker of boundaries between groups – which holds that ethnic intolerance and religiosity are jointly determined by in-group/out-group polarization as a result of competition and conflict over finite resources.

In the North Caucasus, religion is also an important factor in constituting identity formations and axes of conflict across the region, though not in any simple manner. While most titular groups are Muslim (the Ossetians and Russians are Orthodox peoples), significant differences in the strands of Islam can be seen across the localities.

Further, amongst Russians and other groups, high ratios of secularism are evident, partly a legacy of the Communist era. Whether the same expected relationship holds as in Bosnia-Herzegovina is an open empirical question.

3. Support for ethno-territorial separatism is connected to perceptions of relative impoverishment

Materialist political economy theories explain nationalist movements and attendant ethno-territorial separatism in terms of 'internal colonialism' and the particular place of a group within a political economy of opportunity and constraint. Social and cultural differences are magnified by economic factors. An internal colonialism approach applies a core–periphery relations perspective to interterritorial relations within a state in order to explain the rise of nationalism (Hechter 1975). Hechter and Levi (1979) believe that ethnic solidarity among any objectively-defined set of individuals is principally due to the existence of a hierarchical cultural division of labour that promotes reactive group formation. Therefore, political mobilization based on nationalism or ethnicity is formulated according to the nature of core–periphery relations or spatial uneven development. This process is dynamic so ethno-territorial sentiment waxes and wanes.

Woodward's (1995) study of the breakup of Yugoslavia lends support to the argument that the richest republics (Slovenia and Croatia) led the revolt against a re-centralization of the federal state and obligations to redistribute income to the poorest regions of Yugoslavia. The international community has invested considerable resources in trying to reconstruct BiH and make a unified state work, so it is likely that the richest segments of society would only view further separatism as a return to war and inimical to their material interest in state modernization. But perceptions matter most within this perspective, especially perceptions of the relative standing of groups to each other. In those Russian regions with some tradition of autonomy based on their distinct ethnic and religious character, the titular elites were able to mobilize group resources while non-titular populations tended to assimilate and lose their distinct character and group cohesion (Roeder 1991). Overall, this perspective points to perception of prosperity/impoverishment as potentially significant in explaining ethno-territorial sentiment; 'winners' (those perceiving themselves as relatively rich) can, in certain circumstances, potentially be supporters of separatism, but 'losers' (those perceiving themselves as relatively impoverished) are more likely to be inclined to separatism as a means of changing and possibly improving their material circumstances.

4. Support for ethno-territorial separatism is connected to wartime experiences with violence

Grievance mobilization theories explain nationalist movements in terms of the political organization of a population to address an experience of oppression or perception of oppression and unfair treatment. Many accounts focus on the political construction and organization of grievance by political entrepreneurs to serve their own interests. Silber and Little (1995), Gordy (1999) and Gagnon (2004), among others, interpret the wars unleashed by the breakup of Yugoslavia in terms of elite interest in power preservation and augmentation. Treisman (1997), Dowley (1998), and Gorenburg (1999, 2003) conclude that instrumental explanations are better than primordialist ones in explaining nationalism and separatism in post-Soviet Russia.

Our interest in this paper is more with perspectives that point to the power of mobilizing events, traumatic experiences and the power of discursive storylines and belief to create movements which are beyond the instrumental control of elite groups. While political entrepreneurs may organize collective sentiment and perceptions of grievance, the experience of conflict and its translation (or not) into attitudes and political discourse is an important dynamic worth researching. Since the everyday consequences of the war in BiH and ongoing low-intensity conflicts in the North Caucasus are pervasive and widespread, and since our project is specifically interested in 'war outcomes', we asked a considerable number of questions in our surveys about the wartime experiences of our respondents, including whether they were forced to move, whether they witnessed or participated in violence, etc. In a post-war survey in Croatia, Kunovich and Hodson (1999) found that individuals who experienced property damage and violence during the war are less trustful of others, more likely to be ethnonationalists and more intolerant of ethnic minorities. We hypothesize that witnessing wartime violence is a traumatic and radicalizing event and that those who had such experiences are more likely to support separatist sentiment.

5. Support for ethno-territorial separatism is connected to particular geographical locations

Political geographic research on nationalism has a number of themes that are relevant to our concerns, and scholars in this tradition point to processes of *spatial socialization* – acculturation into certain spatial identities and aspirations – and *social spatialization* – the social production of notions of 'homeland', 'region' and 'territory' – that unfold in particular places and geopolitical locations (Paasi 1996). For political geographers, location and place are geopolitical forces in themselves that generate variable attitudes towards ethno-territorial separatism. Regions that are historic bastions of ethnonationalism, that are envisioned as part of imagined separatist spaces, that are ethnically homogeneous, and remote from centres of modernity and commerce, are, we hypothesize, most likely to be strongholds of ethno-territorial sentiment. Whether place overpowers other factors such as wealth, socio-economic status and position is an open question.

Our opinion survey was not designed to 'test' any one theory or definitively 'prove' one account as superior over another. Rather, what we present below are empirical results that allow us to examine our starting hypotheses in greater detail and to see if they have sufficient analytical power to generate consistent results in both conflict regions or not.

The aim of the survey design was to stratify sampling points using thematic data for a wide range of sources: data from aggregate geographic units (*rayoni* in Russia and *opštini* in BiH) derived from government sources (such as the Russian Census 2002) were the primary sources to sample individuals who were chosen to participate in the survey questionnaire based on a geographic design that includes all types of districts in the two study regions. To organize our data collection and to overlay and integrate the spatial coverages for the different types of data, we developed two Geographic Information Systems [GIS] to display and analyse the information collected. The key element of our work is the implementation of a large public opinion survey of 2,000 persons in each region in December 2005. Systematic stratification on the basis of geographical units – in this case, districts (*rayoni/opštini*) and cities/villages – allows for a thorough investigation of the expectations about ethnic territoriality that emerge from the literature. Within the eighty-two primary sampling units in the North Caucasus and the thirty-five sample units in BiH, we surveyed the populations using a random procedure. The numbers per sampling point are not exactly proportional in the North Caucasus and a weight is given to each respondent to adjust for these differences. (Ratios for this region report this weighted value and we used the *svy* option in STATA 8.1 for all these calculations). The response rate in the North Caucasus was 44.9 per cent while that for BiH was 85.9 per cent. Details on the sampling design are included in Ward *et al.* 2006.

Comparing the results from the North Caucasus and Bosnia-Herzegovina

In a series of prompts regarding the best ways to improve ethnic relations in Bosnia-Herzegovina and the North Caucasus, we asked respondents to provide a yes/no/don't know answer to the statement: 'Ethnic relations in my locality will improve when all nationalities (ethnicities) are separated into territories that belong exclusively only to them.' Our assumption is that those who agree are more 'nationalist' in their practices and beliefs. In our BiH sample 50.5 per cent agreed that ethnic relations would improve locally if all nationalities were separated into exclusivist territories. Excluding the percentage figures of 'don't know'/'refuse to answer' from the results (BiH 10.5 per cent and North Caucasus 11.8 per cent), this rises to 55 per cent of those answering yes or no. This bare majority endorsement of ethno-territorialism needs to be contextualized by other results. Other options – when there is a sizeable improvement in economic prosperity (93.2 per cent), when people are more tolerant (92.2 per cent), when everyone cares more about common problems and less about national ones (91.1 per cent), when police enforce the laws against criminality (91 per cent), when leaders are more tolerant (90.8 per cent) and when the government takes stronger action against national prejudice (89 per cent) – obtained a near consensus across Bosnia's three nationalities. Rather than separatism, these results indicate strong potential support for a political order based on the containment and displacement of nationalist antagonism. Economic concerns consistently rate as more important than nationalist issues in Bosnian surveys (see the results from the many UNDP 'Early Warning' surveys; at http://www.undp.ba/). Before the war, BiH had one of the lowest levels of 'ethnic distance' in all of Yugoslavia (Hodson, Sekulic and Massey 1994). Mixed marriage levels were at 16.7 per cent in 1981, with 15.8 per cent of children listed in the census of that year as having parents of different nationalities (Gagnon 2004, pp. 41–2). However, the vicious and brutal nature of the fighting in BiH, driven forward by state apparatuses in Serbia and Croatia, destroyed not only BiH's communities but also the willingness of certain sections of its population to live together (Ó Tuathail and Dahlman 2006).

In dramatic contrast to BiH, only 14 per cent of North Caucasian respondents chose the separatist option, that is, agreed that the best way to improve ethnic relations is by separating groups in exclusivist territories. In this region 51 per cent agreed that the Russian government should take stronger action against 'national exclusivism' and 45 per cent agreed that all people should be 'more tolerant'. Unlike the conflict in BiH in the 1990s, the war in southern Russia is geographically confined to one territory and its border areas, with occasional outbreaks of violence by terrorist strikes. Most people are not nearly as affected by conflict as their Bosnian counterparts were from 1992 to 1995 (Lyall 2006). The Chechen conflict does not threaten to re-shape the Russian Federation in the same way as the Bosnian war did for that state, and in the context of a multi-ethnic region, most respondents in Russia do not see ethnic exclusiveness as a solution but one posing a bigger nationalities problem.

Geographic variations in the levels of support for ethno-territorial separatism

The Bosnian war was not a single war but a series of local civil wars, featuring two- and three-sided fighting by the three main armies, the VRS (Army of Republika Srpska), HVO (Croatian Defence Council) and ARBiH (Bosnian government army). The war is sometimes described as a war of the countryside against the city, with the VRS holding vast swaths of countryside and surrounding ARBiH forces in urban enclaves (Burg and Shoup 1999, p. 33). The dichotomy, however, is a crude one. Our results found that the areas with the highest rates of rejection of ethnic separatism are the cities of Sarajevo, Tuzla (43 per cent) and Zenica (20 per cent) (Figure 1a). But the Sarajevo case is not a uniform rejection as the Stari Grad recorded a 60 per cent level of acceptance of ethno-territorial separatism (45 Bosniacs, 1 Serb and 2 Croats in the sample), the centre of Sarajevo 55 per cent (63 Bosniacs, 8 Serbs and 5 Croats), whereas the Novi Grad, our largest sample point in Sarajevo, had only 34 per cent (110 Bosniacs, 10 Serbs and 7 Croats). Other regions of low support for separatism are somewhat surprising but may be a result of the influence of refugee and displaced person returns: Tomislavgrad (39 per cent, though a centre of Croat separatism at the outset of the war) as well as Foca (30 per cent where 33 of the 38 respondents were Serbs) and Visegrad (37 per cent), regions that saw terrible war crimes committed against their Bosniac residents.

Rejection of ethno-territorialism, thus, is not confined to the Bosnian Federation but also has support in areas of Republika Srpska and western Herzegovina. The highest levels of support for ethnic separation are in regions characterized by intractable local struggles: the Mostar region and Central Bosnian axis of Jajce, Travnik and Gorni Vakuf (100 per cent), with Novi Travnik recording 57 per cent. Having fallen to the Croat army at the end of the war, Jajce has a very poor record of facilitating returns by Bosniacs and Serbs (Dahlman and Ó Tuathail 2005). Travnik was a major Bosniac refugee centre during the war as well as an arms production centre and became a stronghold for Bosniac nationalism. Many Republika Srpska [RS]

Figure 1. *Geographic distribution of preferences for ethnic separatism by sample points: (a) Bosnia-Herzegovina, (b) North Caucasus of Russia*

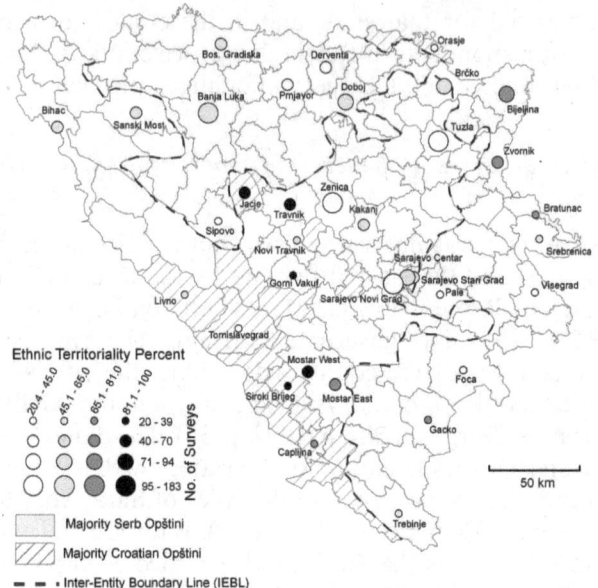

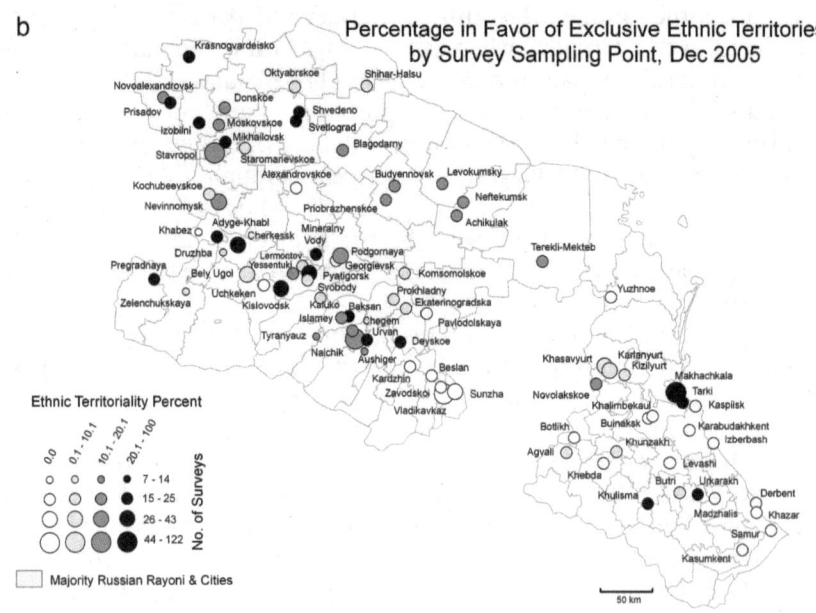

cities like Doboj (59 per cent) and Bosanski Gradiska (52 per cent) as well as the intensely contested city of Brčko (56 per cent) are close to the mean for the country as a whole. The RS capital, Banja Luka, is higher (64 per cent), but the sample in the former capital Pale is, surprisingly, lower (40 per cent).

Though separatism is a minority view overall in the North Caucasus region, its expression varies dramatically from locality to locality, as can be seen from Figure 1b which shows the percentage who favour the separatist option. By superimposing the map of the Russian-majority *rayoni* (counties) and cities, we can observe a general trend – a higher than average percentage of agreement with the separatist option is seen in most of the communities of Stavropol *krai* in the north and west of the region. The highest rejection of separatism is visible in North Ossetia (Vladikavkaz and vicinity), with the four highest values for separatism (at 100 per cent) found in eastern Stavropol (Budyennovsk, scene of a major hostage-taking incident in 1995), the Nogay district of northern Dagestan, and two cities in the southern part of Stavropol (Georgievsk and Yessentuki). Eastern Stavropol and its adjoining regions have seen intensifying ethnic tensions in recent years, resulting in out-migration of ethnic Russians to the north and west (Kolossov, Galkina and Krindatch, 2001; O'Loughlin, Panin and Witmer, 2007). But in remarkable contrast, in another locale of conflict, sample points in the vicinity of Beslan, scene of a 2004 terrorist attack, anchor the other end of the scale. Similarly, most of the sample points in Dagestan, also the scene of growing inter-ethnic competition (Matzuzato and Ibragimov 2005), are lower than average on separatism preferences.

Preference for ethno-territorial separatism by nationality

Given the Bosnian context, one would expect Serbs to have the highest levels of support for ethno-territorialism. The war, after all, was fought over the creation of RS as a separate ethno-territorial home for Bosnia's Serb population, though not all Serbs supported this separatist project in 1992 or support it today. The results, shown in Figure 2, bear this expectation out to a certain degree. Only 44 per cent of self-identifying Bosniacs support ethno-territorialism, and the fact that only 57 per cent of Serbs support ethno-territorialism after the ethnic cleansing, death and sacrifice to create the RS is worth underscoring. Bosnian Serb opinion is heterogeneous, with an evident cleavage between 'paleo-nationalists' (committed separatists) and 'euro-nationalists' (pragmatism within BiH in order to have an 'RS within Europe') (Ó Tuathail, O'Loughlin and Djipa 2006). Also worth emphasis is the finding that Bosnian Croats recorded the highest level of support for ethno-territorial separatism at 58.2 per cent. The geographic variation in this figure is striking. One hundred per cent of respondents in Siroki Brijeg, for example, supported separatism, as did all respondents in Mostar West, uniformly self-identifying Croats. Respondents in the historically Croat region of the Posavina *opština* of Orasje along the northern BiH border with Croatia, by contrast, tended to reject ethno-territorial separatism (38 per cent approval only). Similar forms of variation can be found among Bosniac majority regions (contrast Travnik and Tuzla) and Serb majority regions (contrast Bratunac at 80 per cent and Foca at 30 per cent). On the basis of this survey at least, there does not seem to be support for the contention that 'ethnic enclaves' are likely to be more predisposed to separatism than mixed areas (Massey, Hodson and Sekulić 1999).

A range of responses similar to the geographic variation is visible in the graph of the average agreement level by ethnicity in the North Caucasus (Figure 2). Populations (including Chechens and Balkars) deported from the region by Stalin have higher than average values. While Nogays (a formerly nomadic Muslim group now concentrated in eastern Stavropol *krai* and northern Dagestan) have a two-thirds level of support for the exclusive ethnic territory option, Ossetians (an Orthodox minority) show only 5 per cent support. Muslim groups (e.g. Avars and Lezgins compared to Kabardins and Laks) are found both above and below the regional average of 14 per cent. Neither is there a

Figure 2. *Distribution of preferences for ethnic separatism by ethnic group in the two study areas*

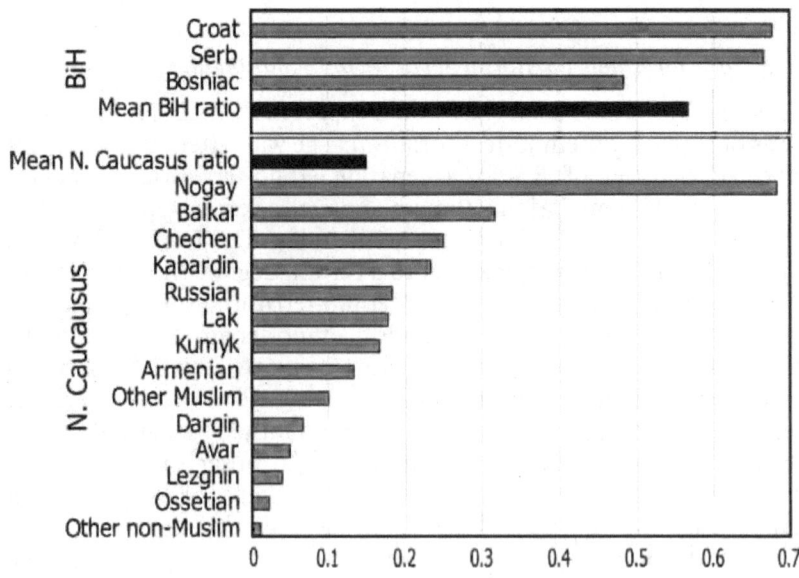

difference by republic: for example, Muslim groups concentrated in Dagestan are both below and above the average.

At first blush, then, it would appear that ethnic accounts trump other alternative explanations of separatist sentiment in the North Caucasus, but, as we will show below, when we examine differences *within* these groups, those contrasts are even more dramatic. A common challenge for researchers on conflict regions, where 'nationality' and 'ethnicity' are politically produced constructions as a consequence of political entrepreneurship and mobilization by local elites, is to avoid reifying these identities or taking them as ciphers which explain all, while grasping that these identities are durable and dominant social facts, institutional categories and political identities that do not have as ready a fluidity and contingency as deconstructionist theory may suggest (Campbell 1998; Brubaker 2004).[3]

Preference for ethno-territorial separatism by nationality and wealth

While the nationalist literature is replete with theories about the effects of cultural, social and political traits of individuals in forming and mobilizing such movements, there is a need to check whether these effects are independent or collinear with other personal characteristics. One of the possible underlying factors is the individual's material status, and our surveys asked respondents to rank their income and material position into categories that we have composed as 'above average' and 'below average' (on a four-point scale, we categorized 'we can buy all we want' and 'we can buy everything except major consumer goods' as above average, and we categorized 'we have only enough money for food' and 'we don't have money even for food' as below average). The results are quite striking and suggest the complexity of the picture of support for ethno-territorial separatism in enlightening ways.

In general, the correlation between reported material status and attitude towards separatism is strong. Those with reported incomes below average register a level of support that is more than double that of those with incomes that are above average. In BiH, all nationalities with below average incomes express high preferences for separatism. Bosniacs with below average incomes record the highest score, followed by Croats and Serbs in this income category. Of those with above average incomes, Serbs are the most positively disposed towards ethno-territorial separatism, though at less than 30 per cent this is well below the overall mean. Interestingly, the discrepancy in attitudes according to perceived income is greatest within the Bosniac community, with almost 60 percentage points separating the separatism attitude of poor Bosniacs from that of rich Bosniacs. Bosnian Croats are the richest of the nationalities in BiH and they too reveal a significant gap between how their richest and their poorest perceive separatism as a 'solution' to ethnic relations.

In the North Caucasus as a whole, individuals rank their material status as low; 35 per cent have only 'enough money for food' and 9 per cent do not even reach that income level. Lezgins, Laks, Avars and Dargins (all concentrated in Dagestan, one of the poorest republics of the Russian Federation) all rank highest in the material well-being self-evaluation, while Ossetians (75 per cent), Russians (48 per cent) and Kabardins (55 per cent) report that they can only afford food, or do not even reach that income threshold. Our expectations for the effects of material well-being are generally met (the poorer segment of each sample has a higher preference for separation), but only the Russian sample shows a significant difference (14 per cent for above average and 24 per cent for below average). Of the independent effects examined in this paper for the North Caucasus region, the difference in the influence of material well-being within the national groups is the weakest, as a comparative glance at Figure 3 and the other graphs shows.

Preference for ethno-territorial separatism by nationality and religious observance

There is a significant correlation between support for ethno-territorial separatism and religiosity in the overall BiH sample. We categorized those who attended a place of workship several times a

Figure 3. *Distribution of preferences for ethnic separatism by ethnic group and material wealth in the two study areas*

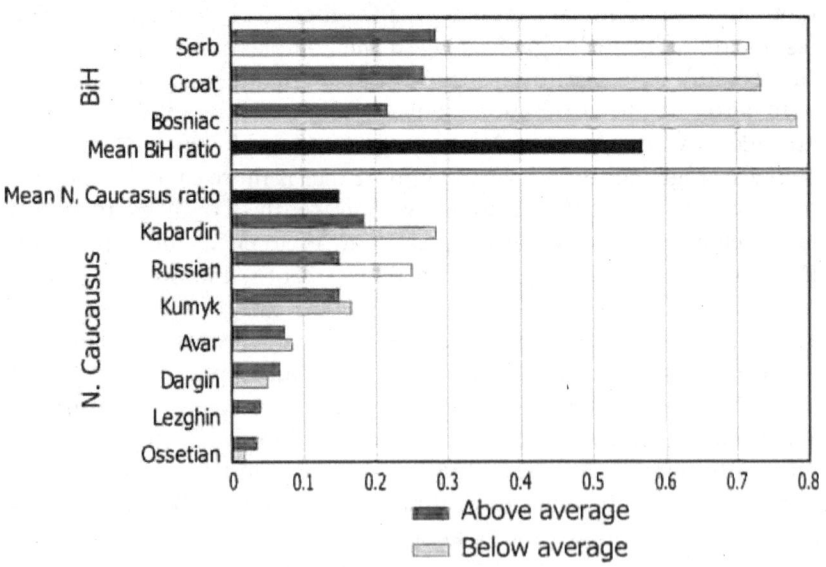

year or more as religious. This is not surprising since religious identity is the ostensible social foundation for the construction of three different nationalities among people in BiH who speak the same language and share so many other cultural traditions and patterns of behaviour. Religious institutions have also partially served as incubators of nationalism historically (Perica 2002). This is most apparent with Serb nationalism which developed closely with the distinctive identity of the Serb Orthodox Church (Cigar 1995; Gordy 1999). The situation is more complex with the Catholic Church and Croatian identity, especially in BiH which historically has been institutionally divided (Ramet 1996). Finally, it is generally held that Islamic religious observation increased significantly after the outbreak of the war in BiH. Religiosity, in all cases, tends to correlate with intolerance and support for ethnonationalism, though it is not necessarily the cause of these attitudes (Kunovich and Hodson 1999).

The most striking correlation between religiosity and separatist sentiment is exhibited by Bosnian Croats where 85 per cent of the 'religious' supported separatism. The scores are slightly lower for religious Serbs and then lower still for religious Bosniacs. The range in support for separatism is slightest for Bosniacs but still considerable at over 40 per cent difference. The greatest range is exhibited by Croats at almost 70 per cent. The results from BiH tend to confirm the importance of a social primordialist approach to understanding political attitudes and preferences. In the wider literature on religion, it has been noted that religious individuals are more socially conservative and more in-group oriented. Regular socialization by durable social institutions like churches tends to produce in-group/out-group polarization (Kunovich and Hodson 1999).

Overall, the North Caucasus sample is not very religious, as measured by attendance at places of worship. Thirty-four per cent have never attended a place of worship, with a further 14.3 per cent attending only rarely; only 12 per cent attend once a month or more often. While there has been a profusion of mosque building in the region, especially in Dagestan, since the end of the Soviet Union, most of these congregations are small (Giuliano 2005; Matzuzato and Ibragimov 2005). As well as the revival of the traditional Sufism of the region, a major attempt to establish Wahhabism has also been evident (Ware and Kisriev 2003; Walker 2005).

A comparison of religious and non-religious respondents for the seven ethnic groups whose numbers in the sample were sufficient to allow such an analysis (more than seventy-five surveys) shows that our expectation was generally upheld. Only in the Ossetian sub-samples do the non-religious show a higher preference for separatism; repeatedly, the Ossetian sample does not line up with either their Russian or Muslim compatriots. Ossetians are predominantly Orthodox and about 13 per cent are Muslim (Roschin 2005). Though generally following our expectation about the role of religion in nationalist discourse and ideology, only the Russian and Kumyk (a Dagestani Muslim group) sub-samples show significant differences, though the respective Ossetian sample differences reverse our expectation. Thus, the evidence is mixed, and overall there is no consistent relationship between the frequency of religious observance and ethnic territoriality in the North Caucasus across ethnic groups.

Preference for ethno-territorial separatism by nationality and ethnic pride

Ethnic pride is a socially constructed and repetitively reproduced 'affect structure' that is held to account for social and political attitudes. Similar to religion, it can be hypothesized that a sense of pride in one's nationality would translate into a greater sense of exclusion and separatism. While pride could be conceived as pride in a group's cultural or sporting achievements or as a general estimation of group self-worth, the evidence suggests that individuals who demonstrate a general sense of pride in their membership of a group are strong identifiers who tend to want, and so construct, clear boundaries between groups. They are, therefore, likely to be positively predisposed to ethno-territorial separatism. We categorized those who answered that they have 'a lot' or 'some' pride in their ethnic group as 'proud'.

The results from BiH confirm this expectation (Figure 4). Those expressing the greatest levels of pride are the most likely to choose ethno-territorial separatism. Like religion, the correlation levels are really quite striking. Those describing themselves as 'proud Bosniacs' are the most predisposed to separatism, followed by Croatians and then Serbs. Bosnian Serbs show the least variation in range and Bosniacs the greatest, with almost 70 percentage points spread between proud and non-proud Bosniacs.

The contrast in ratios with our North Caucasus survey areas is sharp. Again, there, no sub-sample even reaches the 25 per cent threshold of a preference for ethnic separation (Figure 4). Only the differences between the sub-samples of Russians and Ossetians are significant, but the relationships are in opposite directions (proud Russians are more likely to prefer separation, while proud Ossetians are less likely to prefer it – only 2 per cent for this sub-sample). Despite some apocalyptic predictions of large-scale inter-ethnic conflict as a result of an avowedly ethno-political structure (Ware

Figure 4. *Distribution of preferences for ethnic separatism by ethnic group and level of ethnic pride in the two study areas*

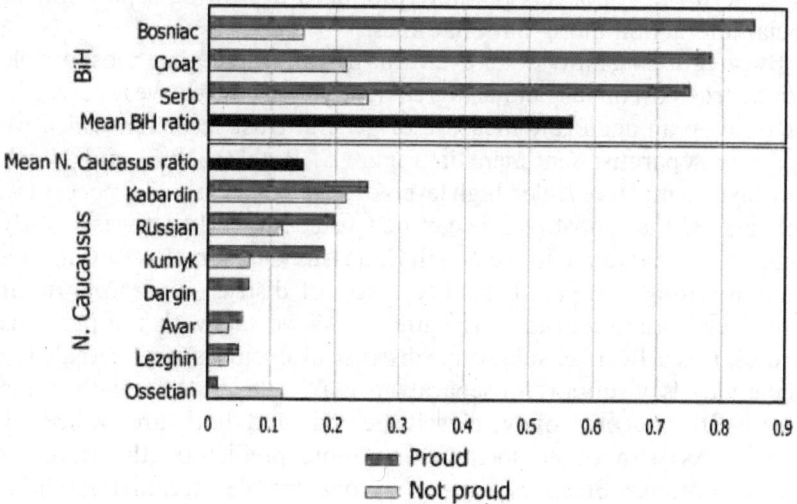

and Kisriev 1997), the beliefs of ordinary Dagestanis do not support this prediction since the vast majority of them, across ethnic lines, do not wish to separate themselves into ethnic enclaves.

Preference for ethno-territorial separatism by nationality and levels of trust/suspicion

In conflict situations, the line between membership of the 'in-group' and the 'out-groups' is typically more firmly drawn. Bonding social networks between co-ethnics tend to become more important than bridging social networks across nationality *qua* ethnicity. One trusts one's own and maintains an attitude of suspicion to other ethnicities/nationalities (Cook, Hardin and Levi 2005). Widner (2004), Woodward (1995) and others note that social relations in conflict and post-war zones are characterized by pervasive levels of suspicion, and more specifically by a lack of bridging social networks (Pickering 2006). Since these last three studies examine the post-Dayton BiH situation, a comparative look at the North Caucasus can be enlightening since the nature of conflict there is of a different scale compared to the large-scale destruction that engulfed Bosnia. Unlike Bosnia more than a decade ago, with the important exception of Chechnya, most people have not had to confront daily violence, the mobilization of able-bodied adults to fight, the possibility of forced displacement, and generalized food shortages. With the general proximity of different nationalities/ethnicities to each other, social networks and attendant levels of suspicion/trust are likely to be quite different. Nevertheless, ethnic-based conflict in specific areas such as North Ossetia, Dagestan or eastern Stavropol has possibly produced a growing separation of social interaction along national lines.

By categorizing individuals overall as trusting (agree that 'most people can be trusted') or suspicious (agree that 'you need to be very careful'), we develop an aggregate measure of general trust/suspicion which we relate to separatist sentiment in Figure 5. Both the BiH and North Caucasus samples revealed high levels of suspicion. Only 22.2 per cent in BiH agreed that 'most people can be trusted', a level that was slightly higher than that found in the North Caucasus. Our survey results in BiH show a strong correlation between level of distrust and support for ethno-territorial separatism (Figure 5). As we saw with the previous figures, it is a Bosniac subgroup (distrustful Bosniacs) that reveals the highest levels of support for separatism as a 'solution'. Serbs in the same distrustful category follow closely behind, and both are trailed by Croats. As with other socio-demographic predictors, the range is greatest amongst Bosniacs, suggesting considerable internal differentiation and cleavages within this group identity. Trusting Bosniacs are the most likely to reject ethno-territorial separatism, followed by trusting Serbs. Croats show the smallest range of attitudes along the trust/suspicion axis, though the divide is a considerable one (over 45 per cent).

In response to the general trust question, which does not refer specifically to ethnicity or nationality, 18 per cent of the North Caucasian respondents believe that 'most people can be trusted'. There are big differences between nationalities. Dagestani nationalities

Figure 5. *Distribution of preferences for ethnic separatism by ethnic group and general level of trust in the two study areas*

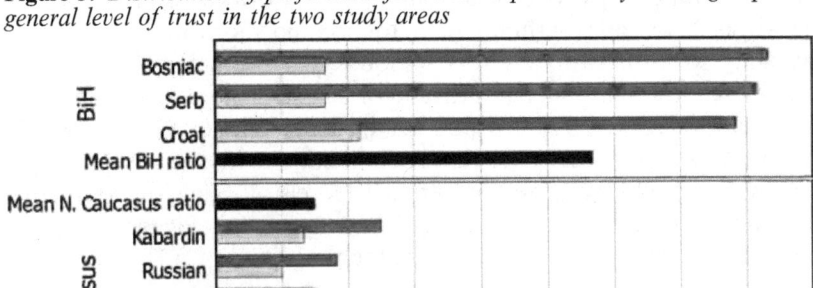

such as the Kumyks (35 per cent) and Nogays (35 per cent) have rates of trust more than double those of Russians (14 per cent) and Ossetians (14 per cent). The literature on generalized social trust has shown a sizeable positive correlation between income and trust, but it also shows that trust is dependent on local contextual circumstances (Secor and O'Loughlin 2005).

Only the Russian and Kabardin samples support our hypothesis about suspicion and separatist sentiment in the North Caucasus; the others are either not significantly different (Ossetians, Dargins, Avars) or reverse the expectation (Kumyks and Lezgins, though the difference is not significant). While it is possible to argue that both Russians and Kabardins are disproportionately exposed to nationalist competition and occasional violence, the same could be said for the other groups in the study. The specific timing of the survey, a couple of months after the major attack in October in 2005 in Nal'chik (capital of Kabardino-Balkaria), in which over 100 died, might have contributed to the results for the Kabardin sample (see also Hahn 2005).

Preference for ethno-territorial separatism by war experiences (witnessing of injury or death)

Even if individuals hold generally tolerant attitudes towards other nationalities, their attitudes can change as a consequence of traumatic events and personal experience with violence, injury and death. During the Bosnian war, an estimated 102,000 people were killed and over half of the 1991 population of 4.4 million were displaced. Few people were left untouched by the violence, for even if they managed to remain in their homes, they likely had an intimate experience with the war through the experience of relatives, through encounters with displaced persons, and maybe even with localized ethnic cleansing which drove neighbours from their community. Some would have directly participated in the fighting. Because the nature of the conflict in the North Caucasus is different – comprised of guerrilla hit-and-run tactics since 2000 – the distribution of violence there is uneven. For some, the key factor is distance from the Chechen war zone. For others, it will be the existence of a localized nationality conflict that cannot be subsumed under a general rubric and concerns the particular structure of governance in that republic or region. In certain cases, the violence will not be ostensibly political but will concern criminal activity and conflicting mafia networks. It was our expectation, in designing the survey, that the experience of individuals with violence would vary considerably and that this experience would colour their attitudes to relations between nationalities. Communities which saw significant violence were expected to show weak cross-ethnic social capital and interactions (Coletta and Cullen 2000). In order to test this relationship, we asked specifically whether the respondents or their close family members had witnessed 'an ethnic incident that involved injury or death'. We found that, contrary to expectations, war experiences influence ethnic nationalist sentiment less than religiosity, education and professional status.

Over 25 per cent of our sample in BiH and 24 per cent in the North Caucasus indicated that they or a close relative had witnessed an 'ethnic incident that involved injury or death'. Unlike the other factors examined above, there was no overall simple correlation between witnessing a death or injury and attitudes towards ethno-territorial separatism (Figure 6). However, there were significant results by nationality, with Croats and Serbs (both sub-samples) above the mean, while the two groups below the mean were Bosniacs who witnessed and Bosniacs who did not witness a violent ethnic incident.

In the North Caucasus, a surprisingly high overall ratio of 24.4 per cent answered in the affirmative about witnessing violence but it varied dramatically from place to place and from group to group. Ossetians (89 per cent), Kabardins (28 per cent) and Laks (26 per cent) have above-average ratios of respondents who said that they or close family members saw violent incidents. In a similar manner, the geographic range of this ratio reaches up to 100 per cent in Beslan, with values greater than 90 per cent in Budyennovsk and Vladikavkaz and 64 per cent in Nal'chik. All of these locations have been the scenes of hostage-taking incidents with large loss of life during the past decade. At the other end of the scale, over twenty sample points have a value of 0 per

Figure 6. *Distribution of preferences for ethnic separatism by ethnic group and experience of witnessing violence in the two study areas*

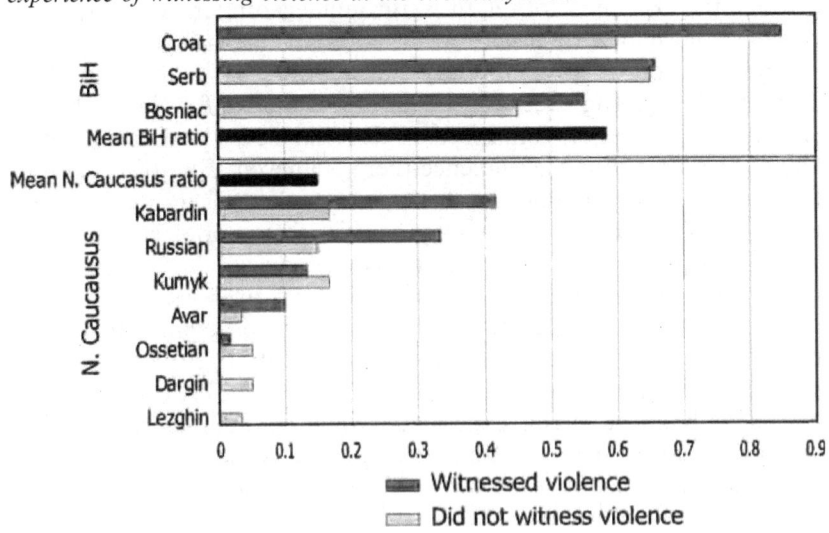

cent on this indicator of localized violence. The ratio of support for the ethnic separatist option has higher values for the Russian and Kabardin sub-samples that witnessed violence than for the other analyses. We attribute the result for the Kabardins to the events in Nal'chik in October 2005 which were fresh in the minds of respondents. The results for the Russians are more intriguing since they are both the largest nationality and the most geographically dispersed in the region. In other survey questions, Russians are more likely than other groups to report deteriorating relations between ethnic groups in the aftermath of the Beslan school hostage tragedy of September 2004. Compared to their Muslim neighbours, Russians are more likely to report a pessimistic outlook on the future of national relations, and are most negative about the (in)actions of the Russian government in reducing violence in the region.

The power of place

This paper has systematically compared attitudes in BiH and the North Caucasus towards ethno-territorial separatism using responses to the same question in large social surveys conducted in both locations at the same time. This type of controlled comparison is rare because the resources required to conduct such symmetrical research are considerable. It creates a unique opportunity to systematically test prevailing hypotheses about the social determinants of, or, at least, the social correlates of, ethno-territorial separatist thinking, using evidence from two distinctive regions. Our overall finding was that BiH had much higher levels of acceptance of ethno-territorial separatism in comparison to the North Caucasus. (It must be remembered that Chechnya and Ingushetia were not included in the North Caucasus survey.) The geopolitical context, demographic structure and conflict experience in both regions are distinctive. Over three years of a brutal war characterized by widespread ethnic cleansing and the imposition of a cartographic fix by the international community has produced much higher levels of acceptance of exclusivist ethno-territorialism in BiH than in our North Caucasus sample region, where conflict is more localized and sporadic.

Traditional social science factors, such as religiosity, perceived income and levels of pride, showed significant results, but more so for BiH than for the North Caucasus. Personal circumstances and personal beliefs are more important in explaining separation preferences than ethnic group membership. Intuitive factors like experience with violence were not consistently revealing and significant. The hypotheses that came closest to accounting for separatist sentiment in both locations were geographical location and levels of trust. Generalizations, however, are hard to make as 'geographical location' is itself something that is conditioned by multiple factors such as the state of local ethnic relations, war damage and experiences, economic prospects, and governmental actions.

In sum, the most salient, yet apparently banal, conclusion may well be the power of place, the power not of the allure of a 'place of one's own' to certain social groups within states, but the power of regional circumstances, cultural distinctions, demographic weight and political opportunity structures in determining the strength of that sentiment. This encompasses the power of geopolitical traditions, socio-economic flows, communication networks and everyday spaces of encounter and mixing in ameliorating exclusionist sentiment and making alternatives to separatism much more appealing, rational and 'natural'.

Acknowledgements

This research was supported by a grant from the Human and Social Dynamics Initiative of the U.S. National Science Foundation, grant number 0433927. Thanks to Vladimir Kolossov for help with the survey and the fieldwork in Russia and to Frank Witmer and Nancy Thorwardson of the Institute of Behavioral Science for preparing the maps and graphs, respectively. We thank Alexei Grazhdankin and his colleagues at the Levada Center, Moscow and Dino Djipa and Marina Francic of Prism Research, Sarajevo for their timely, professional and friendly cooperation that ensured the success of the complex surveys in the North Caucasus and Bosnia-Herzegovina, respectively. Thanks especially to the 4,000 respondents who answered our questions. Detailed census data for the North Caucasus regions were collected with the able assistance and support of Vice-Rector Vitaly Belozerov and Assistant Professor Alexander Panin, Department of Geography in Stavropol State University. We also thank the anonymous and identified (James Sadkovich) reviewers at Ethnic and Racial Studies.

Notes

1. In BiH we used the more common word 'nationality' rather than 'ethnicity'. The wording was: 'Međuetnički odnosi u mom mjestu poboljšat ce se onda kad ... pripadnici svih nacionalnosti budu svaki na svojoj teritoriji.' The Russian text was: 'Chto, po vashemu mneniyu, nuzhno sdelat', chtob' uluchshit'othosheniya mezhdu narodami v vashei mestnosti (vashem rayone)? Vyi mozhete v'bpat' do trekh otvetov u kazhdogo korennogo naroda dolzha b'it' svoya zemlya, a lyudi drugikh narodov dolzhn' uekhat' s etoi zemli.' ('What, in your opinion, is necessary to do to improve relations between the peoples in your locality (your region)? Each defined ethnicity should have its territory and peoples of other ethnicities must leave this territory'). We accept that this Russian wording of the survey question is more explicit and elaborate than that in Bosnia, and that this may well be a factor in accounting for some of the considerable differences of responses across both locations.
2. Due to space constraints, we have had to cut two sections of this paper – one contextualizing ethno-territorialism in the regions under study and one on survey sampling

and design – and condense the discussion. Those interested in the full version can obtain it at the project website: www.colorado.edu/ibs/waroutcomes/
3. In the discussions that follow of the factors underlying the ethnic separatism preferences, we used cross-tabulations to examine the ratios and Chi-square to judge whether the differences with ethnic sub-samples (e.g. Serbs with incomes above and below the mean) are significant.

References

BRUBAKER, ROGERS 2004 *Ethnicity without Groups*, Cambridge, MA: Harvard University Press
BURG, STEVEN and SHOUP, PAUL 1999 *The War in Bosnia-Herzegovina: Ethnic Conflict and International Intervention*, Armonk, NY: M.E. Sharp
CAMPBELL, DAVID 1998 *National Deconstruction: Violence, Identity, and Justice in Bosnia*, Minneapolis: University of Minnesota Press
CIGAR, NORMAN 1995 *Genocide in Bosnia: The Policy of 'Ethnic Cleansing'*, College Station, TX: Texas A&M University Press
COLETTA, NAT J. and CULLEN, MICHELLE L. 2000 *Violent Conflict and the Transformation of Social Capital: Lessons from Cambodia, Rwanda, Guatemala, and Somalia*, Washington, DC: World Bank
COOK, KAREN S., HARDIN, RUSSELL and LEVI, MARGARET 2005 *Cooperation Without Trust?*, New York: Russell Sage Foundation
DAHLMAN, CARL and Ó TUATHAIL, GEARÓID 2005 'Broken Bosnia: the localized geopolitics of displacement and return in two Bosnian places', *Annals of the Association of American Geographers*, vol. 95, no. 3, pp. 644–62
DOWLEY, KATHLEEN M. 1998 'Striking the federal bargain in Russia: comparative regional government strategies', *Communist and Post-Communist Studies*, vol. 31, no. 4, pp. 359–80
GAGNON, V.P. 2004 *The Myth of Ethnic War: Serbia and Croatia in the 1990s*, Ithaca, NY: Cornell University Press
GIULIANO, ELISE 2005 'Islamic identity and political mobilization in Russia: Chechnya and Dagestan compared', *Nationalism and Ethnic Politics*, vol. 11, no. 2, pp. 195–220
GORDY, ERIC 1999 *The Culture of Power in Serbia: Nationalism and the Destruction of Alternatives*, University Park, PA: Pennsylvania State University Press
GORENBURG, DIMITRY 1999 'Regional separatism in Russia: ethnic mobilisation or power grab?', *Europe-Asia Studies*, vol. 51, no. 2, pp. 245–74
——, 2003 *Minority Ethnic Mobilization in the Russian Federation*, New York: Cambridge University Press
HAHN, GORDON 2005 'The rise of Islamist extremism in Kabardino-Balkariya', *Demokratizatsiya*, vol. 13, no. 4, pp. 543–94
HECHTER, MICHAEL 1975 *Internal Colonialism: The Celtic Fringe in British National Development, 1536–1966*, London: Routledge & Kegan Paul
HECHTER, MICHAEL and LEVI, MARGARET 1979 'The comparative analysis of ethnoregional movements', *Ethnic and Racial Studies*, vol. 2, no. 3, pp. 260–74
HODSON, RANDY, SEKULIĆ, DUŠKO and MASSEY, GARTH 1994 'National tolerance in the former Yugoslavia', *American Journal of Sociology*, vol. 99 no. 6, pp. 1534–58
KOLOSSOV, VLADIMIR, GALKINA, TAMARA and KRINDATCH, ALEXEI 2001 'Territorial'naya identichnost' i mezhethnichneskie otnosheniya: na primere vostoch'kh Stavropol''skogo kraya (Territorial identity and inter-ethnic relations: the case of the eastern districts of Stavropol' krai'), *Polis (Political Studies)*, vol. 11, no. 2, pp. 61–78
KUNOVICH, ROBERT and HODSON, RANDY 1999 'Conflict, religious identity, and ethnic intolerance in Croatia', *Social Forces*, vol. 78, no. 2, pp. 643–74

LYALL, JASON 2006 'Landscapes of violence: a comparative study of insurgency in the Northern Caucasus'. Paper presented at the annual meeting of the Midwest Political Science Association, Chicago, IL

MANN, MICHAEL 2004 *The Dark Side of Democracy: Explaining Ethnic Cleansing*, Cambridge: Cambridge University Press

MASSEY, GARTH, HODSON, RANDY and SEKULIĆ, DUŠKO 1999 'Ethnic enclaves and intolerance: the case of Yugoslavia', *Social Forces*, vol. 78, no. 2, pp. 669–91

MATZUZATO, KIMITAKI and IBRAGIMOV, MAGOMED-RASUL 2005 'Islamic politics at the sub-regional level in Dagestan: Tariqa Brotherhoods, ethnicities, localism and the spiritual board', *Europe-Asia Studies*, vol. 57, no. 5, pp. 753–79

O'LOUGHLIN, JOHN, PANIN, ALEXANDER and WITMER, FRANK 2007 'Population change and migration in Stavropol' *kray*, Russia: the effects of regional conflicts and economic restructuring', *Eurasian Geography and Economics*, vol. 48, no. 2, pp. 249–68

Ó TUATHAIL, GEARÓID and DAHLMAN, CARL 2006 'Post-domicide Bosnia-Herzegovina: homes, homelands and one million returns', *International Peacekeeping*, vol. 13, no. 2, pp. 242–60

Ó TUATHAIL, GEARÓID, O'LOUGHLIN, JOHN and DJIPA, DINO 2006 'Bosnia-Herzegovina ten years after Dayton: constitutional changes and public opinion', *Eurasian Geography and Economics*, vol. 47, no. 1, pp. 61–75

PAASI, ANSSI 1996 *Territories, Boundaries and Consciousness: The Changing Geographies of the Finnish-Russian Border*, New York: John Wiley & Sons

PERICA, VJEKOSLAV 2002 *Balkan Idols: Religion and Nationalism in Yugoslav States*, Oxford: Oxford University Press

PETERSEN, ROGER 2002 *Understanding Ethnic Violence: Fear, Hatred, and Resentment in Twentieth-Century Europe*, Cambridge: Cambridge University Press

PICKERING, PAULA 2006 'Generating social capital for bridging ethnic divisions in the Balkans: case studies of two Bosniak cities', *Ethnic and Racial Studies*, vol. 29, no 1, pp. 79–103

RAMET, SABRINA 1996 *Balkan Babel: The Disintegration of Yugoslavia from the Death of Tito to Ethnic War*, 2nd edn, Boulder, CO: Westview Press

ROEDER, PHILLIP 1991 'Soviet federalism and ethnic mobilization', *World Politics*, vol. 43, no. 1, pp. 196–232

ROSCHIN, MIKHAIL 2005 'The role of Islam in North Ossetia', *Chechnya Weekly*, vol. 6, issue 13 (30 March), http://www.jamestown.org/publications_details.php?volume_id=409&issue_id=3282&article_id=2369511

SECOR, ANNA and O'LOUGHLIN, JOHN 2005 'Social and political trust in Istanbul and Moscow: a comparison of individual and neighbourhood effects', *Transactions, Institute of British Geographers*, NS vol. 30, no. 1, pp. 66–82

SEKULIĆ, DUŠKO, MASSEY, GARTH and HODSON, RANDY 2006 'Ethnic intolerance and ethnic conflict in the dissolution of Yugoslavia', *Ethnic and Racial Studies*, vol. 29, no. 5, pp. 797–827

SILBER, LAURA and LITTLE, ALAN 1995 *The Death of Yugoslavia*, London: Penguin

TREISMAN, DANIEL S. 1997 'Russia's"ethnic revival": the separatist activism of regional leaders in a post-Communist order', *World Politics*, vol. 49, no. 2, pp. 212–49

WALKER, EDWARD 2005 'Islam, territory and contested space in Russia', *Eurasian Geography and Economics*, vol. 46, no. 4, pp 247–71

WARD, MICHAEL, O'LOUGHLIN, JOHN, BAKKE, KRISTEN and CAO, XUN 2006 'Cooperation without trust in conflict-ridden societies: Bosnia and the North Caucasus'. Paper presented at the American Political Science Association meeting, Philadelphia, PA, 1 September (available: www.colorado.edu/ibs/waroutcomes/)

WARE, ROBERT BRUCE and KISRIEV, ENVER 1997 'After Chechnya: new dangers in Dagestan', *Central Asian Survey*, vol. 16, no. 3, pp. 401–12

——, 2003 'Political Islam in Dagestan', *Europe-Asia Studies*, vol. 55, no. 2, pp. 287–302

WIDNER, JENNIFER 2004 'Building effective trust in the aftermath of severe conflict', in R. I. Rotberg (ed.), *When States Fail: Causes and Consequences*, Princeton, NJ: Princeton University Press, pp. 222–37

WIELAND, CARSTEN 2001 '"Ethnic conflict" undressed: patterns of contrast, interest of elites, and clientilism of foreign powers in comparative perspective – Bosnia, India, Pakistan', *Nationalities Papers*, vol. 29, no 2, pp. 207–41

WOODWARD, SUSAN 1995 *Balkan Tragedy: Chaos and Dissolution after the Cold War*, Washington, DC: Brookings Institution

From National-Catholicism to Democratic Patriotism? Democratization and reconstruction of national pride: the case of Spain (1981–2000)

Jordi Muñoz

Abstract

Attachment to the nation is often seen as a stable attitude that provides a 'reservoir of diffuse support' for a country, beyond any specific institutional setting. However, I argue that certain deep social and political changes in a country may imply a reconstruction of nationhood that should modify the social bases of support for the nation. I test this hypothesis in the Spanish case, by tracing the changes in the impact of ideology, religion and region of residence on the intensity of national pride during and after the transition from Francoism to democracy. Results show an evolution that is congruent with my theoretical expectations, even if the process seems to be incomplete and, for certain variables, highly mediated by political cycles.

In this article I want to trace the evolution of the social determinants of Spanish national pride from 1981 to 2000, in order to see whether democratization and democratic consolidation processes have modified them. The interest in tracing this evolution lies in the fact that it can shed light on the nature and dynamics of change in citizens' attachment to the nation. Attachment to one's nation is usually considered as a substantially stable attitude, able to grant support for a state beyond political cycles. However, I argue that it is a political attitude and as such is, to some extent, endogenous to the political process. My contention is that a deep political change, such as a regime change, may require a reconstruction of the nationalizing policies and discourses set up by the elites that will, in turn, modify individuals' attitudes towards the nation.[1]

To test this hypothesis I focus on the Spanish case, given that there has recently been a regime change and we have survey data that covers the period of transition and democratic consolidation reasonably well. Moreover, as I show below, Spain is a clear case in which the new democratic elites had to adapt the contents of state-led nationalism in order to accommodate it to the new context, given the strong ideological, religious and cultural biases of the previous regime.

In the first section I discuss the role of national pride as a fundamental component of the political support framework, and advance some theoretical arguments that support my hypothesis. In the second, I briefly review the Spanish case and the evolution of Spanish nationalist discourses during and after the transition to democracy. In the third section, I further refine the hypothesis and discuss the causal mechanisms linking each of my main variables of interest with national pride. In the fourth I present the data, variables and measures used in the analysis, and the next section sets out the empirical analysis itself. The sixth section is devoted to the discussion of the results and the presentation of the main conclusions that stem from them.

Regime change, nationhood reconstruction and shift in national identities

There seems to be a general agreement in the literature around the idea that identification with the political community is an essential attitude for a country, as it may provide a 'reservoir of diffuse support that can maintain a political system through temporary periods of political stress' (Dalton 1998, p. 19).[2] This is so because it grants support for the state beyond the institutional setting of a given moment and, thus, could be the basis for loyalty to the state despite a regime change.

Therefore, the development of a generalized affective attachment to the nation must be (and, indeed, has been) a primary concern of any state wishing to last for long. The wide literature on nation-building processes has clearly shown how states have developed nationalizing policies in order to obtain this diffuse support from its citizens, acting as active agencies of national socialization. The mechanisms used by these policies are educational systems, presence of national symbols in everyday life, development and spread of national languages, and so on. In normal conditions, consolidated democracies do not engage in explicitly nationalistic mobilization of the population, but, even in those cases, there are several daily mechanisms for reproducing nationhood, that have been labelled as 'banal nationalism' by Michael Billig (1995).

However, a deep change in the social or institutional structure of a country (such as a regime change or a massive settlement of immigrants, for example) may imply a shift in the orientation of the nationalizing policies, in order to adapt them to the new context. This new orientation of policies and discourses, alongside changes in the object itself (the nation), are aimed at modifying citizens' perception and attitudes towards it. Two well-known examples of (successful or not) similar processes may be the post-war (and post-unification) debates on the German nationhood that led to formulations such as Dolf Sternberger's and Jurgen Habermas' 'constitutional patriotism' or the much more recent claims that, at the roots of the 2005 riots in the French 'banlieues', there was a failure by the dominant French version of nationhood to incorporate second-generation immigrants into Frenchness. This need for re-elaboration of nationalizing policies and discourses set up by states in order to adapt them to new social and/or political conditions is, as I discuss below, closely linked to the role of state-led nationalism as a fundamental tool for obtaining social cohesion and legitimacy for the state, at least during the twentieth century.

This may seem incongruent with the idea that attachment to the nation is a sort of reservoir of support for the state beyond the specific institutional setting of a given moment. But we must consider that states and elites do not limit themselves to telling their citizens *what* nation they have to identify with, but also aim at influencing people in *how* they have to think that nation and their belonging to it. In normal democratic conditions, the 'official' version of nationhood tends to be constructed in such a way that it can accommodate, at least, the mainstream of the ideological spectrum of the country; but this is not the case in most authoritarian regimes, which tend to monopolize patriotism.[3] The monopolization of patriotism is a process of identification between the ruling group (the regime) and the nation itself (Bar-Tal 1997) that therefore implies a close linkage between attachment to the nation and conformity with the *monopolistic* group or regime.

When the *monopolistic* regime breaks up, the new institutions and elites must reconstruct patriotism in order to adapt it to the new context. The basis of attachment to the nation can no longer be linked to the old regime's ideology, and, if the new regime is a democracy, these bases should be as inclusive as possible, in order to grant stability to the state. Specially when there are relevant actors that call into question the continuity of the state itself (as was the case in Spain), the monopolization of patriotism implies a severe risk to it, so revisiting the 'official' version of nationhood becomes a central concern for the new ruling elites.

We must keep in mind that nationalism as an ideology has as its main goal influencing individuals' attitudes towards the nation by fostering attachment to a given nation and a given nation-ness. So, in addition to the studies on elite discourses and motivations, research on nationalism must turn its view to the individual level in order to capture the effects of these shifts in nationalizing discourses and policies in actually transforming individuals' attitudes towards nations. The general hypothesis that stems from that is that different regimes will develop different kinds of nationalizing policies and discourses, which will exert varying influences on the configuration of the citizens' attitudes towards the nation.

This can be easily illustrated in the case of the members of cultural and national minorities inside a state that can be recognized, assimilated or marginalized by different models of nationalizing policies and discourses. Confronted with these alternative nationalizing models, the members of the minorities will develop different attitudes and strategies, which we could summarize in Hirschman's (1970) famous trichotomy of exit, voice and loyalty. This may also hold for other kinds of groups and, in general, the population of a state: despite a general identification with, or sense of belonging to the nation, the degree of affective attachment with it will depend on the specific foundations of these policies and discourses. For example, if they include ideological or religious biases, we must expect these biases to be reproduced at the individual level and, therefore, citizens with congruent religious or ideological backgrounds will develop more intense attachment to a nation defined in these terms. If this is true, then, when the contents of the discourses and policies change, so will citizens' attitudes. This is precisely the process that I aim at reconstructing empirically in this article by analysing the case of Spain.

Transition to democracy and redefinition of nationhood in Spain

Spain has experienced deep social and political changes in recent decades. The authoritarian and strongly nationalist regime of Franco was followed by the consolidation of a democratic regime that took the form of a constitutional monarchy and a highly decentralized institutional setting, as stated in the 1978 Constitution. Less than a decade later the new Spanish democracy joined the EEC. Since then, Spain has experienced the longest democratic period in its history and an increasing convergence with Europe in terms of economic development.

A central issue faced by the Spanish transition to democracy was, undoubtedly, the so-called 'national question', which had also been crucial during the second Republic and the 1936–9 civil war. In parallel with the democratization process, the definition of the Spanish nation had to evolve from the traditionalist national-Catholicism of the regime towards a new, democratic and inclusive conception of nationhood: after forty years of strong nationalist dictatorship, the common wisdom stated that the democratization of Spain and the resolution of the conflicts with peripheral (mainly Catalan and Basque) nationalisms were intimately linked. The recognition of the internal diversity of Spain, and the decentralization of the state, required a deep redefinition of Spanish nationhood in itself. The long-lasting debates on this issue during the constituent period are enough to demonstrate its crucial role during the years of transition (for a detailed account, see Bastida 1998).

What was at stake, then? Why was the redefinition of the Spanish nationhood so crucial to the transition process? We can say that the Francoist regime had operated, over forty years, a 'monopolization of patriotism' (Bar-Tal 1997) by imposing a specific view of the Spanish nation in the unique, truly patriotic, conception of it as shown by the systematic stigmatization of the opposition as 'anti-Spain'. This monopolization was based on a specific version of Spanish nationalism that had as its main features the identification of the nation with Catholicism and a traditionalist and organicist view of the nation. It emphasized the identification of Spain with its Castilian 'ethnic core' and rejected any recognition of its internal plurality, mainly by reducing the cultural differences to mere folkloristic expressions of regional specificities (Saz 2003; Muro and Quiroga 2005).[4]

National Catholicism as the official ideology of the state was incompatible with the development of a democratic regime, and the incipient Spanish democracy looked for renewed bases of national legitimacy in order to obtain Spaniards' loyalty to the nation beyond the regime change. So a deep redefinition of Spain's nationhood was needed, in order to overcome a profound legitimacy crisis, linked to increasing peripheral nationalist demands, but also to the preferences of democratic forces that claimed a secular, modern and decentralized conception of the Spanish nation.

The reconstruction of the Spanish nationalism has been extensively analysed by several scholars, focused on the parliamentary debates held during the constituent process (Bastida 1998) or on the main theoretical formulations of the 1975–2000 period (Núñez Seixas 2001; Muro and Quiroga 2005; Balfour and Quiroga 2007). This literature shows that the terms of the debate were heavily influenced by the nature of the democratization process. It was not a break-up of the regime, but rather a compromise between its reformist wing and the mainstream democratic opposition (basically constituted by left-wing Spanish forces and the moderate Basque and Catalan nationalists). The need for compromise between the two groups of actors was the main constraint on this bargaining, and left many unsolved issues in this field, as shown by the enduring conflicts between the centre and the peripheral nationalists. That is what Núñez Seixas (2001) has termed the 'unfulfilled renovation' of Spanish nationalism.

In the Spanish case there is a growing literature that tracks this reconstruction at the elite level but, more surprisingly, much less attention has been paid to the individual bases of attachment to Spain and its transformations – even if there are significant exceptions, the most outstanding being the article by Kenneth Bollen and Juan Díez Medrano (1998) that, however, does not adopt a longitudinal perspective.

In this article I want to focus on this level of analysis in order to check whether this process of reconstruction, in more democratic terms, of mainstream Spanish nationalism has effectively transformed the social determinants of individuals' affective attachment to Spain. I contend that, at the end of the Francoism, there were strong religious, ideological and territorial biases influencing the individual levels of national pride as a result of the, until then, dominant version of Spanish nationalism, and want to check whether there has been a reduction in the intensity of these biases due to the transformation, in a more integrative and democratic sense, of Spanish nationalist discourses.

Hypotheses and mechanisms: a dynamic model of pride in Spain

I have so far argued that we should expect certain deep political changes, such as regime changes, to modify the contents of state-led nationalist policies and discourses, and that this was the case in Spain after the Francoist regime. I want to test if, as I expect, these changes had a correspondence at the individual level in modifying citizens' attitudes towards the nation.

As we have seen, in Spain, Francoist nationalism was clearly biased towards the traditionalist, Castilian, right-wing and Catholic segments of the Spanish society,[5] while the renewed, democratic Spanish nationalism had to promote attachment to the nation among all the citizens beyond their religious, ideological or territorial backgrounds. This is why, to test the hypothesis, I will trace the evolution of the impact of ideology, religion and region on national pride.

At the beginning of the democratic period I expect a significant influence of these variables on Spaniards' national pride: the right-wing identifiers, the Catholics and the residents in regions without a distinct cultural background are expected to show higher levels of pride. And, if an integrative version of Spanish nationalism had successfully developed affective attachment among its citizens, we should also find a *progressive reduction in the impact of these variables on the degree of national pride* as time goes on and Spanish democracy becomes progressively consolidated.

The basic model I suggest, then, is as follows:

$$pride_{ti} = b_0 + b_1\ ideology + b_2\ catholicism + b_3\ region + b_4\ cohort \quad (1)$$

$$b_{1,2,3} = b_0 - b_1 time \quad (2)$$

The argument expressed by the formula is that I expect national pride to be a function of ideology, religion, region and cohort, but –and this is my main point – I also expect the coefficients that link ideology, Catholicism and region with national pride ($b_{1,2,3}$) to weaken progressively, as an effect of a renovation of mainstream Spanish nationalism.

However, the mechanisms underlying the relationship among these explanatory factors and national pride may not be so simple, and we should also consider alternative explanations that may be affecting it. We cannot assume the influence of ideology, religion and region on national pride to be exclusively due to 'domestic' mechanisms related to the specific configuration of Spanish nationalism.

On one hand, a certain bias of the right towards nationalism and the left towards 'internationalism' may be a more general phenomenon. On the other hand, majoritarian religion as a bond among members of a nation has been an important criterion of in-group demarcation in many countries, given that religion may act as any other cultural marker used to distinguish among members and non-members of the group. So my expectation is not a complete extinction of the impact of ideology and religion on national pride, but rather a significant weakening of it.

The case of the culturally distinct regions is even more complex. Several comparative studies have established that members of minority ethno-national groups do not tend to develop strong ties with the state (Smith and Jarkko 1998), especially when it is controlled by a 'titular' group that alienates minorities from it, as was the case with Francoist Spain, and could be labelled as a 'nationalizing state' (Brubaker 1996). The decentralization of the state and the official recognition of minority languages had, as one of its main aims, the goal of integrating the minorities into the 'new' Spain, but there are two phenomena that make me cautious about this expectation: on the one hand, the continuous conflicts between peripheral nationalisms and the state that give a sense of incompleteness of this process of redefinition. Some scholars (Núñez Seixas 2001; Muro and Quiroga 2004) have interpreted these conflicts as an enduring trait of Spanish nationalism. On the other hand, alongside the re-installation of democracy, the process of decentralization in Spain permitted the institutionalization of alternative minority nationalisms, which in Catalonia and the Basque Country soon came under the control of the newly established autonomous governments and developed certain policies leading to an 'alternative nation-building' process, opposed to the Spanish one (Linz 1973). These alternative nation-building processes, if successful, will make residents in these territories (especially younger cohorts) feel less attached to Spain as a nation than their counterparts in the rest of Spain (Martínez-Herrera 2002). This process could counterbalance, to some extent, the integrative effects of a new version of Spanish nationalism *vis-à-vis* national minorities. So there are, at least, two processes going on simultaneously that may be affecting the relationship between the variables in opposed directions, and that could counterbalance each other.

Cohort analysis

To understand the dynamics of change and formation of national pride, I also consider the generation variable in the analysis. Through cohort analysis, I intend to approach the issue of how – and when – national pride is constructed and to what extent it is a stable or unstable attitude. The reconstruction of nationhood at the elite level may not have been able to modify attitudes towards the nation among older generations, but it may produce substantially different patterns of attachment among younger generations, as predicted by the well-known 'impressionable years' hypothesis (Krosnick and Alwin 1989).

I expect older generations to show more intense affective attachment to Spain, given that they were socialized in a strongly nationalist environment. Younger cohorts – those that reached adulthood during the regime's crisis, the transition or the democracy – will show lower levels of pride: as already mentioned, the intensity of state-led nationalism substantially decreased after the end of the dictatorship. The increasingly important presence of competitors to the nationalist regime, since the beginning of the protest cycle of late Francoism, may have contributed to a progressive depression in levels of pride among younger cohorts and, furthermore, lower national pride among younger cohorts is a phenomenon already observed by comparative research (Smith and Jarkko 1998).

Data, variables and measurement

In order to reconstruct the evolution of the Spanish national pride, I use data from the World Values Survey and the European Values Survey from the years 1981, 1990, 1995, 1999 and 2000. The first available survey is from 1981. This may be a limit, given that Franco had died six crucial years before, and the Constitution had been put in force in 1978. It could be argued that the process of reconstruction of Spanish national pride may already have been accomplished by then, so we would be missing the crucial years of the transformation. However, it seems difficult to argue that the institutional transformation of the state would have had immediate, direct effects on citizens' attitudes towards the nation. So I treat 1981 as the starting point of the analysis, and assume that the situation by then imperfectly reflects the consequences of Francoism.

The dependent variable

The dependent variable measures pride in being Spanish. It is measured on a 4-point scale, ranging from 'very proud' to 'not proud at all'. There are more sophisticated measures of attachment to the nation, but they are not available for such a long time period in Spain, and this is an essential feature of my design. Moreover, some tests have concluded that this question is a quite good measure of affective attachment to the nation – it approaches reasonably well the results of more sophisticated indicators (Heath, Tilley and Exley 2005). Another strong reason for using national pride to measure affective attachment to the nation is that it has been extensively used by the literature.

Equating 'pride in being Spanish' with national pride could be somewhat misleading given that certain (mainly leftist and peripheral) groups seem to hold a multinational conception of Spain and, so, by declaring their pride in being Spaniards, could be expressing pride in a (multinational) state rather than national pride. However, the consideration of Spain as a nation, as stated by the 1978 Constitution, is widely shared among Spaniards, so I assume – as the literature has done until now – that the question 'how proud are you to be Spaniard?' is measuring national pride.

Another objection that could be made to the use of national pride as a measure of attachment to the nation is that it may also be affected by period effects, given that it does not measure only the affective attachment to the nation but also, up to certain degree, an evaluation of the effective performance of the 'object'. If this is true, we should expect certain contexts (such as economic cycles, political events or sports successes, for example) to depress or exacerbate pride in the nation, or even alter the relationship among our variables of interest and national pride. However, by asking about general national pride (and not, as in other instances, about pride in specific objects, such as the army, sports teams or the social security system), the affective (and supposedly more stable) component of pride gains prominence *vis-à-vis* the evaluation of the nation's performance.

The independent variables

The variable measuring ideology is on the usual 10-point scale ranging from far left to far right. Measuring religious identification is more complex, and there are various approaches to the issue: some surveys use frequency of attendance at religious services, others ask about the importance of religion in one's life, etc. However, I use a simple question asking whether the respondent identifies as a Catholic, a non-believer or a member of another religious group. Using this approach may be problematic to some extent, mainly for two reasons: it is a less fine approach to the issue (we are not able to discriminate among degrees of identification with Catholicism) and, moreover, the variation is quite reduced (on average, around 84 per cent of Spaniards identify themselves as Catholics in the surveys used). However, I contend that using this straightforward measure is useful and interesting because it captures the subjective identification with a cultural trait that has been used as one of the main national markers of Spanish nationalism. For the sake of clarity, and, given that, at the moment, the proportion of people identifying as members of non-Catholic religious groups is negligible in Spain, I dichotomize this variable into two groups: Catholics and non-Catholics.

To cover the regional differences, I use dummies for those autonomous communities with a different official language from Spanish, given that it is a strong marker of cultural distinctiveness.[6] Using territorial location instead of individual traits may lead to somewhat biased results if we intend to infer the effect of cultural distinctiveness: some of those regions are internally heterogeneous and have larger proportions of immigrants than the rest of Spain. In any case, it must be clear that, by using territory as explanatory variable I aim at estimating the role of those regions as differentiated socialization contexts, rather than the effect of individual ethnocultural traits, that would imply the assumption of an essentialist view on the formation of national identities that has been extensively discredited by the literature.

The cohort analysis is based on the cohort division proposed by Montero, Torcal and Gunther (1998, p. 36). Using relevant events or periods of Spanish political history and the age of entrance into political maturity as criteria, they differentiate among six cohorts: the oldest one (Cohort 1) comprises those born before 1922, who arrived at political maturity during the end of the Alfonso XIII monarchy, the Republic or the civil war. The next one (Cohort 2) is the autarchy cohort, comprising those born between 1923 and 1937. Cohort 3 includes those born between 1938 and 1952, who arrived at political adulthood during the years after the autarchy and the first years of economic development of the regime (the 'regime consolidation cohort'). Cohort 4 (born between 1953 and 1962) arrived at maturity during the regime's crisis years, and Cohort 5 (1963–7) represents the so-called 'transition generation'. The youngest cohort (Cohort 6) is the democracy one, and comprises those citizens born after 1968.

Analysis

First of all, in Table 1 I show the distribution of frequencies among the four categories in each year. As we can see, the levels of national pride in Spain are quite high, with around 80 per cent of the sample in the top two categories. There seems to be no specific trend, towards a decline or increase in aggregate levels of national pride, even if some variations may be indicating the influence of certain period effects, as I was expecting above. We must take this into account and see whether these period effects do alter the relationship among our variables of interest.

In order to assess whether national pride in Spain has become less dependent on ideology, religion and region or not, I proceed in two steps: first, I use three waves of the WVS/EVS survey jointly in order to determine whether the profile of proud Spaniards is significantly different at the end of the analysed period or not. Then, I analyse all the surveys separately in order to have a richer picture of the trends and evolution patterns.

I assume that the 4-point national pride scale is measuring a latent, continuous variable that represents intensity of pride in one's country. However, I do not use ordinary least squares regression to model pride, because the 4-point scale is not a continuous variable and, thus, in doing so I would be violating one of the assumptions of OLS regression. To face this problem, and given the ordinal nature of the dependent variable, I use the ordinal logit model, that is suitable for these kinds of variables and, furthermore, it does not force me to assume that the distances among the points in the scale are equivalent. So I model national pride in the following equation as the log odds ratio: $Yi = 1, 2, 3$, or 4. In the function

Table 1. *Frequencies of national pride*

Year of survey	1981	1990	1995	1999	2000	Total
Not at all proud	4.41	4.87	3.13	2.95	2.21	4.01
Not very proud	8.73	8.06	4.66	7.78	5.19	7.41
Quite proud	36.20	41.65	26.76	45.17	30.27	37.62
Very proud	50.67	45.42	65.45	44.10	62.33	50.96
Total	100	100	100	100	100	100
Mean	*3.33*	*2.28*	*3.54*	*3.30*	*3.53*	*3.35*

$$p(Y_i = Y) = a + b_1X_{1i} + b_2X_{2i} + b_3X_{3i} + b_4X_{4i} + e_i,$$

'i' indicates respondent i, Y = respondent i's national pride, X_{1i} = respondent i's religious identification, X_{2i} = respondent i's ideology, X_{3i} = respondent's cohort and X_{4i}, his or her region of residence.[7]

Table 2 shows three merged models that include several interaction terms to test the hypotheses on the evolution of the impact of religion and ideology on national pride (this method is fully described in Firebaugh 1997). The first compares the situation in 1981 with that of 2000, the second compares 1981 and 1990 and the third, 1990 and 2000. These models do not include variables on regions because the 1981 WVS survey did not use the autonomous communities criteria and thus, they are not comparable.[8] Moreover, instead of using dummies for cohorts, for the sake of clarity, I use the birth year as a continuous variable in order to easily introduce interactions with year.

These three models show several interesting results.[9] The first one is that Catholicism, ideology and birth year exert a highly significant influence on national pride in the expected direction for all the models:

Table 2. *Ordinal logit regression models, dependent variable: national pride, coefficients (and standard errors)*

	Model 1	Model 2	Model 3
	1981/2000	1981/1990	1990/2000
Catholicism	0.447 (0.168)***	0.886 (0.099)***	0.433 (0.169)***
Ideology	0.169 (0.040)***	0.156 (0.018)***	0.166 (0.040)***
Birth year	−0.015 (0.002)***	−0.020 (0.002)***	−0.021 (0.002)***
Year	−2.236 (0.280)***	−1.045 (0.207) ***	−1.240 (0.241)***
Catholic*year	0.818 (0.237) ***	0.350 (0.191) *	0.454 (0.196) **
Ideology*year	0.132 (0.049) ***	0.138 (0.034) ***	−0.010 (0.044)
_cut1	−32.983 (4.796)	−39.992 (3.619)	−43.699 (3.880)
_cut2	−31.634 (4.794)	−38.786 (3.618)	−42.568 (3.878)
_cut3	−29.549 (4.789)	−36.642 (3.612)	−40.374 (3.872)
Pseudo R^2	0.076	0.064	0.0601
MK/Z R^2	0.146	0.153	0.142
LR chi^2 (7df)	390.430	624.460	490.430
N	2471	4413	3812

Notes
$p<0.1$, ** $p<0.05$, *** $p<0.01$.
Year is a dummy variable with value 1 for the first year of each model and 0 for the last one.
McKelvey and Zavoina's R2 is the measure of goodness of fit that, in ordinal logit models, better approaches actual R2 in an OLS regression model on the underlying latent variable (Long and Freese 2001, p. 148)

there is a religious, ideological and generational bias in Spanish national pride. Moreover, the coefficients of year indicate that, controlling for the other variables in the model, overall levels of pride have been increasing in these twenty years, despite the substantial reduction in the intensity of the state-led nationalism. This may be reflecting the integration of previously alienated segments of the society. However, in order to test the hypotheses, we have to look at the interactions between year and the two main variables of interest in these models.

Here we can see if, as expected, the impact of Catholicism and ideology has decreased during the time period considered here. In the first model we see a highly significant, positive relationship between national pride and the interaction of year and Catholicism, which indicates a stronger effect of self-identification as a Catholic on national pride in 1981 than in 2000. The same stands for ideology. These results seem to confirm my main hypotheses concerning the progressive (but not complete) *secularization* and *de-ideologization* of national pride in Spain.

In the second and third models I divide this twenty-year period into two ten-year periods in order to approach the dynamics of change with more refinement. The impact of religion on national pride seems to have been decreasing continuously for the whole period. On the contrary, we see that the *de-ideologization* process is located in the 1981–90 period, while in the second decade the effect of ideology on national pride has not changed significantly: it could have reached its limit or, more interestingly, it could be showing a reverse tendency in the last years – if we divide the 1990–2000 period into two five-year periods, we see that between 1990 and 1995 the impact of ideology on national pride continued to decrease (the interaction term has a significant coefficient of .086, with a standard error of .043), while between 1995 and 2000 it increased slightly (−.097, standard error of .055, significant at the 0.1 level). Below I discuss the implications of this finding.

So this first analysis seems roughly to confirm my main hypotheses. However, in order to have more details on what is going on under these results and to test the other hypotheses referring to region and cohort, I have also run a separate regression for each year for which there is an available survey. Table 3 shows the coefficients, standard errors and some statistics of fit for each of the models run for each year.

These results show a quite complex picture. The religion[10] variable is highly significant and has a considerable influence on national pride during the whole period, being one of the most relevant factors in explaining variation in pride. However, as shown by the previous models – and the coefficients of these models – its strength has tended to weaken progressively.

Table 3. Ordinal logit regression models, dependent variable: national pride (1981–2000). Coefficients (and standard errors)

Year	1981	1990	1995	1999	2000
Survey	WVS	WVS	WVS	EVS	WVS
Catholic	1.260*** (.171)	0.824*** (.101)	0.719*** (.201)	0.805*** (.189)	0.442** (.178)
Ideol.	0.300*** (.030)	0.130*** (.019)	0.044 (.042)	0.175*** (.036)	0.148*** (.043)
Cohort1		1.026*** (.173)	1.267*** (.411)	0.946*** (.353)	0.619 (.378)
Cohort2	−0.331** (.161)	0.975*** (.135)	0.980*** (.253)	0.637*** (.211)	0.852*** (.218)
Cohort3	−0.267* (.161)	0.526*** (.127)	0.606*** (.222)	0.497*** (.198)	0.525*** (.202)
Cohort4	−0.743*** (.156)	0.101 (.128)	−0.012 (.229)	0.215 (.209)	0.311 (.206)
Cohort5	−0.240 (.484)	−0.024 (.144)	−0.166 (.240)	0.132 (.244)	−0.006 (.251)
Catalonia		−1.063*** (.106)	0.109 (.408)	−1.329*** (.206)	−1.308*** (.188)
Basque C.		−2.247*** (.170)	−2.195*** (.399)	−2.018*** (.301)	−2.673*** (.362)
Galicia		−0.749*** (.136)	0.093 (.322)	−1.198*** (.244)	−0.190 (.295)
Valencia		−0.421*** (.127)	−0.333 (.255)	−0.264 (.229)	−1.357*** (.216)
Navarra		−1.323*** (.318)	−1.704*** (.522)	−1.187* (.616)	0.019 (.687)
Balears		−0.627** (.256)	0.202 (.540)	−0.213 (.537)	−0.175 (.550)
Canarias		−1.195*** (.194)	−1.268*** (.202)	−0.555 (.336)	−1.326*** (.342)
_cut1	−1.110 (.240)	−1.945 (.166)	−2.910 (.336)	−2.434 (.283)	−3.333 (.319)
_cut2	.281 (.230)	−.723 (.157)	−1.887 (.301)	−.933 (.239)	−2.029 (.266)
_cut3	2.325 (.240)	1.647 (.158)	.180 (.285)	1.739 (.242)	.401 (.248)
Pseudo R^2	0.085	0.096	0.0852	0.093	0.104

Table 3 (*Continued*)

Year	1981	1990	1995	1999	2000
Survey	WVS	WVS	WVS	EVS	WVS
MK/Z R²	0.196	0.219	0.180	0.202	0.212
LR Chi2	286.9	614.23	126.10	166.71	176.55
N	1536	2877	837	855	935

Notes

$p<0.1$, ** $p<0.05$, *** $p<0.01$.

Year is a dummy variable with value 1 for the first year of each model and 0 for the last one.

McKelvey and Zavoina's R2 is the measure of goodness of fit that, in ordinal logit models, better approaches actual R2 in an OLS regression model on the underlying latent variable (Long and Freese 2001, p. 148)

I use Cohort 6 as the reference category, except for 1981, where the reference category is cohort 1 (the oldest cohort), because there are no individuals of the youngest cohort in the sample. In the regions, I compare each of the culturally distinct regions with the rest of the state.

Table 4. *Predicted probabilities of pride in Spain for Catholics and non-Catholics**

	1981		1990	
	Non-Catholic	Catholic	Non-Catholic	Catholic
Not at all	0.10	0.03	0.07	0.03
A little	0.21	0.08	0.14	0.07
Fairly	0.47	0.38	0.53	0.45
Very	0.23	0.51	0.25	0.44
	1995		1999	
	Non-Catholic	Catholic	Non-Catholic	Catholic
Not at all	0.04	0.02	0.04	0.02
A little	0.06	0.03	0.12	0.06
Fairly	0.37	0.25	0.58	0.48
Very	0.52	0.69	0.26	0.44
	2000			
	Non-Catholic	Catholic		
Not at all	0.02	0.01		
A little	0.05	0.03		
Fairly	0.40	0.32		
Very	0.53	0.64		

Note
* Table constructed using the prtab post-estimation stata command (Long and Freese 2001, p. 148).

To clarify the results, in Table 4 I show the predicted probabilities of pride for Catholics and non-Catholics, holding the other variables constant at their means. In this table we can see how being Catholic increases the probability of being very proud of Spain: in 1981, this was more than twice as much for Catholics as for non-Catholics. The differences have decreased slightly but still remain significant. Due to the concentration of an overwhelming majority of the sample in the top two categories, the relevant differences are located between them, so the probability for the three lower categories is always greater for the non-Catholics.

The relationship between ideology and pride is more complex: it was very strong and significant at the beginning of the period (1981), in 1990 it was still significant (albeit apparently weaker) and in 1995 it had lost its significance. Later on, in 1999 and 2000 it retrieved its influence on national pride. These results are congruent with those obtained in the merged models, and seem to suggest that this relationship is mediated by period effects. I will discuss it later on. Again, Table 5's display of predicted probabilities will make it clearer (I show only the extreme and central points in the left-right scale to reduce the size of the table and make it more interpretable).

Table 5. *Predicted probabilities of pride in Spain by left-right self-placement**

	1981			1990		
	1	5	10	1	5	10
Not at all	0.10	0.03	0.01	0.06	0.04	0.02
A little	0.21	0.09	0.02	0.12	0.08	0.04
Fairly	0.47	0.40	0.16	0.52	0.47	0.36
Very	0.22	0.48	0.81	0.30	0.41	0.57
	1995			1999		
	1	5	10	1	5	10
Not at all	0.03	0.02	0.02	0.04	0.02	0.01
A little	0.04	0.04	0.03	0.12	0.07	0.03
Fairly	0.30	0.27	0.24	0.58	0.50	0.33
Very	0.63	0.67	0.72	0.26	0.41	0.63
	2000					
	1	5	10			
Not at all	0.03	0.01	0.01			
A little	0.06	0.04	0.02			
Fairly	0.43	0.32	0.20			
Very	0.48	0.63	0.78			

*Table constructed using the prtab post-estimation stata command (Long and Freese 2001, p. 148).

Territorial differences are especially strong and consistent in the case of the Basque Country, showing huge and highly significant coefficients during the whole period – it is, by far, the variable with the strongest relationship with national pride. Residence in Catalonia also depresses Spanish national pride, but its impact is consistently lower than in the Basque case, and in 1995 it had disappeared. Also residents in the Canary Islands do show lower degrees of pride during almost all the period. The other regions in the analysis show more uneven patterns, although the general tendency is to present negative coefficients that indicate a negative relationship with Spanish national pride. This suggests that cultural distinctiveness exerts some negative influence on affective attachment to the nation-state, but this impact appears to be consistent only in certain cases, after a process of politicization of differences. This process has been successful only in Catalonia and the Basque Country (and partly in the Canary Islands), where minority nationalist parties have been ruling autonomous institutions since they were re-established in 1979. Table 6 shows the predicted probabilities of national pride for residents in Catalonia, the Basque Country and the rest of Spain. The other variables in the model are held constant.

Table 6. *Predicted probabilities of pride in Spain by region**

	1990			1995		
	Rest of Spain	Basque	Catalan	Rest of Spain	Basque	Catalan
Not at all	0.03	0.22	0.08	0.02	0.16	0.02
A little	0.06	0.27	0.15	0.03	0.19	0.03
Fairly	0.43	0.42	0.53	0.26	0.46	0.24
Very	0.47	0.09	0.24	0.68	0.19	0.71
	1999			2000		
	Rest of Spain	Basque	Catalan	Rest of Spain	Basque	Catalan
Not at all	0.02	0.11	0.06	0.01	0.14	0.04
A little	0.05	0.25	0.16	0.03	0.23	0.09
Fairly	0.45	0.53	0.58	0.27	0.50	0.50
Very	0.48	0.11	0.20	0.69	0.13	0.37

*Table constructed using the prtab post-estimation stata command (Long and Freese 2001, p. 148)

In this table it can clearly be appreciated that residence in these two territories substantially depresses pride in Spain. This is especially true in the Basque Country, where the probability of being 'very proud' of Spain has never been greater than 0.2, while in the rest of Spain it has ranged between 0.47 and 0.69. The case of Catalonia is less pronounced than the Basque one, but it still shows huge differences with respect to the rest of Spain.

Cohort analysis, despite some irregularities (that might be due to the reduced numbers of some cohorts), suggests that cohorts that reached adulthood during the regime's crisis, the transition or after the establishment of democracy show lower levels of national pride than the older ones. A quite linear tendency emerges, each cohort being less proud than the previous one.

Due to the well-known age-period-cohort specification problem, we cannot be completely sure that this effect is not due to social ageing rather than political generations. However, there are two reasons that lead me to contend that, despite its apparent linearity, the mechanism linking birth year and national pride is not related to social ageing but rather to cohort effects dependent on different socialization contexts: first, a mechanism linking national pride and social ageing is much less plausible than the cohort effects, determined by the socialization contexts, as stated by previous works (Heath, Tilley and Exley 2005). And, second, as the cohorts age they do not show a strong, linear tendency to increasing national pride nor do we find a progressive convergence among them, as can be seen in Figure 1.

Discussion and conclusions

So the results have roughly confirmed my hypotheses: I have shown that there has been a statistically significant decline in the influence of religion and ideology on Spanish national pride during the analysed period. However, not all the variables behave exactly in the same way and the general picture is rather complex: the details are much more nuanced, and this transformation is neither complete (as I had already predicted) nor homogeneous.

We have observed a constant tendency towards a progressive 'secularization' of Spanish national pride through a reduction of the impact of Catholicism on national pride. This tendency is congruent with the marginalization of the explicit national Catholic discourse from the public sphere since the end of the Francoist dictatorship (Núñez Seixas 2005). However, in the year 2000, we still find a significant impact of religion on national pride, which may be indicating that Catholicism acts as a stable cultural marker for in-group definition in Spain and thus it is not exclusively related to changes in the public discourse. The identification of the Spanish nation with Catholicism has deep roots, and national Catholicism has been a very important component of contemporary Spanish nationalism since its origins in the nineteenth century, even among its liberal exponents (Álvarez Junco 2002).

When Spaniards are explicitly asked about the importance of religion as a national marker, less than a half of respondents consider it important or very important.[11] This may reflect that the explicit identification between Catholicism and nationhood in Spain is slowly disappearing from the public discourse, but it still remains an important marker for individual attachment to Spain. The growing

Figure 1. Evolution of national pride by cohort, 1981–2000 (% being 'very proud' + 'fairly proud')

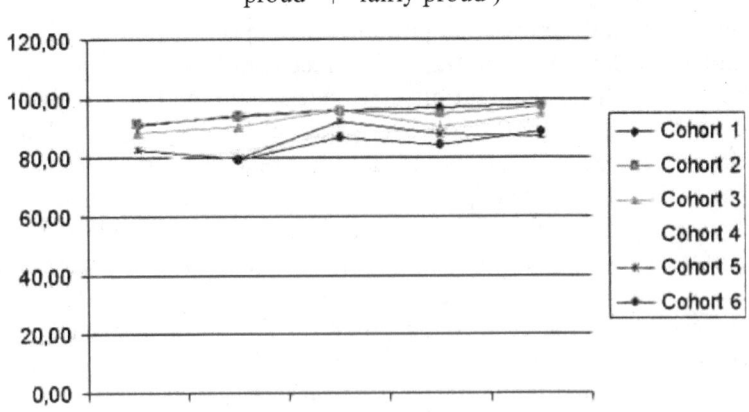

diversity, in religious terms, of the Spanish population (due to the increasing settlement of immigrants and the process of secularization) may contribute, in the near future, to a further loss of impact of religion on national pride. However, some explicit links of the official Catholic church with unitarianist Spanish nationalism, such as the recent consideration by a significant sector of the Spanish bishops of the national unity as a 'moral good',[12] may act as a counterbalancing factor and help to maintain a certain degree of religious bias in the Spanish national pride.

On the other hand, the evolution of the relationship between ideology and national pride in Spain seems to be more complex. From 1981 to 1990 (and 1995) the process of reduction of the influence of ideology on national pride was constant, reaching a point when it had lost its significant impact. The long-lasting left-wing governments (1982–96) may have contributed to this process, by fostering attachment to the nation among left-wing identifiers and, perhaps, also reducing it among rightists.

However, since 1995, ideology has retrieved its influence on national pride, and in 1999 and 2000 it was quite strong again. This change in tendency coincides with the arrival in government of the Popular Party, which may have reversed the de-ideologization of Spain by identifying its right-wing government with the defence of the nation, opposing both external threats (for example, the Moroccan 'invasion' of the islet of Perejil just off the Spanish-ruled northern-African city of Ceuta during the summer of 2002) and internal conflicts with peripheral nationalists that were possibly more intense in the 2000–4 period than ever before since the return to democracy in Spain.

This reversal of the tendency seems to indicate that the relationship between ideology and national pride is mediated by certain period effects, related to changes in mainstream nationalist discourses following short-term political changes. This somewhat surprising result opens room for further research on attachment to the nation, which is usually seen as rather autonomous from short-term political changes.

Finally, residence in culturally distinct territories has an uneven influence on national pride: only in the cases of Catalonia and the Basque Country (and the Canary Islands) does it significantly reduce pride in Spain. In the other cases (Valencia, Galicia, Balearic Islands) the influence is lower or there is no influence at all. Although the lack of data for every time-point on specific cultural practices, such as minority language usage, makes it impossible to estimate the effects of this individual trait, the results suggest that the mechanism that links residence in those territories and lower levels of pride in Spain is not linguistic or cultural distinctiveness by itself but rather the existence of relevant peripheral nationalist elites that have set up alternative nation-building projects, that may hinder attachment to Spain. If the Basque and Catalan cases are commonly referred to as examples of failure of the Spanish nation-building process, the Galician, Valencian and Balearic ones should be considered, at least partially, as examples of successful Spanish nation-building despite the presence of distinctive languages.

These results appear to support the idea that national identities are politically and socially constructed (or 'deconstructed'), and do not derive directly from some *objective* ethnocultural traits of individuals. The lack of data on autonomous communities for 1981 does not allow us to test the hypotheses on the evolution of the relationship between residence in Catalonia and the Basque Country and Spanish national pride. However, the data on 1990–2000 are clear enough in showing that, regardless of the previous evolution, these variables do exert a strong influence in depressing the average levels of pride in Spain, being – especially in the Basque case – by far, the strongest predictor of national pride in the models.

We still cannot be sure whether the lower pride in Spain of residents in Catalonia and the Basque Country is the product of a Spanish nationalism that, by defining the Spanish nation in ethnocultural terms, alienates them from feeling attached to it or, rather, the result of the alternative nation-building set up by Basque and Catalan autonomous governments. Further research would be needed to determine the influence of the distinct forces in shaping the individual attitudes of Catalans and Basques towards Spain. In any case, we have shown that the negative relationship between residence in these territories and pride in Spain has not disappeared at all after more than twenty years of democracy and decentralization of Spain.

Despite the different paths, by the year 2000 the ideological, religious and territorial biases on national pride were still strong and significant. How should we interpret these results? Are they reflecting an unfulfilled, or precarious, process of redefinition of the Spanish nationalist discourse after the end of the Francoism? Or do they simply indicate that the process of change, at the individual level, is slower – and less linear – than predicted? Or has Spain simply reached a 'normal' situation in which the majority religion acts as a national marker just as in other countries, and the relationship between ideology and attachment to the nation is mediated by intervening political variables?

Further research would be needed to provide a satisfactory answer to these questions, and probably all these options are partially true. In any case, in this article I have shown that national pride is not completely autonomous from the political sphere, and that deep political changes such as a transition from an authoritarian regime to a democracy do modify people's attitudes towards their nation.

Attachment to the nation is a political phenomenon and, as such, it is socially and politically constructed (and reconstructed): the agency of the elites and the institutional settings do exert a strong influence in shaping individual attitudes towards the nation, even in the short term.

Acknowledgements

This research was funded by the project *Espacios de competición en gobiernos multinivel. Identidades, partidos y elecciones en el Estado de las Autonomías* (SEC2003-00418) Ministerio de Ciencia y Tecnología (Spain). A previous version of the paper was presented at the first ECPR Graduate Conference, Essex, 7–9 September 2006.

I am extremely grateful to the two anonymous ERS referees, Francesc Pallarés, Javier Astudillo, Ignacio Lago and Luís de la Calle for their useful comments on earlier drafts of this article.

Notes

1. This is not to deny, however, that popular movements and public opinion are strong determinants of the shifts in elite discourses, which acquire a special relevance within the context of democratization.
2. Dalton even goes beyond this general statement and underlines the fact that in Czechosolvakia the levels of national pride in 1990 (three years before its split) were remarkably low. For similar arguments, see also Norris (1999) or the seminal work by Almond and Verba (1963).
3. This is not to say that in democracies conceptions of nationhood are constant and immutable. In some cases, there are groups within democracies that aim at monopolizing patriotism, just as authoritarian regimes do (some examples could be the Israeli religious right wing, McCarthyism in the USA, the BJP's *Hindutva* in India). But also, when there are no such monopolistic attempts, social or political changes (such as integration in supra-national structures or massive settlement of immigrants) may lead to substantial changes in the dominant versions of nationhood.
4. The nature of Francoist Spanish nationalism is certainly more complex: as underlined by Ismael Saz (2003), there were two main components of it: the Fascist (Falangist) one and the traditionalist one. The latter became hegemonic during the regime's consolidation, so we consider it 'the' regime's version of nationalism.
5. We must not forget that the regime had its origins in a civil war, and thus represented the 'winners' of the war. The 1936–9 war was a complex conflict in which several division lines were confronted: democracy vs. authoritarianism, left-wing vs. right-wing, Catholicism vs. anticlericalism, centre vs. periphery, etc.
6. Despite its lack of a distinct language, I also include a dummy for the Canary Islands, given their specificities (geographic distance, presence of movements with an anticolonialist rhetoric during a certain period, etc).
7. Cohort and region are actually introduced in the model as dummy variables for each value.
8. This is a limit, given that the first year in which we are able to test the effect of living in a culturally distinct region is 1990, more that a decade after the autonomous governments' establishment. I will test the effects of regions in the separate analysis.
9. Several variables in the models do violate the parallel regressions (proportional odds) assumption. However, I have run a generalized ordered logit model that does not impose this

assumption, and no substantive result changed: certainly, the coefficients for some variables tend to be greater (and more significant) for the extreme categories (this model computes a separate regression for each Pr (y ≤m)|Pr (y >m) comparison). For the sake of clarity, I go ahead with the ordinal logit models. The same stands for the rest of the models in the article.
10. I have also run the model using a variable that measures intensity of religious practice given that it is a more refined measure of religiosity. However, when using this variable I find significant differences only among those that never attend religious services and those that do attend Mass, but not among different frequencies of attendance.
11. It is considered 'important' or 'very important' to be a Catholic for being 'truly Spanish' by 46.7 per cent in ISSP 1995 and 43.2 per cent in ISSP 2003.
12. See, for example, *El País* (24 June 2006, p. 25).

References

ALMOND, G. A. and VERBA, S. 1963 *The Civic Culture: Political Attitudes and Democracy in Five Nations*, Boston, MA: Little, Brown
ÁLVAREZ JUNCO, J. 2002 'The formation of Spanish identity and its adaptation to the age of nations', *History and Memory*, vol. 14, no. 1–2, pp. 13–36
BALFOUR, SEBASTIAN and QUIROGA, A. 2007 *The reinvention of Spain: Nation and Identity since Democracy*, Oxford: Oxford University Press
BAR-TAL, D. 1997 'Monopolization of patriotism', in D. Bar-Tal and E. Staub (eds), *Patriotism in the Lives of Individuals and Groups*, Chicago, IL: Nelson-Hall, pp. 246–69
BASTIDA, X. 1998 *La nación española y el nacionalismo constitucional*, Madrid: Ariel.
BILLIG, M. 1995 *Banal Nationalism*, London: Sage
BOLLEN, K. and DÍEZ MEDRANO, J. 1998 'Who are the Spaniards? Nationalism and identification in Spain', *Social Forces*, vol. 77, no. 2, pp. 587–622
BRUBAKER, R. 1996 *Nationalism Reframed: Nationhood and the National Question in the New Europe*, Cambridge: Cambridge University Press
DALTON, R. J. 1998 'Political support in advanced industrial democracies', Center for the Study of Democracy, University of California, Irvine
EUROPEAN VALUES STUDY GROUP AND WORLD VALUES SURVEY ASSOCIATION 2006 *European and World Values Surveys Four-Wave Integrated Data File, 1981–2004, v.20060423*, Aggregate File Producers: Análisis Sociológicos, Económicos y Políticos (ASEP) and JD Systems (JDS), Madrid, Spain; Tilburg University, Tilburg, The Netherlands. Data Files Suppliers: Analisis Sociologicos Economicos y Politicos (ASEP) and JD Systems (JDS), Madrid, Spain; Tillburg University, Tillburg, The Netherlands; Zentralarchiv fur Empirische Sozialforschung (ZA), Cologne, Germany. Aggregate File Distributors: Análisis Sociológicos Económicos y Políticos (ASEP) and JD Systems (JDS), Madrid, Spain; Tillburg University, Tilburg, The Netherlands; Zentralarchiv fur Empirische Sozialforschung (ZA) Cologne, Germany
FIREBAUGH, G. 1997 *Analyzing Repeated Surveys*, Thousand Oaks, CA: Sage
HEATH, A., TILLEY, J. and EXLEY, S. 2005 'The decline of British national pride', www.iser.essex.ac.uk/seminars/mondays/2005/spring/papers/heath.pdf
HIRSCHMAN, A. O. 1970 *Exit, Voice, and Loyalty: Responses to Decline in Firms, Organizations, and States*, Cambridge, MA: Harvard University Press
KROSNICK, J. A. and ALWIN, D. E. 1989 'Aging and susceptibility to attitude change', *Journal of Personality and Social Psychology*, vol. 57, no. 3, pp. 416–25
LINZ, J. J. 1973 'Early state-building and late peripheral nationalisms against the state: the case of Spain', in S. Rokkan and S. N. Eisenstadt (eds), *Building States and Nations: Analysis by Region*, Beverly Hills, CA: Sage, pp. 32–116
LONG, J. S. and FREESE, J. 2001 *Regression Models for Categorical Dependent Variables Using Stata*, Stata Corp

MARTÍNEZ-HERRERA, E. 2002 'From nation-building to building identification with political communities: consequences of political decentralisation in Spain, the Basque Country, Catalonia and Galicia, 1978–2001', *European Journal of Political Research*, vol. 41, pp. 421–53

MONTERO, J. R., TORCAL, M. and GUNTHER, R. 1998 'Actitudes políticas de los españoles hacia la democracia', *Revista Española de Investigaciones Sociológicas*, vol. 83

MURO, D. and QUIROGA, A. 2004 'Building the Spanish nation: the centre-periphery dialectic', *Studies in Ethnicity and Nationalism*, vol. 4, no. 2, pp. 18–37

—— 2005 'Spanish nationalism: ethnic or civic?', *Ethnicities*, vol. 5, pp. 9–29.

NORRIS, P. 1999 'Introduction: the growth of critical citizens?', in Pippa Norris (ed), *Critical Citizens: Global Support for Democratic Governance*, Oxford: Oxford University Press

NÚÑEZ SEIXAS, XOSÉ MANOEL 2001 'What is Spanish nationalism today? From legitimacy crisis to unfulfilled renovation (1975–2000)', *Ethnic and Racial Studies*, vol. 24, no. 5, pp. 719–52

SAZ, I. 2003 *España contra España: Los nacionalismos franquistas*, Madrid: Marcial Pons.

SMITH, T. W. and JARKKO, L. 1998 *National Pride: A Cross National Analysis*, Chicago, IL: National Opinion Research Center/University of Chicago

'Exclusive recognition': the new dimensions of the question of ethnicity and nationalism in Turkey

Cenk Saracoglu

Abstract

This article aims to unravel some common aspects of the recently intensifying antipathy towards migrants from Eastern Anatolia in certain Turkish cities. Based on the fact that every manifestation of this antipathy in everyday life involves a logic that recognizes and excludes these migrants as 'Kurdish', the article conceptualizes these sentiments as 'exclusive recognition'. This concept helps us see the fact that the rising anti-migrant discourse is not an ideology that is imposed by the state or any other political organization in Turkey but a historically specific ethnicization process that takes place in the everyday life of cities. As one of the new dimensions of the question of ethnicity and nationalism in Turkey, 'exclusive recognition' shows the insufficiency of reducing the Kurdish question to a problem of democratization of the Turkish political system, and encourages us to turn our attention to the transformation of urban life.

Up until the last ten years, conventional academic literature in Turkey typically rejected seeing issues regarding the Kurds as an ethno-political problem, and reduced it to either a general problem of economic development or an issue of military security. In the late 1990s, however, when Turkey's integration process with the European Union gained a new momentum, a liberal approach emerged as a vigorous alternative to the traditional official perception of the Kurds in Turkey. According to this liberal perspective, it is neither the Kurdistan Workers Party [PKK] terrorism nor economic underdevelopment but the longstanding assimilationist state tradition that is the underlying source of the problem. By 'narrowing the perspectives to the political dimension of the Kurdish "ethnic" problem' this liberal approach has typically limited its focus to the possible political reforms that would regulate the rights and freedoms of the Kurds (Içduygu, Romano and Sirkeci 1999, p. 992). As a result, recently, we have witnessed fierce academic and political debates between a conventional nationalist discourse, which continues to offer stricter security measures as an answer to the problems related to Eastern Anatolia, on the one hand, and a recently growing liberal approach, which considers democratization an indispensable and absolute solution to the 'Kurdish question', on the other.

This article will claim that neither of these approaches is able to present a comprehensive picture of the problems regarding the Kurds in Turkey. Although the recently strengthening liberal discourse seems to fulfil significant missions in terms of challenging the hegemony of the nationalist perception of the subject, it has failed to comprehend some important new dimensions of the Kurdish question in the previous decades. But, what are these new dimensions?

Some recent tendencies in Turkish society, such as (fortunately) sporadic but open ethnic confrontations in some Turkish towns and evident manifestations of an anti-Kurdish discourse in popular media and the internet, indicate that the Kurdish question goes beyond being a problem between the state and the Kurds. Mesut Yegen states that in some social and political circles it is possible to see that the Kurds are no longer seen as a loyal and assimilable Muslim community, but instead they have been perceived as the 'primary Other' of the Turkish nation (Yeğen 2006, pp. 74–143). Tanil Bora also points to the fact that some well-known writers and journalists as well as ordinary people have started to adopt more exclusive language in relation to the Kurds in the last ten years (Bora 2006, p. 78). According to Bora this anti-Kurdish language portrays the Kurds as culturally backward, intrinsically incapable of adapting to the 'modern city life', naturally criminal, violent, and separatist people. He also notes that there are a considerable number of people who regard the increasing number of Kurds in Western Turkish cities as the 'Kurdish invasion'. It is quite ironic but meaningful to observe that at a time when the Turkish state is taking some 'historical' steps towards recognizing certain political and cultural rights of the Kurds, some scholars underscore the rising antagonist discourse towards the Kurds in Turkey.

This newly rising anti-Kurdish discourse, as a new dimension of the Kurdish question, reveals itself in different facets of social life, such as in internet forums, websites, the media, and daily life (Bora 2006). This article aims to unravel some common aspects of the different manifestations of the anti-Kurdish discourse in Turkish society and thereby draw a general preliminary framework that can help us understand the reasons for its occurrence. While doing this, my research material will be made up of the concrete expressions of anti-Kurdish sentiments on the internet and in the media, and also in ninety in-depth interviews that I conducted in İzmir between July 2006 and June 2007.

The field study that I conducted in İzmir aimed to understand the changing nature of ethnic relations in the city since the 1980s.[1] The in-depth interviews that I conducted with the people who live close to the shanty towns of the Kurdish migrants were an important part of this study. The most fundamental insight that I gained from these interviews is the following: that, despite the divergences in form and intensity, it is possible to consider all recent manifestations of anti-Kurdish sentiments under the concept of 'exclusive recognition'. I have constructed this concept based on four common features of the recent anti-Kurdish discourses revealed in different spheres of social life. First of all, in contrast to the conventional assimilationist discourse of the state, which sees the 'Kurds' as a part of Turkish nation, the recent anti-Kurdish discourse *recognizes* the 'Kurds' as a separate 'people group'. Secondly, this recognition necessarily accompanies a logic that *excludes* the Kurds, because in the cognitive world of anti-Kurdish people, the Kurds have been distinguished by negative traits such as being ignorant, culturally backward, and separatist. Thirdly, the agents of anti-Kurdish discourse derive the negative stereotypes primarily from their superficial contacts with and observations of Kurdish migrants in the everyday life of Turkish cities. In other words, only after they *recognize* the Kurds in the urban space do these people develop their own conception of what is meant to be 'Kurdish'. This shows that the negative perception of Kurds is not a 'false consciousness' that is directly imposed by some external agents such as an organization, party, or class. Rather, it is a discourse that has been primarily developed independently within the circle of everyday life social relations. The word 'recognition' here implies that Kurds refer to an 'experienced Other' rather than an 'imagined Other' in the cognitive world of anti-Kurdish people (Miles 1982, pp. 121–150; 1989, pp. 11–40). Fourthly, the people who use such negative labels to identify the Kurds do not *necessarily* exhibit an antagonistic attitude towards other ethnic groups. In other words, these pejorative labels are generally used *exclusively* against Kurdish migrants. Indeed, the metropoles such as Istanbul, Izmir Mersin, Antalya include many people from other non-Turkish ethnic origins such as Bosnians, Albanians, Circussians, Georgians or Laz, but most people are almost indifferent to their ethnic origins and generally do not tend to 'group' and categorize them based on their ethnic origins. In other words, the exclusive discourse under consideration targets Kurdish migrants *exclusively*. Regardless of the divergences in form and intensity, the recent manifestations of anti-Kurdish discourse necessarily exhibit these four characteristics. Here, the concept of 'exclusive recognition' is very instrumental in conveying and highlighting these four common characteristics of anti-Kurdish sentiment.

This exclusive recognition can be considered a novel dimension of the Kurdish question today. Although it is hard to find out the level of prevalence of this discourse in Turkish society, it might be possible to trace its social origins. If so, where to look for the sources of 'exclusive recognition'? The typical liberal approach, which sees the Kurdish question as an 'inveterate illness' that stems from the Turkish state's traditional authoritarian policies or as an extension of the long-standing nationalist political culture in Turkish society, is deprived of the necessary analytical tools for answering this question. Indeed, 'exclusive recognition' is in compliance neither with the state's official ideology nor with the discourse of any civil political actor within Turkish politics. On the contrary, 'exclusive recognition' seems to be a historically specific phenomenon that develops independently of the manipulation of the state or of any established political actor in Turkish politics. In order to make this point more clearly, I would like to present a discussion on the ways the Kurds have been viewed in different facets of mainstream Turkish nationalism. By doing so I want to show that the discourse of 'exclusive recognition' is so unique and novel that its sources cannot be found only in historical discourses and practices of mainstream Turkish nationalism as revealed by the state or any non-state political actors.

The Kurds in mainstream nationalist discourses

In accordance with assimilationist practice, the state discourse in Turkey has long denied the presence of a separate Kurdish ethnicity in Turkey. It has been far from being overtly racist in the sense that its long-term objective was to assimilate the Kurdish people into larger Turkish ethnicity rather than systematically excluding them on a racial and ethnic basis (Bora 2006, p. 32). In official nationalism, the confines of the 'Turkish nation' have been open to the Muslim peoples in Anatolia such as the Kurds, Circussians Balkan Muslims etc., while it has been closed to the non-Muslim peoples such as the Armenians and Greeks who have been considered to be minorities (Özdoğan 2001; Yegen 2006, pp. 8–69). The recently popularizing exclusive recognition is qualitatively different from this official discourse in the sense that the former recognizes and excludes the Kurds, whereas the latter denies the existence of a separate Kurdish ethnicity and opens the doors for the assimilation of the Kurds into the 'Turkish nation'.

After Turkey was considered a candidate member of the EU in the 1999 Helsinki Summit, the state, to some extent, liberalized its Kurdish policy, since the recognition of certain cultural and political rights of the Kurds was seen as a precondition of being a part of the EU. In 2002, private institutions that teach in Kurdish and private media that broadcast in Kurdish language under state control were both legalized. These reforms were followed by some debate-provoking statements by the current prime minister Tayyip Erdogan, who on many occasions proclaimed that there are different ethnic sub-identities in Turkey and that 'being a citizen of Turkey' is the real common bond between these different ethnic groups. The ultimate aim of this new 'multiculturalist' discourse was to integrate the Kurds within the existing social establishment rather than excluding them. In this sense, it is obvious that neither the current multiculturalist nor the conventional assimilationist discourse exhibits any similarity to exclusive recognition. As such, it would be a futile effort to trace the sources of this sentiment in the state's conventional as well as current projects.

Besides the official state discourse, the realm of political parties and organized political movements, have been long closed to any *systematic, explicit and coherent* anti-Kurdish discourse. Turkey's oldest and most radical ultra-nationalist party, the Nationalist Action Party [MHP] has generally reproduced the official denialist and assimilationist approach throughout its history. This party has always claimed that the Kurds are not a separate ethnic group but actually a part of the Turkish nation. Recently, although the leadership of the party recognizes the fact that a segment of the Turkish nation speaks the Kurdish language, it strictly opposes any political and legal reform that would recognize the political and cultural rights of Kurdish people. Despite this rigid attitude, the official leadership of the party has never employed an explicitly racist anti-Kurdish discourse. According to some Turkish specialists on nationalism, an anti-Kurdish, racist sentiment has recently become popular especially among the youth of the MHP movement but we should also note that this has never represented the official line of the party (Bora and Can 2004, p. 402)

This does not mean that anti-Kurdish sentiments remained completely anathema to Turkish society before. Rather, it is possible to see some examples of a racist attitude towards the Kurds in the writings of some Turkish 'intellectuals' in the 1960s and 1970s. Nihal Atsız, for instance, a Turkish novelist, can be considered a prominent racist figure, who still continues to inspire some Turkish nationalists, especially the youth of the MHP (Saraçoğlu 2004, pp. 100–18). However, it is important to note that the recent rise of 'exclusive recognition' seems to be qualitatively different from Nihal Atsız's racist antagonism. The reason for this is that Nihal Atsız's discourse was based on a hatred towards all non-Turkish components of Turkish society as well as a glorification of the Turkish race (Özdoğan 2001;

Bora and Can 2004), whereas exclusive recognition involves an exclusive discourse directed specifically towards the Kurds. In fact in the interviews I conducted in Izmir I came across some individuals who regard Jews and Greeks in Izmir with a kind of nostalgia, while revealing a crude antagonistic and exclusive discourse against the Kurds in the city.

Therefore, based on these preliminary observations, it can be argued that the nature of 'exclusive recognition' has been so specific that it cannot be seen as the continuation of already existing nationalist currents or an ideology that was imposed from 'above' i.e. a higher authority in Turkish politics. This is not to deny that this discourse also borrows some ideas and symbols from conventional Turkish nationalism. However, it is also clear that this discourse situates these symbols and motives within a completely different framework, which is indeed at odds with the basic mentality of conventional nationalist approaches. Then, it seems necessary to consider some other independent dynamics that have contributed to the emergence of exclusive recognition.

The social sources of exclusive recognition

Given that exclusive recognition does not emanate from traditional nationalist currents, we need to turn our attention to some other areas of social life to trace its origins. A closer analysis of the logic of 'exclusive recognition' might help us to develop a perspective on the origins of this sentiment. As was stated before, the discourse of exclusive recognition is not based on the 'imagination' but the 'recognition' of Kurds in the everyday life of Turkish cities. This means that rather than passively repeating an already existing pejorative perception of Kurdishness that was imposed from 'above', the agents of 'exclusive recognition' produce and reproduce a particular image of the 'Kurds' based on their individual experiences and interactions in everyday life of Turkish cities. In this sense exclusive recognition refers to an ethnicization process (Brubaker 2004).

A concrete example from the stereotypes that constitute exclusive recognition will clarify these points further. The word 'ignorant' (*cahil* – in Turkish) is one of the most common expressions used to identify Kurdishness in the urban space. Such a pejorative expression is used in two main interrelated meanings. On the one hand, it implies that the level of Kurds' school education is generally insufficient and that is why they can hardly ever obtain good jobs and get disintegrated from the rest of the city. According to this reasoning, it is the Kurds' ignorance that caused their poverty, unemployment and other social problems. The word 'ignorant' is used also in a way to signify the

Kurds' alleged inability to comply with the basic rules of good manners as well as their difficulty in internalizing the so-called *etiquette* of the city. When the word 'ignorant' is used in this way, it refers to Kurdish migrants' alleged lack of necessary *cultural capital* to get integrated with the rest of the city. According to the agents of the 'exclusive recognition', the lack of *cultural capital* of Kurds or their alleged 'ignorance' manifests itself on different occasions of everyday life, such as being disturbed by a Kurdish teenager while walking downtown at night, hearing some swear words or noisy talk on public transport vehicles or coming across a poor Kurdish migrant throwing garbage into the streets. These particular experiences of 'Kurds' in everyday life play a vital role in the construction or reinforcement of the notion that 'all Kurds are ignorant'.

Here the 'ethnicizing' logic starts by labelling the migrants' alleged lack of education and cultural capital with such a pejorative word as ignorant and continues with regarding this 'ignorance' as one of the integral characteristics of being 'Kurdish'. As this logic has been continuously reproduced in the everyday life of metropoles, this 'ignorance' becomes one of the ossified labels used to define and distinguish the 'Kurdish' in the city. Other labels that are used to define 'Kurdish' – such as aggressive, separatist, living by ill-gotten gain – are also generated from and reproduced via limited observations and experiences with 'Kurds' in the everyday life of cities. At this point, then, it is important to analyse those elements of everyday life that make possible the formation of 'exclusive recognition', as a new dimension of the Kurdish question today.

This analysis should go beyond a criticism of the Turkish state's treatment of the Kurds in history because exclusive recognition in Turkish urban space seems to emanate from changing everyday life and ethnic relations in the Turkish urban context. In this sense, assessing the issue as a *direct product* of so-called authoritarian Turkish 'state tradition' or of the intensification of longstanding but submerged ultra-nationalism in Turkish society cannot fail to be a superficial interpretation. Therefore, in order to provide a preliminary alternative framework, in the rest of this article, I will briefly look at the factors that have transformed the structure of everyday life in Turkish metropoles and have thereby prepared the convenient milieu for the formation of exclusive recognition. At this point, it is important to note that we need to consider all these factors relationally and as a whole as they work in unison to constitute the everyday-life context of exclusive recognition.

a) The exodus from Eastern Anatolia since the early 1980s

The mass migration of Kurds from Eastern Anatolia has been happening in Turkey for roughly 50 years. However, after 1980 it gained some qualitatively different characteristics. The first difference lies in the socio-economic context of migration that has been taking place since the early 1980s. The migration before 1980 occurred in a social and economic context in which the national developmentalist model or the strategy of import substitution industrialization was predominant. This strategy created surplus labour in rural areas of Turkey because of the mechanization of agriculture and a demand for labour in the Western cities due to rapid industrialization. The natural result of this process was large-scale internal migration from rural to urban areas. In this sense, the emigration of the Kurds in the 1960s and 1970s was rather a part of a general trend that has taken place in almost all 'rural' regions of Turkey, where employment opportunities were limited. Unlike the case in the 1960s and 1970s, however, the Kurdish migration of the last twenty years has not been necessarily motivated by industrialization of the metropoles. On the contrary, it has taken place at a conjuncture when most of the Western cities have been rather deindustrialized, since the strategy of capital accumulation has no longer rested on domestic industrialization (Odekon 2005). Therefore, it was not the employment opportunities in the industrial sector of Western metropoles, but mainly the skyrocketing unemployment rates and deteriorating living conditions in Eastern Anatolia which have played a major role in the exodus from Eastern Anatolia after 1980 (Kurban, Çelik and Yükseker 2006, p. 2).

The second specific characteristic of Kurdish migration since the early 1980s was the role that security concerns played in the process of emigration. The continuous conflict between the PKK and the state, a factor that was absent in the 1960s and 1970s, has been an independent dynamic that has triggered the exodus from Eastern Anatolia. Thus, it is important to highlight that it is no longer possible to explain the dynamics behind Kurdish outflow solely with economic factors.

Extensive research, conducted by Hacettepe University in 2005, has estimated that between 953,680 and 1,201,200 people had to leave their villages or cities in Eastern Anatolia for security reasons (HÜNE 2005, pp. 57–61). In fact, it is difficult to distinguish the forced migrants from those that have emigrated for economic reasons, since the provinces that have been exposed to the conflict are also the ones which have the lowest scale in the human development index, namely in adjusted income, education and life expectancy (Zucconi 1999, p. 22). In other words, most of the migrants from Eastern Anatolia have been the victims of both extreme economic deprivation and high insecurity.

As a result of the huge migration waves since the early 1980s, some Turkish cities such as Istanbul, Adana, İzmir, Antalya, Mersin and Bursa have undergone a rapid demographic and socio-cultural transformation. Two specific characteristics of these cities rendered them amenable to the deep structural influences of migration. Firstly, unlike some other small cities in Anatolia, in the mid-1980s and throughout the 1990s these cities had greater employment opportunities in sectors such as tourism, finance, industry and construction. This situation led many Kurdish migrants to flow primarily into these cities. Secondly, these cities (with the exception of İstanbul) did not contain a considerable Kurdish population up until this recent immigration wave (Mutlu 1996, pp. 539–40). Because of these two specific characteristics, the people living in these cities witnessed deep social effects of a rapid increase in the number of Kurdish migrants in their everyday lives. In the last twenty years they have found more chances of experiencing occasional encounters with Kurdish migrants in common life spaces such as bazaars, grocery stores and public transportation.

In the wake of increasing Kurdish nationalism in Turkey, which will be discussed in the following pages, such a rapid change in the ethnic composition of these cities has triggered the notion among some people that the growing number of Kurdish people in Turkish Western cities is an important step towards realizing the long-term 'secret' plan of Kurdifying all Anatolia and establishing a free Kurdistan in Turkey. In this conjuncture, it was even possible to see some political magazines openly warning against a so-called 'Kurdish invasion' of Turkish cities.

At this point it is important to note that the Turkish state's longstanding assimilationist perception of Kurdish ethnicity, albeit indirectly, contributed to the emergence of such a discourse. In the aftermath of the 1980 coup, the Turkish state had abolished the use of the Kurdish language in different spheres of social life with the claim that the free use of other ethnic languages could harm national unity. Therefore, even though there are no longer any legal barriers against the use of Kurdish in everyday life today, the previous restrictions on the use of such a right transformed the Kurds' use of their mother tongue in their everyday life into a controversial political issue and a divisive threat in the eyes of many Turkish people living in Western cities.

The gigantic Kurdish migration in the last twenty years has also made possible the intensification of the Kurdish nationalist movement's activities in Western cities as well. The big demonstrations organized in the 'Newroz' (Spring festivity) celebrations, considered a 'national' day by the Kurdish nationalist movement in Turkey, indicated that Kurdish nationalism has a strong social base among the Kurds living in the Western cities as well. Weakening the hitherto dominant perception that the PKK is completely a marginal illegal organization whose power rests on certain international actors that want to divide the country, this situation made Turkish people realize that this organization obtains some considerable support from ordinary Kurds as well.

However, this 'disillusionment' has prepared the ground for the emergence of another 'illusion' of seeing all Kurds as PKK sympathizers. This tendency is clearly revealed in the interviews I conducted in Izmir in which most of the respondents expressed the opinion that while they thought in the 1990s that the PKK took its support not from the Kurds but from some European countries, now they believe that the Kurds themselves aspire for an independent Kurdistan and that they are openly or latently sympathetic to the PKK. This represents an abrupt shift from an extreme position of seeing the Kurds completely unaffiliated to PKK to another extreme position of seeing all of them as loyal sympathizers.

B) Neo-liberal transformation of the Turkish cities

Today researchers increasingly draw attention to the role of neo-liberal economic and social transformation in the recently rising ethnic confrontations. This approach is based on the assumption that social and economic conditions and injustice deepen social polarization and exclusion in cities (Young 1999, p. 51; Öncü and Weyland 2005, p. 10; Gough, Eisenschitz and McCulloch 2006). This general proposition seems to be true for Turkey too.

Since 1980 Turkey has been experiencing a rapid economic and political transformation along the lines of the neo-liberal structural adjustment policies. As has been the case for other social contexts experiencing a neo-liberal stage of capitalism, social and economic relations and class structure in Turkish cities have been deeply transformed (Balkan and Savran 2000; Yeldan and Sakallioğlu 2000). The economic and political reforms that ensured the further incorporation of the Turkish economy into global capitalism marked the decline of social state policies and the concentration of financial and commercial capital in the developed Western regions of Turkey, which are relatively appropriate for international investment (Sönmez 1998). This process has led to profound social transformations especially in the Eastern regions of Turkey, where increasing poverty and unemployment have gone hand in hand with the acceleration of low-intensity conflict between the PKK and Turkish state forces. As I have said earlier, the result of these interpenetrated dynamics has been a huge Kurdish migration into the Western urban areas where Turkish people comprised the majority of the population.

The urban areas of Turkey have been restructured in accordance with the premises of neo-liberalism as well. Although the rate of national and international financial flows received by Western urban areas has been higher, there has been a striking stagnation and even shrinkage in the labour-intensive industrial sectors (Aydin 2005). As economic growth has been dependent on short-term international financial flows rather than investment in new industrial sectors, Turkish cities have had to face growing unemployment, increasing economic inequality and declining social security, which are the standard social problems that emerge in almost all social formations that go through a neo-liberalization process (Boratav 1991; Aydin 2005; Bağimsiz Sosyal Bilinciler 2007). This was not the case, however, in the 1960s, since, in that period, the rapid growth of labour-intensive industrial sectors made some work opportunities in the formal sector at least possible if not guaranteed (Demirtaş and Şen 2007).

These conditions have influenced especially those Kurdish migrants who fled from Eastern Anatolia for security reasons, because an overwhelming majority of these involuntary migrants (78 per cent) came from the rural areas of Eastern Anatolia and did not have the 'necessary skills' to find a job in the formal employment sectors (HÜNE 2005, p. 60). In a country where primary school education is compulsory, 81.8 per cent[2] of the involuntary migrants did not have a primary school diploma (HÜNE 2005, p. 76). Under these conditions, it has become almost impossible for the Kurdish migrants of the last twenty years to find a job in the formal sectors of Western cities, where industrial employment opportunities have been already contracted as a result of neo-liberal policies (Bagimsiz Sosyal Bilimciler 2007, p. 42).

This situation has compelled most of the newly arrived Kurdish migrants to look for employment exclusively in the informal sectors, where ethnic or *hemşehri*[3] based patronage relationships play a decisive role (Doğan 2002; Pinarcioglu and Işik 2002). Indeed, finding a job even in the informal sector was not an easy thing for these Kurdish migrants, as can be seen from the fact that 44 per cent of the involuntary migrants are unemployed, 49 per cent of them work in informal sectors without any social security, and only 6 per cent of them work in a formal job with social security (HÜNE 2005, p. 76). These numbers are striking enough to highlight the extremely wide socio-economic gap between migrants from Eastern Anatolia and the rest of the city population (Kurban, Çelik and Yükseker 2006, pp. 26–7).

As a result of this situation, in some Western cities everyday life has been socially and spatially polarized between those who have been at best employed in unsecured and temporary informal markets and those who have enjoyed certain relative advantages of being employed in formal jobs. This situation manifested itself clearly in cities such as

İzmir and Mersin. In order to get closer to these Kurdish circles in these cities, recently arrived migrants have ended up concentrating on specific areas of these cities where they have been able to find cheaper housing opportunities as well as temporary job opportunities in informal job circles. In the daily life of these cities, these migrant-concentrated areas have been typically labelled as 'Kurdish districts'.

In İzmir, the *Kadifekale* region and *Onur Mahallesi* and in Mersin, *Demirtaş Mahallesi*, have clearly exhibited these characteristics, in that, they are typically inhabited by Kurds migrating from the same province who are closed to outside cultural influences and have their own social routines and practices (Kaygalak 2001; Ünverdi 2002). The life of the migrants in these jerry-built slums has been incomparably different, especially from the life of middle- or upper-class people in Turkish cities. This is not a surprising phenomenon when it is considered that most of them have been employed in the informal economy of the city and been deprived of a regular wage as well as most of the social security benefits of the state, whereas the better-off sections of society work in formal jobs, and get regular pay and benefits from the social security system of the state (HÜNE 2005). These circumstances, in the end, have separated and differentiated the recently arrived Kurdish migrants in terms of housing and standards of living, and segregated them from not only the rich segments of the city but also from other labourers employed in formal sectors.

Despite this residential and socio-economic segregation, however, Kurdish migrants can also find frequent occasions to interact with people outside their neighbourhood. The encounters between Kurdish migrants and other sections of labourers has been possible in the everyday life of the city since both sections of society, due to their economic constraints, frequently meet at such places as cheap vegetable and fruit bazaars, discount supermarkets, and on public transportation vehicles. An encounter is also always possible between a Kurdish migrant working in the informal economy and a Turkish labourer who buys services or products from informal markets. It is primarily through these encounters in common life-spaces that the agents of exclusive recognition engage in some observations about migrants, and produce or reproduce a negative perception of 'Kurdishness'.

The difficult conditions surrounding Kurdish migrants living in the slums of Turkish metropoles can apparently be seen from their housing conditions and work environment. However, despite these apparent indicators of economic deprivation and social exclusion, the agents of exclusive recognition typically complain that it is not the Kurdish migrants but themselves who are the real 'victims' in the city. They justify this sentiment by referring to the differences in the ways the Kurds earn a living. From their standpoint, their own property and savings or *better* living conditions were deserved because they have spent a lot of labour and effort in a 'formal' or 'legal' work process, paying regular taxes to the state and being loyal and respectful to the law for many years. However, what the Kurdish migrants already possess are ill-gotten gains. The slums in which they currently dwell are gained through occupation of the state's territory. They steal electricity and water from the municipality. More importantly, they work in informal work sectors and do not pay any taxes to the state. From their point of view some of them could get rich very quickly through accumulating the ill-gotten money gained in the informal work processes. In the discourse of exclusive recognition the people living in the slums or shanty towns of the city represent not the urban poor suffering from increasing poverty and exclusion but the 'Kurds' who make their living by ill-gotten gain. This is how the image of the Kurdish migrants 'as the mass of people living by ill-gotten gain' has been constructed.

Here, the so-called 'Kurdish mafia' phenomenon plays a great role in rationalizing and reinforcing this stereotype. It is known that by using their strong network and solidarity ties, some sections of migrants from Eastern Anatolia have managed to establish monopolies in certain formal and informal economic sectors, and developed some mafia-like structures in the cities to preserve or enlarge these monopolies. This situation has given an ethnic and political colour to already existing and increasing economic struggles for the control of the informal economic market. The people that express the discourse of exclusive recognition present this reality, i.e. the phenomenon of so-called Kurdish mafia, as another justification of the negative image of the 'Kurdish' in their mind.

Neo-liberal transformation of Turkish cities has also manifested itself in the increasing crime rates in Turkish cities. As has been the case in other places exposed to neo-liberal policies (Young 1999), increasing poverty and inequality go hand in hand with skyrocketing crime rates and rising insecurity in Turkish cities. Dwellers in the cities can easily feel the influence of increasing insecurity in their everyday lives by experiencing, witnessing or hearing of more frequent incidences of theft from apartments and houses, of robberies in public places, of sexual harassment and even of rapes. The increasing insecurity and crime rate in Turkish cities is a complex phenomenon, which can only be adequately comprehended when it is contextualized within the rapid socio-economic transformation that Turkish society has undergone since the 1980s. However, according to the people revealing the discourse of exclusive recognition, the reason for the sharp increase in insecurity is not the 'social structure' but the migrants themselves. Most of them identify the neighbourhoods where the Kurdish migrants live as centres of crime and violence, and believe that the real threat to order and peace in the city comes from the neighbourhoods where migrant Kurds are living. What we see here is the ethnicization of the 'allegedly' high crime rates among Kurdish migrants, since the subjects of the ethnicizing discourse consider a social fact (high crime rates) one of the essential elements of what is meant to be Kurdish.

This discussion as a whole shows that an analysis of the social ramifications of neo-liberalism is vital to take into account the social and historical context on which exclusive recognition has been constructed and gained popularity. The reasons for this are that it is neo-liberalism: a) which lies behind most of the 'push' factors that induced large-scale Kurdish migration into Western urban areas; and b) which has deeply transformed social relations and everyday life in urban areas.

C) Changing political balances in the Middle East after the US occupation in Iraq

It is true that the agents of 'exclusive recognition' construct the pejorative images, stereotypes and labels that are directed towards the Kurds primarily within the social relations of everyday life. However, some political dynamics at the regional and national level also play a significant role in the reinforcement and ossification of an anti-Kurdish perception engendered in everyday life processes. Today, it is not difficult to see that the split between the Turkish state and Kurdish nationalist projects further provokes and reinforces the negative image of the Kurds and Kurdishness that was created originally within the circle of everyday life. An analysis of the tendency to perceive every Kurdish citizen as a separatist or a PKK sympathizer will be useful for clarifying this point.

The logic that sees the Kurds and PKK as identical is actually more recent than the conflict between the PKK and the Turkish state. The so-called low-intensity warfare between the PKK and the Turkish state continued throughout the 1980s and 1990s and its social costs were tragic – as many as 30,000 people died and nearly one million people were forced to emigrate from Eastern Anatolia. It is critical to note that the impacts of this bloody conflict did not remain limited to the regions where armed conflicts took place. The thousands of soldiers who lost their lives in the armed struggle against the PKK were those young people (between the ages of 18 and 24) who came to Eastern Anatolia from different cities of Turkey in order to fulfil their compulsory military service. As a result, in every city of Turkey, by the late 1990s, there were many families mourning for their young people who lost their lives in the war.

The situation was already tragic enough to create deep and widespread rancour against the PKK, but the reactions and sentiments of people were heightened further by an intense state and media campaign, in which the PKK and its leader Abdullah Öcalan were portrayed in images such as 'baby-killer', 'rogue', 'satan', 'blood-sucker' 'betrayer' etc. (İbrahim and Gürbey 2000, p. 8). Despite these conditions, the armed conflict between the PKK and the state never took the form of an ethnic tension between ordinary Kurds and Turks. Throughout the 1990s, in the media and state discourse, the PKK was pictured as an externally supported organization that actually lacked the support of people living in the region (Kirişçi 2004, p. 290). Taking advantage of the historically established and popularly adopted hostility towards Armenians, the media and the state went too far in declaring that the leader and even the militants of the PKK were Armenian rather than Kurdish. In the 1990s, this tendency of differentiating the Kurds from the PKK seemed to be so internalized by the Turkish public that, even in the most hectic days of the conflict, the Kurds living in the Turkish cities were not subjected to any collective violence or widespread racist reaction. Assuming that the link between ordinary Kurds and the PKK was rather weak, even the families of the soldiers did not react against the Kurds but directed their rancour against the PKK, its leader Abdullah Öcalan, and the countries that were believed to support PKK such as Greece, Italy and France.

In this sense, the roots of the discourse that identifies the Kurds as PKK sympathizers is such a novel phenomenon that its roots cannot be reduced to the relatively longstanding bloody conflict between the PKK and state. At this point, it is critical to ask the question why, despite the fact that PKK actions were no less intense in the 1980s or mid-1990s, it was not until early 2000 that the agents of 'exclusive recognition' started to see an overt attachment between the Kurds and the PKK separatism?

I think there are two answers to this question. Firstly, as I stated earlier, the huge Kurdish migration made it possible for Kurdish nationalist currents to transfer their organized actions to Western metropoles especially in the late 1990s and this has indicated to the public that the PKK is not solely a marginal group that owes its existence only to the support of international actors but is an organization that has been popularly supported by a considerable number of the Kurds as well. In other words, in the everyday life of Western metropoles the link between the Kurds and the PKK has become more visible. Secondly, the nature of Kurdish nationalist politics in general, and that of conflict between the PKK and the Turkish state in particular, has undergone a profound transformation since the US occupation of Iraq in 2003. I would like to elaborate on this second point in more detail.

The US occupation of Iraq has redefined the role of Kurdish nationalism in the Middle East and this has deeply influenced Turkey's Kurdish problem too. The collaboration of the Kurdish nationalist parties of Iraq, the Patriotic Union of Kurdistan [PUK] and the Kurdistan Democratic Party [KDP], with the American occupation forces, and the increasing possibility of an independent Kurdish state in northern Iraq have produced a well-established public concern about the territorial integrity of Turkey as well. During the Iraqi War, the Turkish government did not actively oppose the occupation but still repeatedly declared that the Turkish state would consider any independent Kurdish entity in Iraq a *casus belli*. The Turkish state has always been concerned about a scenario in which an independent Kurdish entity beyond the borders of the Turkish Republic would encourage the Kurds of Turkey to rebel for independence.

Such concerns of the Turkish state and general public were intensified when the leadership of the Kurdish movement in Turkey jettisoned its project for the 'democratization of the Turkish Republic' and replaced it with the goal of establishing a Kurdish confederation. In contrast to the project of 'democratization' that proposed to find a solution to the Kurdish question within the borders of Turkey, the project of confederation was based on a Kurdish nationalist agenda which aspired for the unity of Kurdish people in all Middle Eastern countries. Through this new strategy, the Kurdish movement in Turkey has inclined to extend its hands to pro-American Kurdish groups in Iraq and endeavoured to take advantage of the occupation rather than condemning and opposing it. The rapprochement between the Kurdish movement in Turkey and pro-American Kurdish nationalists in Iraq became more evident in the Newroz festivities of 2007, when Leyla Zana, who is a prominent and symbolic figure of the Kurds in Turkey, publicly declared that

> The Kurds have three comrades. All of them are very precious. They occupy a significant space in Kurdish hearts. First of these is Uncle Jalal [Jalal Talabani] the president of Iraq. He is a Kurdish leader and a believer in brotherhood, he accepts all of us. The second one is Uncle Massoud [Massoud Barzani], the leader of the Kurdistan region [in Iraq]. The third one is the one you call the guide, the leader: he is the will of the Kurdish people as we all know in our hearts, Ocalan. All three are our pride, ears, hearts and brains. They are etched in our hearts. (quoted in Karabat 2007)

As such, the picture is clear enough to understand how the changing political balances in the Middle East have prepared a convenient milieu for the reinforcement of the logic that sees all Kurds as separatists. On the one side, anti-American sentiments in Turkey have reached their highest ever level because of the atrocities of the occupation in Iraq. These sentiments have been intensified with speculations in the Turkish media, such as that the PKK has been endorsed by US forces in the region and also that the USA has been planning to establish an independent Kurdistan, which would involve the territories from Turkey as well. On the other side, there emerged popularly attended Newroz demonstrations, in which Barzani and Talabani (the biggest enemies of Turkey in the eyes of many Turkish people) were proclaimed to be the friends of the Kurdish nation. These kind of occasions reinforced the image of Kurds as separatists who want to divide the country with the help of the USA and thereby constituted a strong justification for those who employ the discourse of exclusive recognition.

Under these circumstances, there is every reason to believe that the recently intensifying armed conflict between the PKK and the Turkish state has the strong potential to ossify the discourse of 'exclusive recognition' in Turkish cities even further. It seems that in the near future the course of macro-political developments in the Middle East in general and PKK activities in Turkey in particular will continue to *reinforce* exclusive recognition. In the wake of current intense armed conflicts between the PKK and the state, the possibility of a new wave of security-based migration towards the Western metropoles would also complicate the social relational dynamics of the Kurdish question further (Kurban, Çelik and Yükseker 2006).

Conclusion

The recently popularizing 'exclusive recognition' is not the only, but a very important, aspect of nationalism and the Kurdish question in Turkey. Considering that scholarly or political discussions about the Kurdish question have been confined to democratic reforms at the political level, this article aims to provide a general framework for an alternative conception of the Kurdish question by highlighting one of its social-relational dimensions. Before attempting to present accurate solutions to the Kurdish question and proposing policies for ensuring the fraternity of the peoples living in Anatolia, extensive research and analysis of the social relations of the Kurdish migrants is necessary. Through presenting and examining some possible social factors that might have prepared the ground for the rise of exclusive recognition in Turkish society, this paper can constitute a preliminary framework for such an analysis.

Acknowledgements

I am grateful to Neşe Özgen from Çanakkale University and Daniele Belanger from the University of Western Ontario for their help in the writing process. I also thank the two anonymous reviewers of this article, whose comments helped me to improve my ideas.

Notes

1. This field study yielded many important results pertaining to the changing social relations in Turkish cities, which need to be evaluated in a much larger-scale study.
2. These statistics are extracted from the interview-based researches conducted by HÜNE in 2005.
3. This Turkish word refers to the social bond created on the basis of being from the same town or region.

References

AYDIN, ZÜLKÜF 2005 *The Political Economy of Turkey*, Michigan: Pluto Press.
BAĞIMSIZ SOSYAL BİLİMCİLER 2007 *IMF Gözetiminde 10 Uzun Yıl*, Yordam: İstanbul
BALKAN, NEŞECAN and SAVRAN, SUNGUR 2002 *The Ravages of Neo-liberalism: Economy, Society and Gender in Turkey*, New York: Nova
BORA, TANIL 2006 *Medeniyet* Kaybi, İstanbul: İletişim
BORA, TANIL and CAN KEMAL 2004 *Devlet ve Kuzgun: 1990'lardan 2000'lere MHP*, İstanbul: İletişim
BORATAV, KORKUT 1991 *1980'li Yıllarda Sosyal Siniflar ve Bölüşüm*, İstanbul: Gerçe.
BRUBAKER, ROGERS 2004 *Ethnicity Without Groups*, Cambridge, MA: Harvard University Press
DEMİRTAŞ, NESLİHAN and ŞEN, SEHER 'Varoş identity: the redefinition of low income settlements in Turkey', *Middle Eastern Review*, vol. 43, no. 1, pp. 87–106
DOĞAN, ALİ EKBER 2002 *Birikimin Hamallari: Kriz, Neo-Liberalizm ve Kent*, İstanbul: Donkişot.
GOUGH, JAMIE, EISENSCHITZ, ARAM and McCULLOCH, ANDREW 2006 *Spaces of Social Exclusion*, London: Routledge
HÜNE (HACETTEPE ÜNİVERSİTESİ NÜFUS ARAŞTIRMALARI MERKEZİ) 2005 *Turkey Migration and Internally Displaced Population Survey*, Ankara: İsmat
İBRAHİM, FERHAT and GÜRBEY, GÜLİSTAN 2000 'Introduction', in Ferhat İbrahim and Gülistan Gürbey (eds), *The Kurdish Conflict in Turkey: Obstacles and Chances for Peace and Democracy*, Hamburg: LIT, pp. 7–17
İÇDUYGU, AHMET, ROMANO, DAVID and SİRKECİ, İBRAHİM 1999 'The ethnic question in an environment of security: the Kurds in Turkey', *Ethnic and Racial Studies*, vol. 22, no. 6, pp. 991–1010
KARABAT, AYSE 2007 *Diyarbakir's Nevruz Celebrations*, http://www.worldbulletin.net/news_print.php?id=2793, Accessed on 20.05.2007
KAYGALAK, SEVİLAY 2001 'Yeni Kentsel Yoksulluk, Göç ve Yoksulluğun Mekansal Yogunlaşmasi: Mersin/Demirtaş Mahallesi', *Praksis*, no, 2, pp. 124–72
KİRİŞÇİ, KEMAL 2004 'The Kurdish question and Turkish foreign policy', in Lenore G. Martin and Dimitris Keridis (eds), *The Future of Turkish Foreign Policy*, Cambridge, MA: MIT Press, pp. 277–315

KURBAN, DİLEK, ÇELİK, BETÜL AYŞE and YÜKSEKER, DENİZ 2006 *Overcoming a Legacy of Mistrust: Towards Reconciliation between the State and the Displaced*, İstanbul: TESEV
MILES, ROBERT 1982 *Racism and Migrant Labor*, London: Routledge
—— 1989 *Racism*, London: Routledge
MUTLU, SERVET 1996 'Ethnic Kurds in Turkey: a demographic study', *International Journal of Middle East Studies*, vol. 28, no. 4, pp. 517–41
ODEKON, MEHMET 2005 *Costs of Economic Liberalization in Turkey*, Bethlehem, PA: Lehigh University Press
ÖNCÜ, AYŞE and WEYLAND, PETRO 2005 *Mekan, Kültür, İktidar: Küreselleşen Kentlerde Yeni Kimlikler*, İstanbul: İletişim
ÖZDOĞAN, GÜNAY GÖKSU 2001 *Turan'dan Bozkurt'a*, İstanbul: İletişim
PINARCIOĞLU, MELİH and IŞIK, OĞUZ 2001 *Nöbetleşe Yoksulluk*, İstanbul: İletişim
SARAÇOĞLU, CENK 2004 'Ülkücü hareketin bilinçalti olarak Nihal Atsiz', *Toplum ve Bilim*, vol. 100, pp. 100–35
SÖNMEZ, MUSTAFA 1998 *Bölgesel Eşitsizlik*, İstanbul: Alan
ÜNVERDİ, HAYAT 2002 'Sosyo-Ekonomik İlişkiler Bağlaminda İzmir Gecekondularinda Kimlik Yapılanmaları', PhD dissertation, Department of City and Regional Planning, Dokuz Eylul University, Turkey
YEĞEN, MESUT 2006 *Müstakbel Türk'ten Sözde Vatandaşa*, İstanbul: İletişim
YELDAN, ERİNÇ and SAKALLIOĞLU, ÜMİT CİZRE 2000 'Politics, society and financial liberalization: Turkey in the 1990s', *Development and Change*, vol.31, no.2, pp. 481–508.
YOUNG, JOCK 1999 *The Exclusive Society: Social Exclusion, Crime an Difference in Late Modernity*, London: Sage
ZUCCONİ, MARIO 1999 'The Kurdish question and migration in Turkey', *Ethnobarometer Working Paper Series*, no.4, pp. 1–44

The politics of war memory in radical Basque nationalism

Diego Muro

Abstract

This paper examines how war memory has been appropriated, interpreted and domesticated by radical Basque nationalism. The so-called patriotic left presents an interesting case study because of its need to justify ETA's use of unconventional methods and political violence. The politics of war memory places violent conflicts in a historical continuum where Basques and Spaniards stand against each other. The memory of the Carlist Wars, the Spanish Civil War and ETA's violent campaign are all used both as an ethnic boundary between Basques and Spaniards and as a powerful mobilizing agent. The conflict between the Basque insurgents and the Spanish state is celebrated as a narrative of heroic past wars and redemptive sacrifices, hence removing the need to reflect on the usefulness of the armed struggle.

Introduction

The social construction of collective memory has become the subject of intense scholarly debate. Contributions from the fields of psychology, anthropology and history, most notably Pierre Nora's grand project, *Les lieux de mémoire*, have all developed the study of collective memory, first pioneered by Maurice Halbwachs in the 1930s. The study of war memory has also been consolidated with well-researched episodes such as the Shoah, the Vietnam War and the two World Wars. Surprisingly, the role of war memory in Spain, and, in particular, of memory of the Civil War, has been absent from many of these international studies. This is probably due to the fact that most studies take a state-centred approach and find internal wars and authoritarian pasts to be intricate cases to deal with.

This paper examines the war memory of radical Basque nationalism defined as both a political ideology and a social movement. As a doctrine, radical Basque nationalism advocates the political independence of the Basque homeland through violent means. As a social movement, it takes the form of the Basque Movement of National Liberation (*Movimiento de Liberación Nacional Vasco* or MLNV), a self-named network of organizations founded in 1974. This complex system is informally known as the patriotic left (*izquierda abertzale*) and it is made up of a number of interconnected political organizations, social agents and NGOs with interests in the fields of feminism, environmentalism, internationalism, Basque culture, youth, students' and prisoners' rights. The most important members are the trade union LAB (*Langile Abertzaleen Batzordeak*), the political party Batasuna (previously called *Euskal Herritarrok* and *Herri Batasuna*) and the terrorist group ETA (*Euskadi Ta Askatasuna*), the undisputed head of the movement. The key characteristic of all the satellite organizations is their ideological and strategic dependency on ETA. ETA sets the violent means to achieve the final goal (an independent Basque socialist state), and it establishes a link between ethnicity and violence as Basqueness is derived pre-eminently from active participation in the liturgy of national struggle (Muro 2008).

The paper is structured as follows. The first section explores the role of history, memory and public commemoration in the construction of a national narrative. The following section is devoted to the impact of warfare on the national community. This section argues that the experience of war is a powerful socialization agent which is remembered by the national body in commemorative rituals and repetitive practices. The third section analyses the importance of both the Spanish Civil War and other conflicts in the shared memory of radical Basque nationalists. As will be explained, war memories are presented in a historical continuum where Basques and Spaniards have always opposed and fought each other. This narrative of war memory is functional as it serves to reinforce both the doctrine and movement of radical Basque nationalism. The fact that a lineage of Basque ancestors fought foreign invaders in the past helps justify the current use of political violence and terrorism. Hence, the politics of war memory in radical Basque nationalism is based on the notion that violence is an indicator of a historical problem (not a problem in itself). Finally, the fourth section argues that the practice of war memory is structured around acts of remembrance and patriotic rituals, especially the cult of the war dead.

Memory and the nation

The relationship between the nation and its past first attracted the attention of the French historian and theologian Ernest Renan (1823–92). In a famous lecture, '*Qu'est-ce qu'une nation?*', delivered at the

Sorbonne in 1882, he suggested that the nation's existence was founded upon the desire to live together or, in his famous phrase, 'a daily plebiscite'. He defined the nation as 'a soul, a spiritual principle' and at once linked this definition of the nation to the existence of shared memories (Renan 1990, p. 19). For Renan, it was the existence of a shared history, which he defined as 'a rich legacy of memories', that forged the national community. The large aggregate of individuals that make up a nation is bound together by these common memories. The cement of their group identity is not the past itself (what actually happened) but what members of the community tell one another in the present (what they remember). 'Getting history wrong', in Renan's words, is a precondition of nationalist history. In his view, a national history is an act of both collective remembering and collective amnesia. It is not the scientific history that binds together the historically formed community. Rather, it is the ritual observance of myths, symbols, legends, ballads and epic songs that binds the national body. The content of these might not be entirely true and, in fact, they might have fictitious elements and historical errors, but they are genuine insofar as they are perceived as original and authentic.

The extent to which a 'legacy of memories' could be fabricated was researched by Eric Hobsbawm and Terence Ranger in *The Invention of Tradition* (1983). This collection of essays was concerned with the role played in modern societies by constructed versions of 'the past' and examined the 'mass-producing' practices that emerged in the period between 1870 and the outbreak of the Great War in 1914. The contributors to the volume examined rituals such as the royal Christmas broadcast, the British coronation ceremony or the Highland tradition in Scotland and argued that these 'invented traditions' were 'highly relevant' to the analysis of the nation. Indeed, during the course of the nineteenth century most European states indulged in the fabrication of historical re-enactments and the recording of their national memory. Nations began to worship themselves through the ritualization of their pasts and the establishment of holy sites, public commemorations and national days, which created the illusion of historical continuity from time immemorial. For example, in France, the Third Republic adopted 'La Marseillaise' as the national anthem in 1879 and a year later, in 1880, Bastille Day was added to the annual cycle of commemorative holidays. The Spanish state-building process too culminated with the adoption of the 'Royal March' as the national anthem in 1908 (Muro and Quiroga 2005). The building of this new ritual and commemorative agenda was not free of challenge and controversy. Some refused to participate in these newly created cultural practices, which took time to be consolidated. In Philadelphia, the city where the American Declaration of Independence was signed in 1776, there was no consensus on how the founding document of the USA should be honoured until the 1850s (Gillis 1994, p. 9).

The period studied by Hobsbawm and Ranger (1870–1914) was characterized by secularization, the emergence of mass politics and the consolidation of electoral politics. The turn of the nineteenth century was also a time when the state felt the need to imbue its citizens with virtues through the building of commemorative monuments. In Spain, statues of (dead) individuals who embodied a worthy social value or patriotic fervour were erected by state institutions to instil an idea of a common heritage. Official monuments found their purpose in teaching the past to the illiterate masses. Each one of these 'glorious statues' spoke for themselves and were examples of the nation's splendid annals. Inspiring individuals who were worth a statue included past monarchs (Isabella of Castile, Don Pelayo, Alfonso X the Wise), explorers and conquistadors (Columbus, Elcano, Hernán Cortés), as well as painters (Velázquez, Murillo, Goya), writers (Cervantes, Lope de Vega, Quevedo) and a few politicians (Castelar, Cánovas del Castillo). Among the victims of war, those who had heroically perished in the War of Independence against the French (1808–14) figured prominently in these places of memory (Los héroes del Dos de Mayo, Agustina de Aragón) (Reyero 1999, pp. 389–94).

It could be argued that throughout the nineteenth century the state's pre-eminence over public space was growing in parallel with control of the citizen's own past. The development of myths and symbols was often sponsored by state institutions in order to convey the national ideal. But what can one say about the characters and topics chosen? Were they picked arbitrarily? Were these fabrications forcefully imposed on lifeless masses? How can we explain the potency and resonance of certain nationalist narratives over others? A possible explanation is that state officials were careful enough to select topics and characters that could evoke a reaction from both the credulous and the well-informed. The monument designed by the artist had to strike a chord with the masses if any long-lasting effect was to be accomplished. Or, in the words of Hobsbawm, the political rituals had to be 'broadcasted' 'on a wavelength to which the public was ready to tune in' (Hobsbawm and Ranger 1983, p. 263).

Renan's most perceptive observation was that, as the collective memory of the nation was constructed (and more stories were left behind), there would be a rise of counter-discourses. Marginalized groups, Renan warned, would become aware of their origins, defeats and injustices. The dominant national history (and its chief architects) would be contested by disadvantaged groups and repressed memories would surface. The twentieth century offered ample evidence for this pluralization of commemorative narratives that offered alternative interpretations on the multiple roots of collective identity. Entire social groups first challenged and then gained admission to national memories: from women, Jews, homosexuals, workers and exiles to indigenous communities and various ethnic groups. All these organized collective actors had a common grievance: their experiences of inequality and injustice did not appear in the so-called 'official histories' and they actively demanded their ordeal be documented and celebrated in museums, textbooks and holiday parades. These disadvantaged groups also shared a common interest in studying and learning their 'lost past' in order to avoid exclusion in the future. For all these social movements who had fought for social change, celebrating present success or well-being was as important as studying their past losses and defeats. 'Getting history right', it could be argued, was seen by activists to have political importance.

Warfare and the nation

Among the different recollections of the past available to nationalist elites, war memories tend to occupy a prominent position. This is probably due to the fact that during war the nation may experience glory and suffering as a collective, and, as Renan reminded us, 'this is the social capital upon which one bases a national idea' (1990, p. 19). The experience of war has never been greater for nations than in the modern epoch. With the Napoleonic wars, large citizen armies began replacing mercenary troops and warfare affected people from all social backgrounds. The nationalization of the masses and the perception of the nation as a community of sacrifice intensified as the century progressed and culminated in the total wars of the last century (Mosse 1975, 1990). Whereas nineteenth century warfare was a powerful agent of socialization which greatly shaped those who participated in volunteer armies, the great wars of the twentieth century had a much more significant impact. During the last century, war increasingly targeted civilians as military objectives and more genocides were committed in that century than ever before in history. Moreover, through air-raids war was experienced not only at the front but also at home and the nation gradually became a community of sacrifice. For those in the line of fire the feeling of camaraderie greatly increased as their identity was posed against a stereotyped image of the enemy.

But there is more to war than the strengthening of identity, the maintenance of ethnic boundaries and the polarization of stereotypes. Warfare, and more importantly sacrifice, is crucial to the nation-building process. Through ceremonies, the nation reflects upon heroic times of sacrifice and this provides a reference point for future generations. During the nineteenth century, on the other hand, ordinary soldiers who fell for the nation were quickly forgotten and those who were wounded on the battlefield suffered from a lack of care

– so much so that the Swiss philanthropist Jean Henri Dunant decided to found the Red Cross in order to assist the injured who had been abandoned to their fate on the battlefield. Similarly, Florence Nightingale decided to assume direction of all nursing operations during the Crimean War (1853–6) after reading reports of the poor treatment wounded British soldiers were receiving on the front line. Besides, only officers had their graves marked and their names inscribed on European war memorials. There is a monumental lion at Waterloo that stands on the hill where the Prince of Orange was wounded in 1815 but there is no *monument aux morts* for the French casualties (40,000) or for the Prussian (7,000), British and Dutch (15,000). This military practice of remembering military elites changed with the Great War of 1914–18 when countries felt the need to leave traces of the terrible injuries suffered by their citizen-armies by consecrating military cemeteries (Gillis 1994). The state also paid tribute to those who had encountered a violent death by selecting an unidentified soldier, symbol of the ultimate sacrifice, and building the Tomb of the Unknown Soldier.

It is usual for the victors to commemorate military successes and for political elites to try to instrumentalize these past glories. It is in this way that past victories and the high status of the armies can boost pride in the military tradition, as can be observed in the USA, France and Britain. About the latter, Martin Shaw has argued that the militarism in British culture is built on a 'century or more of successes', not only in the First World War, he argues, 'but before that in South Africa, the Crimea and even the Napoleonic Wars, not to mention countless colonial conflicts'. In fact, one needs 'to go back to the American War of Independence to find a major British defeat' (Shaw 1997, p. 192). France poses more of a peculiar case. Despite having had its territory invaded by the Wehrmacht, France successfully reconstructed a war memory that celebrated the role of the Resistance, described the Vichy government as alien and argued that the Fatherland had been saved through Republican values. Hence, one could conclude by saying that the existence of a victorious military record *and* the unproblematic commemoration of these events are what allow some countries to engage in new military enterprises. Defeated states that have been discredited internationally have greater difficulties in joining foreign campaigns and, in the cases of Japan and Germany, they have constitutional arrangements that prevent them from participation in an intervention mission.

There are also times when defeats may be marked and remembered. After all, traumatic loss and mass death are a large part of what war is about for soldiers, families and national communities. These acts of remembrance are less common but not impossible to find in some nations' memorial calendars. This is the case of the Battle of Kosovo for Serbs (1389), the fall of Constantinople for Greeks (1453), the Battle of Culloden for the Scots (1746), the Easter Rising for the Irish (1916), the battle of Tel Hai for Zionists settlers (1920) and September 11 for both Catalans (1714) and Americans (2001). These downfalls might seem like the end of national splendour but they tend to be remembered as sublime images of heroic resistance (Turner 2006, p. 206). It seems it is only in defeat that uncompromising love for the nation, expressed in personal sacrifice, can occur, as war provides the zealous nationalist with the perfect stage for an apotheotic end. History is not short of episodes where love for the motherland has been dramatically expressed in martyrdom. Examples of extreme sacrifice can be found in most nationalist histories: the Jews of Masada, Lieutenant Colonel Custer of the 7th Cavalry Regiment, the allies in the Battle of Normandy, the kamikaze pilots of the Japanese Air Force, the hero of Cascorro in the 1898 Hispano-American war or the fire-fighters of the World Trade Centre in New York. In all of these cases, the martyrs willingly accepted suffering and death rather than renounce a belief, principle or cause.

War memory in radical Basque nationalism

The role of war memory in the Basque provinces has received little attention. Interest in the Basque nationalist's memory of the Civil War (1936–9) initially stemmed from a need to explain why the transition to democracy in the Basque Country had been so 'peculiar' (Aguilar 1998; Edles 1998). The process of political reform of the late 1970s had different characteristics in the northern provinces of Spain. Between 1975 and 1982 there were more strikes and killings in the Basque Country than anywhere else in Spain. However, the explanatory power of war memory goes beyond revealing the different character of democratization in the Basque Country. In fact, the 'war memory' of radical Basque nationalists provides crucial clues for understanding the current use of political violence. The emergence of ETA has often been explained by the oppressive character of the Franco dictatorship (1939–75) which created objective grievances in the population (Jáuregui 1981). A combination of grievances and other factors, such as resources and political opportunity structures, explains why political violence was chosen by ETA as a cost-effective means of pursuing a given set of interests (Sánchez-Cuenca 2001). Although the rational choice explanation has several merits, it sheds very little light on the reasons why ETA continued to use extra-institutional means after the authoritarian polity disappeared. A meaningful explanation of the armed group's survival in recent decades needs to go beyond the restrictions of the rational choice paradigm and must incorporate an examination of the building blocks of the violent culture. Hence, it is necessary to incorporate an analysis of the long-lasting beliefs, rituals and memories which facilitate the reproduction of radical Basque nationalism as both a social movement and an ideology.

The process by which people are persuaded to mobilize is not always apparent, especially when there are incentives for individuals to free ride on the efforts of others (Olson 1998). On the one hand, radical leaders often appeal to emotion and passion in order to sustain individual and group identity and frame their message in ways that will rally support for their interests and goals. On the other hand, their strategic use of culture is constrained by prevailing norms, cultural beliefs and historical traditions. This means that a 'pick 'n' mix' narrative will not have an immediate effect on mobilization and affective loyalties. Opportunities for collective action and a moral obligation to act will come when the narrative appeals to a shared set of beliefs and a sense of belonging. When told in an appropriate discursive context, the radicals' narrative on war memory will be effective in reinforcing their violent subculture and mobilizing an increasingly divided movement on fronts beyond the political one.

The remainder of the paper is structured as follows. First, I will analyse how Basque nationalists establish a binary opposition of adversaries, provide a justificatory discourse for the social movement and establish a moral vision that needs to be realized in the future. Second, I will argue that this particular memory of martyrdom and heroic victimization can be understood only by framing it within a long-term cultural frame which allows well-intentioned individuals to be integrated into a radical movement, not as irrational protestors or selfish calculators, but as human beings with values, beliefs and moral visions (Jasper 1997, pp. 1–16). From this perspective, radical nationalists identify the injustice of the situation, assert the capacity of the Basque people to bring about the changes they seek and turn an anti-systemic movement into a 'moral protest'. Their view of the past therefore becomes a motivational story with a clear moral conclusion: Basques have been forced by others to use all means necessary to end their unjust situation. The role of the violent vanguard is to show the way and lead a much larger movement that will eventually end the unjust situation. Third, I will argue that the success of the overall struggle depends on ritual mobilization and on the level of social support received by the elites of the violent movement. The function of 'war memory' is to engage existing members, persuade others to participate and reproduce a discursive process that makes ETA a necessary solution to an obvious injustice.

There can be little doubt that the Civil War of 1936–9 is the most noteworthy historical event in modern Spanish history, as it continues to attract continuing, even obsessive, attention from Hispanists. From the Basque Country, the Civil War has always been seen with different eyes. This was the argument presented by Paloma Aguilar in a seminal article about the war memory of the Basque Nationalist Party [PNV]. According to Aguilar, the 'civil' or 'fratricidal' dimension of the war was denied by Basque nationalists and a particular memory of what happened between 1936 and 1939 was passed down to new generations of nationalists. In the Basque lands, Aguilar points out, people were told that the Civil War was a war 'between Spaniards' in which Basques were obliged to fight against their own will, and then only to safeguard the interests of their homeland. Both the PNV and ETA later came to argue that Basques had suffered a bloody war which did not concern them and an oppressive dictatorship that occupied their land for forty years (Aguilar 1998).

This nationalist recollection is a clear distortion of what actually happened. The same cleavages that cut across Spain cut across the Basque lands. This fragmentation was clearly seen in the first days of the insurrection. The provinces of Navarre and Alava immediately sided with the Francoist rebels whereas Biscay and a part of Gipuzkoa sided with the Second Republic. Echoing Largo Caballero's famous remarks, many scholars have pointed out that these two provinces sided with the Republic in exchange for the 1936 statute of autonomy and only in order to protect it. This argument is backed by the way the Basque autonomous government and its army (*Euzko Gudarostea*) behaved in two crucial events during the war. The first happened after 13 August 1936 when General Mola had successfully blocked the Basques' escape route to France by gaining control of San Sebastián and Irún and the war moved in the opposite direction, to neighbouring Santander, where the Basque soldiers (*gudaris*) surrendered in the infamous Pact of Santoña. Shortly after the *gudaris* had left their homeland the Basque government ended the fighting instead of integrating their units into the Republican army. The second event was the Basque government's refusal to practise a policy of scorched earth, a military tactic that would have left no transportation, communication or industrial resources to the rebel forces. As is well-known, Basque soldiers protected the Biscayan industries until the Francoist army took control of the situation.

The brutality of the Civil War was epitomized by the bombing of cities such as Durango and Gernika. However, the repression continued in Basque lands well into the 1940s and 1950s. Apart from the well-documented artistic and educational repression, which some scholars have hyperbolically described as 'cultural genocide', Gipuzkoa and Biscay were labelled 'traitor provinces' until 1967, and the Basque Country suffered more 'states of exception' (a suspension of civil liberties) than any other region of Spain. The defeat of the Republican project signalled the end of the PNV's hegemonic position and its replacement by a new generation of nationalists who decided to create ETA (*Euskadi Ta Askatasuna* – Basque Homeland and Freedom).

ETA combined a pre-existing tradition of radicalism with the abandonment of confessionalism, the fusion of socialism with nationalism and the strategic use of violence. However, the most notable addition was the changing character of 'Basqueness'. Unlike the founding father of Basque nationalism, Sabino Arana (1865–1903), who was fixated on racial purity and genealogy, ETA members preferred to define the nation in cultural terms while emphasizing the importance of using the Basque language (Euskara). Hence, Basqueness evolved from being an organic and genealogically based concept to a more inclusive and voluntary one. One did not have to be *born* Basque, it was possible to *become* one. This identity option could take the form of speaking Euskara or, more importantly, devoting one's time to the Basque cause, expressed in the likelihood of being imprisoned or killed by the Spanish police and security forces. As Jeremy MacClancy has correctly pointed out, 'to sympathisers of ETA and Herri Batasuna, Basque patriots should be *abertzales*, a status not defined by birth but by performance: an abertzale is one who actively participates in the political struggle for an independent Basque nation with its own distinctive culture' (1997, p. 114).

The new generation of nationalists that founded ETA in 1959 interpreted the Civil War as yet another example of the Spanish state's aggression against the Basque people. During the 1940s and 1950s the writings of Arana, in which he described the colony-like nature of *Euzkadi*, made more sense than ever before. It is thanks to this combination of Arana's nationalism, which argued the Basque Country was an occupied nation, and Francoism, which made that occupation very real, that the birth of the insurgency can be explained. The works of Aguilar (1998) and Edles (1998) concluded that the memory of the Spanish Civil War had been instrumentalized by both the PNV and ETA. However, at no point did these scholars try to incorporate this 'peculiar' understanding of the war within a wider framework of war memory. And this is the truly intriguing point: the fact that the Civil War does not occupy a unique and exceptional place in the war memory of radical Basque nationalism. It is important for being the latest but not necessarily the most significant. In fact, the Civil War occupies just another point in a historical continuum of warfare which extends in both directions: going back in time one encounters the Carlist Wars and going forwards, ETA's war. This social construction of historical continuity reminds some Basques of their alleged bellicosity and allows them to reinterpret the current use of political violence. As Eviatar Zerubavel has suggested elsewhere, representations of lineages invoke the image of a 'succession of individuals carrying, as if in some imaginary relay race, the same symbolic baton throughout history' (2003, p. 57).

Radical Basque nationalism has developed a war memory that justifies ETA's use of political violence. This canonical narrative establishes what the group dislikes, identifies the goals and behavioural strategies of the group and narrows down the available repertoires of action in the hope of mobilizing people. According to Eric Hobsbawm, the 'politics of memory' is an exercise in 'social engineering' made by elites or, in his words, 'from above'. The central point of any 'politics of memory' is that it is not made of what the popular memory considers the history of the nation but from 'what has been selected, written, pictured, popularized and institutionalized by those whose function it is to do so' (Hobsbawm and Ranger 1983, p. 13). Following Hobsbawm, one can argue that the politics of war memory in radical Basque nationalism is based on a careful selection of facts which responds to a logic of reproduction and strengthening of the social group. The selection of facts that need remembrance and commemoration is mainly functional as it fulfils the current political need to justify the use of unconventional methods.

The politics of war memory in radical Basque nationalism is a clear attempt to domesticate the past by 'remembering' some facts and 'forgetting' others. Members of the radical community seem to retain information about the 'war of 1936' and they are able to present current levels of violence as a continuation of the conflict that has opposed Spaniards and Basques for centuries. At the same time, this representation of the past disregards the civil character of the 1930s war and neglects the fact that more than half of the territory that constitutes the Basque homeland sided with the Francoist rebellion. The need to present a coherent use of violence throughout history also forces radical Basque nationalism to see its own movement in monolithic terms. During Francoism, the use of violence was, in itself, a subject of controversy capable of producing outright schism. Between 1966 and 1975 ETA suffered three splits and, on each occasion, the hardliners who defended the use of terror tactics managed to keep control of the organization (Muro 2008, p. 109). Since the history has been re-told by those who kept control of it, the existence of less intransigent members has been continually forgotten when not physically eliminated. This was the case of Dolores González Catarain, known as YOYES, a former ETA leader who was shot by her comrades in 1986 after publicly abandoning the armed struggle. No-one has explained better the organization's firm internal discipline than the journalist Luciano Rincón when arguing that 'ETA does not change, *etarras* do' (1985, p. 13).

A nostalgic way of looking at the past is not new in Basque history (Muro 2005). The nineteenth-century Carlist Wars, for example, were romantically seen by some as wars of national liberation. Or, at least, that is how they were seen by the French-Basque writer Joseph-Augustin Chaho (1811–58). In his book, *Voyage en Navarre*, Chaho did not interpret the struggle between '*carlistas*' and '*isabelinos*' as a dynastic dispute, a nineteenth century civil war or as a confrontation between liberalism and traditionalism, but as a war of national emancipation. Arana, too, put a lot of effort into emphasizing that one of the areas in which Basques had *traditionally* excelled was that of warfare. For him, the unique characteristics of Basques could be identified by any observer. In fact, it was thanks to their skills on the battlefield that they had managed to protect the essential qualities that made them Basque: language, race, religion, etc. Arana's particular fixation with the fighting spirit of Basques can be seen from his early years. In his first ever political writing, *Bizkaya por su independencia* (1892), he articulated a narrative of how Basques had lost their ancient independence and noble freedom. Despite their glorious military past, Arana explained, Basques had lost their most important battle against Spaniards. However, this was not a battle lost on a front line but in the field of culture. Arana concluded his text by saying that it was not the military victory of the Hispanic monarchy over Basques but the increasingly hispanophile evolution (*españolización*) of their culture that signalled the end of their ancient independence.

One could argue that an element common to Chaho, Arana and radical Basque nationalism was the construction of a reductive narrative of binary opposites that emphasized the unjust situation of the Basque nation, defining it against Spain, while asserting the capacity of the people to bring about the necessary changes. It seems that, if enough offences caused by wars could be recollected, the nationalist programme would be seen as a rightful reaction to an undeserved series of humiliations. In extreme cases, as is the case in marriages, the nation would have the right to secede as the last resort or form of self-defence against an abusive partner.

Fallen soldiers

In order for any 'politics of war memory' to be preserved and reproduced, mechanisms for its promotion have to be established. Pierre Nora suggested that 'sites of memory', such as monuments, cemeteries, museums, streets, but even flags, anthems, uniforms, stamps and coins, help maintain an already existing communal identity. The institutions of a nation-state periodically organize large-scale commemorative events and ceremonies to foster a sense of nationhood. Stateless nations, on the other hand, have fewer resources at their disposal and tend to use more modest ritual instruments to mark their identity. In the case of radical Basque nationalism, political rallies and ceremonies of remembrance have revolved around the figure of the fallen soldier.

The quasi-religious cult of the fallen soldier is important in reproducing a tradition of martyrdom, nourishing an image of common identity and generating further recruitment for the resistance cause. Beyond the creation of group solidarity, the role of war commemorations is to absorb death into a collective political ritual characterized by standardization and repetition. The public commemoration of the war dead allows societies to purge themselves emotionally and to argue that the self-sacrifice of their idealistic youth has not been unnecessary. The actual performance of a commemoration provides death, any death, with a meaningful narrative that explains an altruistic personal sacrifice as the pursuit of a higher, more sacred or transcendental goal. In the eloquent formulation of Benedict Anderson:

> the nation secures its symbolic continuity through time, and mobilises the willingness of current generations to die in its defense, by interpellating them as members of an imagined community which transcends death. War commemoration is a vital moment in that process of interpellation. (Anderson 1983, pp. 9–10)

In the American case, the flag is the emblem of the group's agreement to be a group but it is also used as a ritual instrument of cohesion and social co-operation. As Carolyn Marvin and David W. Ingle (1999) have argued, the Stars and Stripes is the central totem of the American civil religion and the preservation of group solidarity depends on periodical blood sacrifice in warfare. Arguing in a typically Durhkeimian fashion, Marvin and Ingle pronounce that, just as religion is a system of beliefs and practices which unite those who adhere to them in a single moral community called a church, nations are also moral communities based on shared beliefs and participation in common rituals.

In radical Basque nationalism, the fallen soldier is an ETA member who can be either arrested or killed 'in action'. In both scenarios, the *etarra* is seen by his or her community as a hero of the *herria* (nation), a frontline martyr who imbues the other members of the community with his/her example (Mata 1993, pp. 80–3). However, this is not just any kind of fallen soldier; this is a fallen *gudari* who contributes to the national cause by encouraging others to follow his or her example. As will shortly be explained, by taking the name of the Basque soldiers who fought in the Civil War, the sacrifice of an ETA member is placed, yet again, in a long list of sacrifices in their historical opposition to the Spanish state (Casquete 2006b, p. 171).

Being arrested is an essential rite of passage for ETA members but also the most common form of ending to the clandestine militancy of the armed group. In comparative terms, many more militants are made prisoners than killed. When the *etarra* is arrested, he briefly enjoys a period of media attention and glorification in the radical press. After his time in the judicial organ that deals with terrorism charges, the Madrid-based *Audiencia Nacional* (National Court), the *etarra* joins a community of 'prisoners of war' dispersed around Spain. The time spent in prison is often represented in radical nationalist rhetoric as the 'final front of struggle' because the member of ETA lives alongside 'the enemy', in the form of prison guards (Hamilton 2007, p. 125). The community of ETA prisoners has considerable moral weight in the world of radical Basque nationalism. Despite having lost any direct control over the armed group, they remain sublime examples of a sacrificial act and their opinions are deemed to be highly influential.

Acts of remembrance for ETA prisoners and demands for their release are not difficult to find in the Basque Country. Radical nationalists have established a calendar of standardized, symbolic and repetitive practices which place the ETA prisoner at the centre of a radical imaginary. One example of such ritual action is the peaceful demonstration of relatives of ETA prisoners in the main squares of numerous Basque towns and cities. Civil society organizations in support of amnesty also organize rallies and marches against 'Spanish repression' and in favour of the inmates' release from prison. At the iconic level, posters of deceased and imprisoned ETA members are usually hung in *abertzale* bars and social centres (*Herriko Tabernak*) and many balconies exhibit *Euskal Presoak Euskal Herrira* posters (Basque prisoners to the Basque Country), a black map with two red arrows pointing to the seven Basque provinces which represents the claim for the return of 604 ETA prisoners (in September 2007, 452 in Spanish jails and 152 in French ones) to Basque jails. The poster also acts as a symbolic protest against the Spanish government's dispersion policy, which was first implemented in 1989.

Radical Basque nationalism has often venerated ETA prisoners as rallying symbols that the nature of the Basque conflict is undeniably 'political'. As Sáez (2002, p. 225) has rightly pointed out, the Basque Movement of National Liberation [MLNV] has presented the circumstances of their prisoners as analogous to that of members of the public kidnapped by ETA. Both sentenced prisoners and abducted citizens (expected to pay extortion money known as 'revolutionary tax') are presented as unwilling participants in a larger theatre of war. What unites these two collectives is both being deprived of their individual freedoms and being unwilling characters in a political drama beyond their control. As a result, their hardship cannot be solved by individual measures but only by a law of amnesty framed in a comprehensive political settlement between the Spanish and Basque nations.

ETA prisoners are a central symbolic element of the MLNV's iconography but their importance in reproducing the radical cause cannot be compared to the sacrifice of those who have fallen in the course of an *ekintza* (action). Whereas imprisoned insurgents need to go through a lengthy process of validation, the status of martyr is granted almost immediately to ETA members upon a violent death. Important examples are the first death of an ETA member, Txabi Etxebarrieta (1959), the capital punishments of Jon Paredes (Txiki) and Ángel Otaegi (1975), the assassination of the ETA leader José Miguel Beñaran (Argala) at the hands of the Batallón Vasco Español (1978) and the death in a car accident of Txomin Iturbe (1987), ETA's chief negotiator during the Algiers peace negotiations. Being killed by the Spanish security forces (José Antonio Lasa and José Ignacio Zabala, 1983), while in police custody (Xabier Galparsoro, 1993) or while manipulating explosives (Patxi Rementería, 2000) are also considered to be dignifying examples of the nation's fighting spirit. Even suicides in prison (José Angel Altzuguren, 2005; Igor Angulo 2006) are interpreted by the radical community as altruistic and inspiring acts which can activate feelings of kinship more effectively than mass political action. On occasions, town councillors or MPs of *Herri Batasuna*, the political branch of ETA, have also received *gudari* honours in their funerary rites. When Telesforo Monzón, one of the founding fathers of Herri Batasuna, died in 1981, his funeral was widely attended by nationalists from other political parties. On 20 November 1984, the tenth anniversary of Franco's death, the paediatrician and *Herri Batasuna* leader, Santi Brouard, was gunned down by members of the state-funded paramilitary group GAL (*Grupos Antiterroristas de Liberación*) in his Bilbao surgery and his funeral was attended by hundreds who regarded him as a martyr (MacClancy 1997, p. 120). Five years later, the journalist and MP for *Herri Batasuna* Josu Muguruza was killed in Madrid by GAL on the same date as Brouard. The death of these individuals has been interpreted as a symbolic offering to the nation, an example of the fighter's devotion and readiness to sacrifice for a supreme national ideal. The social value and political impact of the heroic death is not in the sacrifice in itself but in the ritual remembrance of an act of martyrdom where the individual has a special role to play in collective redemption. In the radical calendar, the *Gudari Eguna* or day of the Basque soldier has been held on 27 September since 1975 to pay homage to the executions of Txiki and Otaegi and the death of subsequent *gudaris*.

The central role played by the martyrdom of the ETA activist (and his or her ritual commemoration) in the social reproduction of the militant uprising was first examined by the anthropologist Begoña Aretxaga (1988). The cemetery is usually the central space where fallen soldiers are remembered in rites of martyrdom but revolutionary movements are often prevented by states from mourning collectively in public spaces. Since radical Basque nationalists do not have control over inhumation at the cemetary, the preceding funeral becomes the theatre where the ETA member's heroic life and martyrdom is worshipped. According to Aretxaga, the day after an *etarra*'s death the *abertzale* newspapers publish accounts of the deceased's life, his personality, his interests, the fluency of his (usually learnt) Euskara and, above all, the depth and length of his commitment to the Basque cause. Nothing in any way reproachable about his or her character is mentioned. The funeral service is conducted in Basque in an open space and it is followed by a series of speeches, also in Euskara. The burial of the coffin (often covered with a Basque flag or the ETA logo of the axe and the serpent) is preceded by an *aurresku* (Basque honorary dance) and the playing of the *txistu* (Basque flute) or the *txalaparta*, a traditional percussion instrument made of two wooden boards held horizontally and then beaten vertically with special drumsticks. Between 1968 and 2005, radical Basque nationalists performed funerary rituals to honour the heroic deaths of 160 *gudaris* and, on most of those occasions, the funeral ended with the nationalist anthem of the Spanish Civil War, *Eusko Gudariak* (Basque soldiers), sung ritually with the hand raised in a clenched fist salute (Casquete 2006a, pp. 195–205).

In radical Basque nationalism death in war is not absent of meaning. What George L. Mosse called the 'Myth of the War Experience' is the process by which war is seen 'as a meaningful and even sacred event' (1990, p. 7) and it is fully internalized by the national community. The *etarra*'s death is seen as the ultimate sacrifice given for the sake of his homeland. This idealistic act is meant to be understood in almost sacramental terms, as a sacred event whose personal transformative power is approximate to that experienced by religious martyrs. If the taking up of arms is a rite of passage marking the transition from boyhood to manhood, then violent death in the course of duty is to be seen in similarly ritualistic terms, as the transformation of a human into a new, more permanent state, one which approaches sainthood (Zulaika 1988, pp. 283–7). Besides, the heroic death is not the end of the war but the beginning. The fallen soldier allows the cycle of violence to re-start itself. Fallen *gudaris* are seen to be the ultimate expression that there is 'a problem' and that the spiral of action-repression-action is needed. As Begoña Aretxaga points out in her study of funerary proceedings, the dead have made their sacrifice and the living have to accept their debt and act on it.

After the memorial service to one dead *abertzale*, the mayor of his home village told the gathered crowd:

> At times we ask ourselves it if is worth the trouble to go on fighting and working, if this is nothing more than banging our heads against (established) power, which is so meticulous and which always wants to deceive us. But one must say Yes, that it is necessary to go on fighting, because Mikel fought, and we have to work and fight, as he did, loving the Basque people, as he did. (Aretxaga 1988:53)

There is, of course, a pressing need to make sense of the death of an *etarra*. An armed organization cannot constantly reflect on the use of political violence. Otherwise, how can one make sense of the recent death of the dedicated militant? There are, then, large incentives to continue with the armed struggle and glorify the sacrifice of ETA members. Unless this is done, their remembrance as *gudaris* might be endangered. As Telesforo Monzón once put it, 'if we lose, the martyrs of ETA will be terrorists, but if we win, they will be heroes' (Herri Batasuna 1999, p. 426).

Conclusion

The memory of a nationalist movement is a conglomerate of individual experiences that has been deliberately appropriated and shaped to mark social boundaries and define a sense of belonging. The process by which this collective memory is formed is complex and many times unpredictable. Memories are sustained by national traditions, myths and symbols which are constantly renewed by nationalist elites. Often, a new political and ideological setting urges nationalist leaders to fabricate or distort the past in order to define a new political project. In clear contradistinction to history though, the nation's narrative, to borrow Bhaba's phrase, involves forgetting as well as remembering. The politics of war memory in radical Basque nationalism are characterized by the inclusion of facts that the *abertzale* left considers to be worth remembering in order to portray the recent past as an unambiguous story of moral success. There is nothing new about the omission of actual facts to construct a national memory. As both Renan and Hobsbawm suggested, the social memories of all nations have been constructed in this way.

National memories are important because they outlive individual participants of history and influence the way new generations look at their past. In the case of radical Basque nationalism, the main purpose of the politics of war memory is to strengthen the emotional bonds of the radical community, identify the villains and heroes of the age-old Basque drama and glorify the sacrifice of ETA militants. In the same way as state bureaucracies do with their fallen soldiers, the public remembrance of fallen *gudaris* serves the ritual of uplifting active *etarras*, recruiting future members and persuading them to lay down their lives for the Basque homeland. The current cycle of political violence is seen by radical nationalists as the last stage in the long-term conflict opposing Basques and Spaniards. Such an ethnohistory and the need to glorify past sacrifices make the use of force a tactical, strategic and moral need. The living are seen to have an obligation to the dead lineage of *gudaris* who have willingly sacrificed their lives against the invader since the times of Charlemagne. Radical nationalists define the hardship endured by young Basques as political martyrdom in order to maintain popular support for its violent cause and provide a powerful and emotive symbol for new generations of militants. Through martyrdom, the arrest or death of an ETA militant is no longer a defeat, but a sublime example of symbolic power, a resource used by members of the radical community to generate strong emotions for a 'good cause' and recruit new members. For existing members, their duty is to emulate the example set before them and lead the fight for Basque independence in the hope they will be followed by the masses at a later stage.

A successful national narrative often allows for the personal memories of the individual to be interpreted and understood as part of a wider communal narrative. When there is a continuous disagreement between the individual and the collective, the national message fails to be effective and needs to be revisited or abandoned. At the moment, the politics of war memory continue to persuade young Basques who willingly join the armed group. Whether they join for patriotism, love of adventure, to prove their manliness, for social advancement or because they are looking for camaraderie, their arrest or death is currently being interpreted in the same way. Their will to sacrifice is inserted in a grand narrative whereby the nation is energized and the hero is for ever remembered for fulfilling his duty.

References

AGUILAR, PALOMA 1998 'The memory of the civil war in the transition to democracy: the peculiarity of the Basque case', *West European Politics*, vol. 21, no. 4, pp. 88–109
ANDERSON, BENEDICT 1983 *Imagined Communities: Reflections on the Origin and Spread of Nationalism*, London: Verso
ARETXAGA, BEGOÑA 1988 *Los funerales en el nacionalismo radical vasco: Ensayo antropológico*, San Sebastián: Baroja
CASQUETE, JESÚS 2006a 'Música y funerales en el nacionalismo vasco radical', *Historia y Política*, vol. 15, pp. 191–215
—— 2006b *El poder de la calle: ensayos sobre acción colectiva*, Madrid: Centro de Estudios Políticos y Constitucionales

EDLES, LAURA DESFOR 1998 *Symbol and Ritual in the New Spain: The Transition to Democracy after Franco*, Cambridge: Cambridge University Press
GILLIS, JOHN R. 1994 *Commemorations: The Politics of National Identity*, Princeton, NJ: Princeton University Press
HAMILTON, CARRIE 2007 *Women and ETA: The Gender Politics of Radical Basque Nationalism*, Manchester: Manchester University Press
HERRI BATASUNA 1999 *Herri Batasuna 20 años de lucha por la libertad: 1978–1998*, San Sebastián
HOBSBAWM, ERIC and RANGER, TERENCE 1983 *The Invention of Tradition*, Cambridge: Cambridge University Press
JASPER, JAMES M. 1997 *The Art of Moral Protest: Culture, Biography, and Creativity in Social Movements*, Chicago, IL: University of Chicago Press
JÁUREGUI BERECIARTU, GURUTZ 1981 *Ideología y estrategia política de ETA: Análisis de su evolución entre 1959 y 1968*, Madrid: Siglo XXI
MACCLANCY, JEREMY 1997 'To die in the Basqueland: martyrdom in northern Iberia', in Joyce Pettigrew (ed.), *Martyrdom and Political Resistance: Essays from Asia and Europe*, Amsterdam: VU University Press, pp. 111–33
MARVIN, CAROLYN and INGLE, DAVID W. 1999 *Blood Sacrifice and the Nation: Totem Rituals and the American Flag*. Cambridge: Cambridge University Press
MATA LÓPEZ, JOSÉ MANUEL 1993 *El nacionalismo vasco radical: Discurso, organización y expresiones*, Bilbao: Universidad del País Vasco
MOSSE, GEORGE L. 1975 *The Nationalization of the Masses*, New York: Howard Fertig
────── 1990 *Fallen Soldiers: Reshaping the Memory of the World Wars*, Oxford: Oxford University Press
MURO, DIEGO 2005 'Nationalism and nostalgia: the case of radical Basque nationalism', *Nations and Nationalism*, vol. 11, no. 4, pp. 571–90
────── 2008 *Ethnicity and Violence: The Case of Radical Basque Nationalism*, London: Routledge
MURO, DIEGO and QUIROGA, ALEJANDRO 2005 'Spanish nationalism: ethnic or civic?', *Ethnicities*, vol. 5, no. 1, pp. 9–29
OLSON, MANCUR 1998 *The Logic of Collective Action: Public Goods and the Theory of Groups*, Cambridge, MA: Harvard University Press
RENAN, ERNEST 1990 'What is a nation?', in Homi K. Bhabha (ed.), *Nation and Narration*, London: Routledge, pp. 8–22
REYERO, CARLOS 1999 *La escultura conmemorativa en España: La edad de oro del monumento público, 1820–1914*, Madrid: Cátedra
RINCÓN, LUCIANO 1985 *ETA (1974–1984)*, Barcelona: Plaza & Janés
SÁEZ DE LA FUENTE, IZASKUN 2002 *El Movimiento de Liberación Nacional Vasco: Una religión de sustitución*, Bilbao: Instituto Diocesano de Teología y Pastoral/Desclée de Brouwer
SÁNCHEZ-CUENCA, IGNACIO 2001 *El Estado contra ETA: las estrategias del terrorismo*, Barcelona: Tusquets Editores
SHAW, MARTIN 1997 'Past wars and present conflicts: from the Second World War to the Gulf', in Martin Evans and Ken Lunn (eds), *War and Memory in the Twentieth Century*, Oxford and New York: Berg, pp. 191–205
TURNER, CHARLES 2006 'Nation and commemoration', in Gerard Delanty and Krishnan Kumar (eds), *SAGE Handbook of Nations and Nationalism*, London: Sage, pp. 205–13
ZERUBAVEL, EVIATAR 2003 *Time Maps: Collective Memory and the Social Shape of the Past*. Chicago, IL: University of Chicago Press
ZULAIKA, JOSEBA 1988 *Basque Violence: Metaphor and Sacrament*, Princeton, NJ: Princeton University Press

The patrimonial state and inter-ethnic conflicts in Nigeria

Ukana B. Ikpe

Abstract

Conflicts of various kinds in Nigeria have often been attributed to ethnicity. For instance, communal clashes, electoral violence and so on have all been rooted in ethnicity. However, there is an indirect relationship between, say, inter-party competition and ethnicity. What intervenes between ethnicity as independent variable and conflict as a dependent variable is the patrimonial character of the Nigerian state. Patrimonialism emphasizes personal and clientelist rule in which state officers dispense resources to clients in exchange for loyalty and services. The ease with which state offices are personalized, commoditized and commercialized increases their stakes. This calls for utilization of all imaginable strategies including mobilization of ethnic solidarity by political elites. Ethnic acrimony engendered by one instance of mobilization keeps recurring in other instances to entrench inter-ethnic conflict.

Introduction

Several scholars and political leaders have used ethnicity as a primary analytic variable for explaining some fundamental aspects of political behavior in Nigeria. Even today, the most dependable strategy for mobilizing political support by political elites in Nigeria is appeal to ethnic solidarity. Consequently, political competition in Nigeria usually takes the form of ethnic or communal rivalry for the control of state power, which is often privatized, commoditized and commercialized for the benefit of officials and their communal/ethnic groups, and to the disadvantage of those who lose out or are not sufficiently strong in the contest. As a result, these competitions are consistently tempestuous and considered in zero-sum terms. Ethnicity is often blamed for this systemic chaos. However, although this may seem true, the relationship is not primary because the cardinal factor is located, not in ethnicity itself, but in the activator of ethnicity, which this essay identifies as the patrimonial character of the Nigerian state. Hence, the thesis of this essay is that the patrimonial state in Nigeria shapes and conditions inter-ethnic relations.

Theory of ethnicity and the socio-political environment of Nigeria

Ethnicity is a social phenomenon associated with interaction among members of different ethnic groups within a political system of which language and culture are the most outstanding characteristics (Nnoli 1978, p. 5). Thus, ethnicity is congenital in a political society comprising diverse ethnic groups, which suggests that interactions between ethnic groups within the same political system produce ethnicity. This interrelationship tends to generate 'a common consciousness of being one in relation to the other relevant ethnic group'. In turn, this creates in-group/out-group boundaries, which, over time, the various ethnic groups come to guard jealously (Nnoli 1978, pp. 6–7). From this perspective, ethnicity therefore becomes a process for politicizing ethnic identities (Hendricks 1995; Eriksen 1996, p. 30).

Ethnicity as a political problem, invariably, is inescapable in a multi-ethnic state. According to one popular view, politicization of ethnicity 'occurs because of two overlapping factors: interest of the elites and groups competition for scarce resources' (Rothchild 1986). This is the focus of two prominent schools of thought on ethnicity and conflict: the rational choice theory and the radical theory. The rational choice theory postulates that conflict will occur when two or more ethnic populations come to compete for the same valued and scarce resources of the society, such as allocation of national revenue, normal benefits and largesse of state – employment, education, election, representation and, most of all, the control of power (Osaghae 1992, p. 49; Olzak and Nagel 1986). What makes politicization of ethnicity dangerous is inequality among the contesting groups: some of them are advanced, while others are backward; some dominating and others are dominated; and, because of its zero-sum strategy in which the winner sweeps the stakes, conflict based on it tends to be cut-throat, with the persistent danger of violence (Osaghae 1992, p. 49). Inter-ethnic conflicts occur when groups feel denied of access to what they consider as their right and they interpret this exclusion as domination and discrimination by the stronger and more advantaged group (Ibrahim 1994).

On the other side of the theoretical fence is the radical or the critical school, which has a largely Marxist orientation. Its focus is on the link between class and ethnicity. According to this school, ethnicity, far from being the result of inter-ethnic competition for scarce resources, is a tool of class struggle for the ruling or the dominant classes. In Nigeria and Africa in general, Nnoli (1978), p. 130) observed that ethnicity has a class character and its major function in the political system is to obscure class differences within a communal group as well as to mobilize mass support for the contending factions of the same privileged classes. From a similar radical position, Yolamu Barongo (1987) argues that, in Nigeria, ethnicity and its accompanying problems result from the antagonistic material interests of individuals and the various groups, which, for the most part, are generated by the existing capitalist economic system. Furthermore, ethnic or tribal identities are the most favoured means of mass mobilization for elite members of ethnic groups for corporate actions against other groups when they are competing for resources in the forms of political power, jobs and other material rewards (Barongo 1987, p. 72).

The position of the radical school has come under severe criticism by the rational theorists and other scholars who accord ethnicity an independent existence. According to Osaghae 'to say that it [ethnicity] does not exist outside the class context is to deny it any amount of relative autonomy' (1994, p. 140). Besides, ethnicity is not a monopoly of the elite class. Non-elites who seek material and social advancement also frequently employ the ethnic strategy by establishing dependent ties with highly placed members from their communities in the national political arena (Young 1976, p. 303; Osaghae 1992, p. 48).

However, both the rational and radical theories are apposite for the explication of ethnic politics in Nigeria. It would be irrational to deny that inter-ethnic contestation for resources produce ethnicity, which sometimes results in open inter-ethnic conflict. Similary, it would be unrealistic to reject that ethnicity is a manipulative tool of political elites in Nigeria in their struggle to control state power. It is common for Nigerian politicians to engage in 'categoric politics' whenever they compete for power. This, according to Margaret Peil (1976, pp. 66–98), means the mobilization of ethnic groups and other primordial sentiments by political leaders right from formation of parties to canvassing for votes. Indeed, the political pertinence of ethnicity lies in its capacity to create and sustain groups' consciousness with significant potentials for political mobilization of its members, which when actualized could threaten the stability of the state (Ganguly and Taras 1998; Ibrahim 1994, p. 16).

Nevertheless, the common, yet highly pernicious, effect of ethnic mobilization is the escalation of groups' exclusiveness, which, according to Nnoli (1978), p. 8), results in nepotism and corruption and a situation where merit is sacrificed on the altar of ethnic chauvinism and solidarity. The appropriateness of radical and rational theories notwithstanding, Milton Esman (1994) has cautioned that the political effects of ethnicity may not be fully grasped unless the focus is shifted from group conflict and class struggle to environmental factors that shape and condition ethnicity; that is, the examination of the threats and opportunities that ethnicity affords its users. Hence, attention should be paid, particularly, to the state because the strategies it adopts to accommodate ethnic demands are elemental in shaping inter-ethnic relations within the country. Besides, states sometimes selectively confirm, co-opt, reinforce or even create ethnic and other identities (Campbell 1997, p. 74). It is for this reason that this essay will focus on the Nigerian state and its patrimonial character, and the pattern of inter-ethnic relations it generates.

Patrimonialism and ethnicity: a symbiotic relationship

Patrimonialism as a concept was developed by Max Weber to describe a system of government based on personal rule in which the ruler dispenses offices and other benefits to subordinates in return for loyalty, support and services (Weber 1978, p. 1031). This also applies to sub-types such as neo-patrimonialism, prebendalism and clientelism in which support for the government or the political regime is generated and maintained through distribution of state largesse such as offices, grants, licenses, contracts and so on (Roth 1968; Theobald 1982). What distinguishes prebendalism from patrimonialism is the absence of authority of the personal ruler and the existence of a feigned legal-rational order and, sometimes, a democratic facade. Neo-patrimonialism describes personal rule that operates under a democratic cloak but continues to retain basic patrimonial characteristics such as 'hierarchical particularistic exchanges, patronage, nepotism and favors for official actions' (O'Donnell 1996, p. 40). According to Rene Lemarchand (1972, p. 69, 1988), clientelism is a personalized relationship between a set of actors (i.e. patrons and clients) commanding unequal wealth, status or influence, based on conditional loyalties and involving mutually beneficial transactions. Clientelism is therefore more of a strategy of patrimonialism than a system of government because prebendalism, patrimonialism and neo-patrimonialism are all particularistic systems, which operate through patron-client networks. Besides, they all describe and study the same socio-political phenomenon: privatization and commoditization of political power and state offices for the benefit of the rulers and office-holders. From these discussions, it would appear that a patrimonial system has five principal characteristics:

1. political power is controlled by a personal ruler or a cabal of patrons or both;

2. there is an absence of separation between public and private realms for state officials;
3. political offices are regarded as personal rewards and benefits for officials;
4. the exercise of public authority is utilized to serve rulers and officials, and;
5. the system operates through numerous patron-client networks and relationships.

The symbiotic relationship between patrimonialism (and its subtypes) and ethnicity was first demonstrated in Rene Lemarchand's seminal work:

> It is less obvious; however, that clientelism and ethnicity have seldom operated independently of each other. ... Just as ethnicity has sometimes been credited with integrative properties that really belong to the realm of clientelism, so, clientelism as an integrative mechanism has often developed out of exigencies of ethnic fragmentation. (Lemarchand 1972, p. 69)

Furthermore, ethnicity and clientelism may have overlapping memberships, with some individuals solidly anchored in the ethnic sub-structure and others acting as intermediary links between this substructure and the higher reaches of the clientelist pyramid. Therefore, what may be taken for clear example of ethnicity at one level may be nothing more than lower reticulations of a more extensive clientelist network (Lemarchand 1972, p. 69).

This relationship is also highlighted when ethnicity is considered as a tool of manipulation for political elites. As Nigeria is a dependent capitalist state with underdeveloped productive forces, the bulk of the bourgeoisie do not produce wealth by engaging in productive ventures but rather they accumulate from state resources. The ease with which this is done has created a ravenous ruling elite class, which has come to depend entirely on state power for private accumulations. For this class, capturing state power through which access to state resources is secured has come to be highly prized. In the process, political elites rely extensively on mobilization of ethnic sentiments and solidarity for electoral support or political blackmail. Political elites assume the role of ethnic/communal patrons who compete with other communal patrons for their communities' shares of the 'national cake' and their own personal rewards as patrons.

The response of the masses to ethnic calls by their elite members is positive even though they (masses) are not convinced about the rectitude and sincerity of their leaders in pursuing selfless interest for the benefit of the community. Yet still, they want their communal members to be part of the government even if all they do is embezzle public funds. In fact, there is a strong belief in Nigeria that communities without their kinsmen in government can hardly benefit from government patronage, which comes through amenities such as electricity, portable water, schools, hospitals and award of contracts to individual communal members (Joseph, 1987, p. 175; Ikpe 1999). Thus, elite members have a three-fold interrelated responsibility: representing their communal/ethnic groups in the struggle for state power and resources against other communal groups; being the conduit through which state largesse flows to their respective groups; and acting as a two-way channel of communication between the communal groups and the state, and between the state and the communal groups. The struggle for linkages between ethnic/communal groups and the state, through their patrons, is the fundamental problem underlying the frequent conflicts between the majority and minority ethnic groups at the local, state and national levels. The partialness of state interest is inherent in a patrimonial state like Nigeria, such that the state easily becomes an instrument of private and sectional interest (Williams 1980, p. 48; Ake 1985; Falola and Ihonvbere 1985, pp. 241–3). Important state policies often respond to interests of ethnic patrons. For instance, government created some new states and local governments to give political fiefdoms to some ethnic patrons. However, when patrons' demands are not widely accepted, especially by other affected ethnic groups, they generate inter-communal/ethnic conflicts, which can be violent. Such were the cases of the Ife-Modakeke crisis in Osun State; the Eket-Ibeno crisis in Akwa Ibom State; the Ijaw-Itsekiri crisis in Delta State; and the Zangon-Kartaf crisis in Kaduna State. In all these crises, creation of local government or the location of its headquarters was the predominant cause of disputes.

The ethnic situation in Nigeria is comparable to that in many other African countries especially after independence. For instance, in Liberia, Rwanda, Burundi, Uganda, Zaire, Angola, Sudan and Ethiopia, Carlene Edie observed that political parties were all ethnic based because 'political dominance translated into control of political offices and better access to jobs, housing, and other valued services. Competitions for increased access to such scarce resources favor mobilization and collective actions along ethnic lines' (2003, p. 84). Edie argues further that the winner-takes-all style of politics at this period also encouraged collective actions based on ethnic identity because the practice perpetuated economic deprivation among, or denied overall opportunity to, losers in election. In the political realm, this meant that only members of the ethnic-based regime controlled the best access to jobs, housing and other valued resources. This was the reason that political parties tended to be ethnic based, that particular ethnic groups would support candidates from their own ethnic groups and that violence during elections has frequently been along ethnic lines. Thus, competitive party politics affected ethnic groups by fomenting ethnic insecurity and increasing the potential for mobilization on a large scale spearheaded by ethnic power elites.

These ethnic power elites constitute ethnic intermediaries, who channel and present the demands of their ethnic groups to national political leadership and transmit demands and expectations of that leadership to their constituents (Chazan *et al.* 1999, p. 112; Schraeder 2000, p. 140). According to Chazan *et al.* (1999, pp. 112–13), ethnic intermediaries are the patrons who promote collective ethnic political and economic interests at the centre within the network of political clientelism. Ethnic patrons lead their groups in the contests against other ethnic groups. They are important in all regimes, democratic or military, but appear to be more important in military regimes because of the absence of formal institutions of political participation and representation.

Patrimonial rule and ethnicity in Nigeria

Colonial administrations created and politicized ethnicity in Africa when they changed the dynamics of ethnic relations by placing particular resources in the hands of one or another of the ethnic groups within a state, and dictated policy in favour of, or inimically to, one or another of the ethnic groups (Nnoli 1978, 1989; Samatar 1997, p. 695; Edie 2003). In Nigeria, for instance, ethnicity emerged with the British policy of indirect rule, which emphasized separate administration of the respective ethnic groups according to their traditional political systems (Crowder 1978, pp. 191–2). The colonial powers consistently discouraged intermingling of ethnic groups, while vociferously propagating their separateness, culturally and historically, and the advantages of maintaining these demarcations, which was an effective way of checking coordinated groups' dissidence against colonial rule (Campbell 1997, p. 62). This colonial policy heightened groups' senses of exclusiveness and distinctiveness. The most devastating aspect of this separatist policy was isolating the North administratively from the rest of the country from 1900 to the 1951 Macpherson Constitution. In the process, the North, being predominantly Muslim, was encouraged to protect itself against the morally bankrupt Christian South. This separatist policy and indoctrination was so intense that it even strained the relationship between colonial officers in the Northern and Southern Provinces (Kirk-Greene 1967). This idea of North-South dichotomy has persisted in Nigeria until today, and it is the biggest hindrance to national integration (Ikpe 2004, p. 104).

The patrimonial state in the First and Second Republics

When the colonialists decentralized the administration of the country, a three-region structure based on the three major ethnic groups was created. The Northern Region had the Hausa/Fulani as the dominant group, with such minorities as Nupe, Idoma, Gwari, Igala, Tiv and so on. The Western Region had the Yoruba as the major ethnic group with minorities like Itsekiri, Urhobo, Edo and others, while Igbo was the major ethnic group in the Eastern Region with the Ibibio, Efik, Ijaw, Ekoi and others constituting the minority groups. Related to this were the sizes of the regions. The Northern Region was twice as large as the two southern regions (Eastern and Western Regions). Conflicts between the North and South became more flagrant as independence approached, particularly when the 1954 constitution provided for appointments of federal and regional ministers, and power to control regional resources vested in the regional governments. In the course of competing for these offices and resources, political elites mobilized forces of ethnicity for support. Consequently, the major political parties that emerged as the official vehicles of competition had ethnic identities in the three regions (Osuntokun 1979, p. 101). Due to this regional structure, conflict was perennial, based on disputes over the sharing of power and resources within the regions between the majority groups and their respective minorities, and at the inter-regional level between the majority groups of the three regions.

With power to control resources vested in local political leaders, political competition in the regions became brutal, normless and ruthless. In the process, politicization of ethnicity increased because it was the only ideology espoused by the competing parties (Anifowose 1982, pp. 187–8). Accordingly, each party was identified with a majority section, which used political power to enhance the economic and social positions of their kinsmen and communities to the conspicuous neglect of the minority groups, thereby creating an environment characterized by ethnic tensions, political instability and social mal-integration (Post and Vickers 1973, p. 42; Barongo 1987, p. 69).

In the Second Republic, patrimonial rule took the forms of neo-patrimonialism and prebendalism because it operated with an elaborate democratic façade. Nevertheless, there were several changes in the political and socio-economic environment, which strengthened ethno-patrimonial politics in Nigeria's Second Republic. First, the four large regions were broken into twelve, then later, nineteen states. The implication of this for the Second Republic was that new majorities and minorities emerged, thereby increasing and complicating the problem of inter-ethnic relations as the new minorities began agitation for new states. This was a major source of conflict between ethnic groups in the respective states. In addition, creation of new states meant the emergence of new patrons on the political scene, who would also begin to mobilize ethnic solidarity to gain prominence at the centre. Rivalry between intending patrons in these new states was a potent source of conflict.

The second factor was the replacement of cash crops by petroleum, which increased the revenue of the state tremendously. The availability of oil revenues accompanied a new revenue allocation formula, which gave all incomes earned to the federal government. Concurrently, the state markedly expanded into economic and social arenas, with such instruments as the Land Use Decree, Indigenization Policy and so on. The Indigenization Policy, for instance, gave the federal government the power to acquire controlling shares in all foreign companies and appoint chairpersons, directors and board members to the newly nationalized companies. These positions largely went to relatives, friends and other clients of top government functionaries. Similarly, with the Land Use Decree, the state, through its officers, could acquire lands anywhere they wanted in the country (Ake 1985, p. 22). These changes provided more bounteous resources for private accumulation by state officers than were available in the First Republic. Because resources concentrated at the centre, the focus of politics in the Second Republic also shifted from the regions or states to the federal government. Consequently, politics to control the centre was bound to be more desperate and unscrupulous than was the case in the First Republic. This was apparent in the 1979 election but quite egregious in 1983 when the soldiers were no longer on the political scene.

The product of a ferocious struggle to control state power and its resources has always been the mobilization of ethnic solidarity by the contestants. Therefore, in the Second Republic, ethnic-oriented parties, as in the First Republic, also emerged. As it turned out, the National Party of Nigeria (NPN), representing the Hausa-Fulani, won the 1979 election and took control of a patrimonial government. This government functioned through a pyramid of patron-client clusters and networks, which incorporated sectional identities into the state. This was the soul of the popular zoning system: a clientelist system in which the state related with the society through the affiliation of individuals acknowledged as patrons of their particular communities (Joseph 1987, pp. 58–60). Unfortunately, not every communal group could have patrons to act as conduits for their shares of amenities; as such, communal groups without representatives on the board of patrons were bound to feel neglected, deprived and discriminated against.

Military rule, patrimonialism and inter-ethnic relations

The military has controlled the Nigerian state for a greater period of its existence as an independent nation, so, if ethno-patrimonial exchanges dominate state-society relations in Nigeria, then the military has contributed immensely to this. Politicization of the military began very early in the history of Nigeria. In fact, by 1960, the North got 50 per cent enlistment of officers in the army to reflect its size, which they claimed was twice that of the two southern regions (Luckham 1971; Miners 1971; Ademoyega 1981). Thus, being an officer in the army came to depend on one's ethnic group/region, which promoted inter-ethnic disharmony within the officer cadre of the army. It was this problem, combined with those of the larger society, which ignited the first coup led by Southern officers in January 1966, which, in turn, inspired a Northern-led coup as retaliation (Dudley 1973, p. 134). This crisis, as is well known, culminated in the civil war, which lasted for nearly three years.

It is significant to note that Northern officers were conscious of their dependence on their ethnic/regional political patronage, and, therefore, had immense interest in sustaining that system of domination. At this time, the military had degenerated into what could felicitously be described as 'ethnic soldiers' (Enloe 1980). Officers like T. Y. Danjuma, Murtala Muhammed, Yakubu Gowon, Hassan Katsina and a host of others were fervent believers in the primacy of the North in Nigerian politics. Muhammed masterminded the counter-coup of July 1966, and Yakubu Gowon, who later became the head of state, gave his blessing, while Danjuma was actually the man who killed the incumbent head of state, General Aguiyi Ironsi (Kurfi 1983).

Despite the prevailing equal quota in military recruitments for all states, feelings of ethnic domination in the army have remained high because some ethnic groups, particularly the large ones, have more states, which mean that they also have larger numbers of military officers. Besides, a disproportionate majority of officers who have grown in the profession to be service chiefs, division commanders and so on were from the former Northern Region. Hence, Northern domination is even more glaring during military rule because of the dominant number of military officers from the region. This position supports our earlier argument that 'when a pluralist state is weak and lacking in autonomy, like Nigeria is, the ruling class becomes factionalized and the most advantaged of the factions strives to establish, maintain and recreate its domination' (Oyewole and Ikpe 1994).

The high level of ethnic consciousness in the military suggests that military regimes were susceptible to ethno-patrimonialism (Ikpe 2005). The first military government headed by General Ironsi did not last long but traces of ethno-patrimonialism were obvious. First, his position as head of state and supreme commander marked him out as a personal ruler. Second, the General was accused of surrounding himself with advisers who were his kinsmen. His unification policy was seen by the North as an attempt to promote Igbo ascendancy and domination in Nigerian politics. This, coupled with the loss of their civilian and military leaders in the January 1966 coup, sparked off the counter-coup of July 1966. After this coup, conflict was inevitable between the Northern-led federal government and the Eastern Regional government whose indigenes constituted the bulk of the victims of the July counter-coup.

General Yakubu Gowon headed the next military government. He came to power in the period of crisis and his successful prosecution of the war turned him into a charismatic leader, which converted to being a patrimonial ruler with ease. Gowon's administration was quasi-patrimonial because it was not only brazenly corrupt, but relied upon the 'disposition of offices and shared material rewards to obtain the support of those both within and outside the military which he thought he needed to stay in power' (Ojo 1987, pp. 157–8). According to Richard Joseph (1987, pp. 72–3), this regime was the very best of prebendalism because officers were busy serving their private, ethnic and communal interests, while state governors enjoyed a monopoly of legitimate use of force, and 'acted like provincial chiefs in a decentralized patrimonial order'. Murtala Muhammad who ruled next was a principal beneficiary of political patronage in the First Republic and Gowon's regime. His position as a defender of Northern interest was flagrant. First, he led the Northern counter-coup of July 1966. Second, he reintroduced an imbalanced federal structure in favour of the North. That is, his administration created ten states for the North and nine for the South. Third, his administration initiated the removal of the seat of government from Lagos in the South to Abuja in the North. Although he came to power as a transformed reformer, his past corrupt life and the fact that he had become a charismatic leader made him precariously vulnerable to ethno-patrimonial forces. Moreover, like Ironsi and Gowon, he was primarily a personal ruler.

General Olusegun Obasanjo came to power in February 1976 after the death of Muhammad. This regime is always joined to that of his predecessor as the Muhammad/Obasanjo regime, obviously because he was determined to complete the programmes initiated by the Muhammad administration, and so inherited a substantial legitimacy that Muhammad had gained. However, it was under this regime that the Nigerian state expanded more rapidly and forcefully into economic and social arenas of Nigerian society. As stated already, the prominent instruments of this expansion were the Indigenization Policy, Land Use Decree, universal primary education, Festival of Black and

African Arts [FESTAC 77], the First Lagos International Trade Fair, Operation Feed the Nation, construction of barracks for soldiers and building of a new federal capital at Abuja. All these projects meant spending huge sums of money and patronizing clients and kinsmen with offices, contracts and grants. In effect, this regime increased the proclivity of the state to patrimonialism by engendering the conception that politics is an unremitting and unconstrained struggle for possession and access to state offices with the chief aim of procuring direct material benefits to oneself and one's acknowledged communal and other sectional groups (Joseph 1987, p. 75).

By and large, the most fitting examples of ethno-patrimonial regimes in Nigeria are the Babangida and Abacha regimes. General Babangida came to power in 1985 and ruled until 1993, while General Abacha took over in 1993 after a brief interlude of Interim National Government. The Babangida administration initiated the 'politics of settlement', which, technically, is a strategy combining patrimonialism and incorporation (Ikpe 2005). This strategy depended on identifying and gratifying leaders and powerful members of strong groups capable of generating legitimacy, or precipitating trouble, for the regime. Incorporation extended to such groups as serving and retired army officers, prominent academics and intellectuals, labour leaders, communal political and opinion leaders, and traditional rulers (Amuwo 1990; Ihonvbere 1992, p. 120). At the communal level, Babangida demonstrated the power of government patronage at its best. His home state, Niger State, became a model in terms of infrastructural development because its son was the head of state. And, like all patron-client relationships with dual exchanges, the people of Niger State showed their appreciation by according him a grandiose reception on his retirement, which could best be described as 'Babangida's triumphant entry into Minna'. It is important to note that this event occurred at a time Babangida's popularity had waned in other parts of Nigeria, especially after the annulment of the 12 June 1993 election. Babangida was a strong supporter of Northern dominance in Nigerian politics and government, and he used his regime to foster this project. Certainly, nothing demonstrates the plausibility of this argument better than the annulment of the 12 June election. The major reason for the annulment was that the presidency was moving to the South with the victory of M. K. O. Abiola, and this was unacceptable to a powerful clique of Northern political and military elites (*African Concord* 1993, p. 22; *Tell 1993*). The Abacha administration continued where Babangida stopped with politics of settlement, and the patrimonial characteristics common to personal rule were obvious. Only favourites of the junta were military administrators in the states, federal ministers, state commissioners and even local government functionaries.

The significant thing to note is that, whether it is a military or civilian regime, Nigerian masses and elites see officers of the regime as representatives of their respective communities (Ikpe 1999, p. 150). A typical case occurred when Abacha removed Rear Admiral Allison Madueke as the chief of naval staff and as member of the Provisional Ruling Council [PRC], which most Igbo saw as a conspiracy against them. There was spontaneous Igbo agitation, however, not for reinstatement of Madueke, but for 'another Igboman to represent us in the PRC' (*Sunday Vanguard* 1994). Thus, for Igbo elites and masses, the issue was not the rightness or wrongness of Madueke's dismissal, but having an Igbo representative in the PRC.

Patrimonial politics and the Fourth Republic

Three major political parties contested the transitional election of 1999. The People's Democratic Party [PDP], the All Nigeria People's Party [ANPP] and the Alliance for Democracy [AD]. Both PDP and ANPP were northern-based parties, but had successfully incorporated other sections of the country. The AD's base was the south west – a Yoruba enclave. In that election, there was a consensus to appease the Yoruba for the annulment of 12 June 1993 presidential election which a Yoruba man, M. K. O. Abiola, won. The PDP adopted Olusegun Obasanjo while ANPP and AD combined to present Olu Falae for the election. Thus, either way it would be a Yoruba president. The AD won almost all the offices in Lagos, Oyo, Osun, Ogun, Ondo and Ekiti – all Yoruba states. Nevertheless, it was the PDP that won the presidential election, although its presidential candidate, Obasanjo, did not win even in Ogun, his home state. Thus, Obasanjo had a tenuous hold on the PDP, as it was widely known that he had no 'home-base support', an essential factor in Nigerian politics. However, with careful manipulation of the patronage system at individual and group levels, Obasanjo was able to strengthen his hold on both the party and government, and the Yoruba came to accept him, although they could not help him much politically as most of them were in AD.

Consequently, in the 2003 election, Obasanjo got into a secret agreement with the AD leadership for the AD to contest all the offices except the presidency, which would compel the Yoruba to vote for Obasanjo. The plan succeeded for Obasanjo but backfired for the AD governors. Since the gubernatorial and presidential elections were held simultaneously, with very similar ballot papers, most voters could not distinguish between the presidential and the gubernatorial ballots. Thus, the widely publicized decision to support the PDP presidential candidate (Obasanjo) led to most people picking both the presidential and gubernatorial candidates from the PDP. Apart from Lagos State, PDP won the governorship of all other Yoruba states. This is a classic case of manipulating ethnicity and patronage to win power. However, some analysts have chosen to describe this as the weakening of ethnicity because AD, a Yoruba party, has disintegrated. This argument appears rather presumptuous. If in the 2011 election the Yoruba still vote overwhelmingly for the PDP with Obasanjo gone, then the observation would be correct. Otherwise, if the AD or any other Yoruba-based party suddenly resurrects, then it means the Yoruba voted for the PDP in 2003 and 2007 only to strengthen Obasanjo's position in both the party and national politics to ensure largesse from the state.

Indubitably, the most outstanding feature of patrimonial politics in the Fourth Republic is the emergence of godfatherism. Godfathers are political investors who sponsor candidates to political offices in return for the right to control major appointments, award of contracts and some percentages of revenues allocated to those offices. Politics of godfatherism operates in many of the states of the federation, but it is in Anambra and Oyo States that the typical models exist. Lamidi Adedibu sponsored Governor Ladoja of Oyo State, while Chris Uba sponsored Governor Chris Ngige and almost all other elected officers in Anambra State. When the governors breached the contracts, the godfathers mobilized all their political forces to ensure their removal from office. The resistance by the governors meant large-scale violence between their supporters and those of the godfathers. The magnitude of these conflicts made Anambra and Oyo States almost ungovernable (*Tell 2003, 2004*; Odion 2006, p. 56).

The patrimonial state and ethnic-communal conflicts

The most destructive consequences of patrimonial politics in Nigeria are the local communal conflicts it generates in most of the states. These conflicts follow the same logic of exclusion or inclusion for cornering state resources by elites of these communal groups. For instance, at the root of the Tiv-Jukun conflict in Taraba State, which had persisted intermittently from the colonial period (1959) to its most atrocious stage between 1999 and 2001 (*IRIN News* 2007), was struggle for political power between the Jukuns (majority and indigenes) and Tivs (minority and settlers). Although the immediate causes of conflicts, each time they occur, are land disputes between Tiv farmers and Jukun landowners, nevertheless it is enmity in the political arena that conflagrates petty squabbles into large-scale violence. Jukuns have forcefully thwarted Tiv demands for routes of access to state resources such as political appointments in Taraba State, participation in the control of Wukari Local Government Council and participation in Wukari Traditional Council (Best, Idyorough and Shehu 1999).

Similarly, the Ife-Modakeke conflict became more ferocious when political elites in the two communities began to compete for access to state resources. Land disputes had generated and sustained acrimonies between the Ife (landlords) and the Modakeke (tenants/settlers) in the past, but it was agitation for a separate local government by the Modakeke elites and the opposition by their Ife counterparts that escalated and magnified the brutality of the conflict intermittently between 1981 and 1997 (Albert 1999). In the Zangon-Kataf crisis in Southern Zaria in Kaduna State, the supposed settlers (Hausa/Fulani) were in the dominant position, while the indigenes, the Atyap, alleged discrimination in both the local government and traditional council politics. The creation of Zangon-Kataf Local Government in 1989 in which the Atyap now dominated was obnoxious enough to the Hausa to be a source of tension, which found outlet in February 1992 resistance to the relocation of the Zangon-Kataf market, which the Hausa controlled. Because the Atyaps are mostly Christians while the Hausa are predominantly Muslims, the crisis easily took the form of a religious conflict, which claimed hundreds of lives and several millions of naira worth of property (Akinteye, Wuye and Ashafa 1999).

The Jos conflict also followed the indigenes-versus-settlers pattern, with the settlers appearing to dominate the indigenes. The Hausa (settlers) right from the colonial period had comparative economic and political advantages over the indigenes and, coupled with the fact that majority of the Hausa/Fulani are Muslims while the indigenes are mostly Christians, presented a situation for constant rivalry and conflict. Nevertheless, the levels of these conflicts were minimal until 2001 when indigenes challenged the Hausa/Fulani dominance of the rich Jos North Local Government and some other political appointments in the state. The conflict that had smouldered for a long time burst into open flames in the form of religious/ethnic conflict in September 2001 and destroyed many lives and property. Subsequently, violence-prone tensions became permanent features of Plateau State, waiting for slight provocation. This came in May 2004 with the killing of a Tiv farmer and a Biron man by Fulani herdsmen in Yelwa. As in previous conflicts, this one also assumed a religious dimension, especially after the killing of forty-seven Christians in a church. Violence spread quickly to other towns in the North, particularly Kano, Kaduna and Bauchi (*Newswatch 2004*). In the process, many Igbo settlers and Christians from the South were killed, leading to retaliatory attacks on Hausa/Fulani settlers in Igbo towns like Onitsha and Owerri. The magnitude of the crisis led to the declaration of a state of emergency in Plateau State (*Newswatch 2004*, p. 24).

Although competition for access to state resources remotely caused the Hausa-Yoruba communal conflict of 2 February 2002 in the Idi Araba area of Lagos, nevertheless it constituted a deep-seated source of animosity between the two groups, which was bound to erupt when ignited. This source of animosity was the annulment of 12 June 1993 presidential election won by Chief M. K. O. Abiola (Yoruba) by the Babangida (Hausa-Fulani) regime and, the suspected murder of Abiola and his wife by the Abacha-led (Hausa-Fulani) military junta (*The Week 2002*). The Yoruba felt deprived of opportunity to lead Nigeria after several years of domination by Hausa/Fulani. This led to the creation of a pan-Yoruba organization, O'dua People's Congress (OPC), with a militant youth wing, to sustain agitation for the realization of the Abiola/Yoruba mandate (*The Week 2002*). Thus, a minor dispute over defecation led to a fight, and, with the involvement of the OPC, the tempo of the conflict escalated (Anugwuom, 2002). As the news of the conflict reached the North, reprisal attacks on Yoruba settlers in Northern cities, particularly Kano, occurred.

Summary and conclusion

The task of this essay was to explain how the patrimonial nature of the Nigerian state engenders inter-ethnic conflicts. It has shown that Nigeria is an underdeveloped capitalist state with underdeveloped productive forces and a malformed bourgeois class, which shifts wealth accumulation from commodities and services productions to amassment of private wealth from state resources. The control of state power therefore becomes a cardinal factor in this contest. To ensure victory, political elites mobilize ethnic solidarity in electoral contests. In these competitions, large groups in the national, state or local governments have overt advantages over the smaller groups, which are also reproduced in the accumulation process by the elites of the respective groups and in the provision of amenities to communal groups. This inequality of access to state largesse between groups is largely responsible for inter-ethnic tensions which could be expressed in the forms of secession threats (as is the case with the Ogonis), agitation for new states and local governments, and outright violent inter-communal clashes.

The situation is not different under military regimes because the same patronage and ethnic considerations dominating civil politics also control the military. In fact, all military regimes in Nigeria have exacerbated rather than attenuate ethnic tensions. Excessive patrimonialization of state power has increased the potential for inter-ethnic conflict. The frequent calls for sovereign national conference are an indication that many ethnic/communal groups are not satisfied with the state of the nation. Hence, there is a need for reconstruction and reorganization of the Nigerian state. In the present Fourth Republic politics, there is a need gradually to elevate the status of the citizens above communal groups. That is, the direct focus of policies should be on citizens and not the communal groups, which will necessitate the emergence of ethnic patrons and political acrimony. The fight against corruption should be thorough and sustained, together with the quest for accountability. All these will discourage abuse of office by state officers, lack of distinction between public and private resources, political and bureaucratic corruption and normless competitions for political offices. If there is nothing to gain, political patrons and godfathers will cease to be relevant and their role in mobilization of ethnic solidarity will diminish.

References

ADEMOYEGA, A. 1981 *Why We Struck: The Story of the First Nigerian Coup*, Ibadan: Evans Brothers (Nigeria Publishers)
AFRICAN CONCORD 1993 5 July, Lagos
AKE, CLAUDE 1985 *Political Economy of Nigeria*, Lagos: Longman
AKINTEYE, A., WUYE, J. M. and ASHAFA, M. N. 1999 'Zangon Kataf crisis: a case study', in O. Otite and I. O. Albert (eds), *Community Conflicts in Nigeria: Management, Resolution and Transformation*, Ibadan: Spectrum Books, pp. 222–46
ALBERT, I. O. 1999 'Ife-Modakeke crisis', in O. Otite and I. O. Albert (eds), *Community Conflicts in Nigeria: Management, Resolution and Transformation*, Ibadan: Spectrum Books, pp. 142–83
AMUWO, K. 1990 'Soldiers-rulers and military academic advisors: notes on constitutionalism and democracy in Nigeria with specific reference to the Babangida administration', paper given at Nigerian Political Science Association, 17th Annual Conference, University of Jos, 21–3 November
ANIFOWOSE, REMI 1982 *Violence and Politics in Nigeria: The Tiv and Yoruba Experience*, New York: NOK Publishers International
ANUGWUOM, EDLYNE 2000 'Is democracy really the answer? State of ethnic conflict in Nigeria', paper given at Ethno-Net Africa Conference (UNESCO/MOST Project), Yaounde, Cameroun, 18–21 March
BARONGO, Y. R. 1987 'Ethnic pluralism and democratic stability: the basis of conflict and consensus', in S. E. Oyovbaire (ed.), *Democratic Experiments in Nigeria: Interpretive Essays*, Benin City: Omega Publishers, pp. 65–80
BEST, S. G., IDYOROUGH, A. E. and SHEHU, Z. B. 1999 'Communal conflicts and possibilities of conflict resolution in Nigeria: a case study of the Tiv-Jukun conflicts in Wukari Local Government Area, Taraba State', in O. Otite and I. O. Albert (eds), *Community Conflicts in Nigeria: Management, Resolution and Transformation*, Ibadan: Spectrum Books, pp. 82–117
CAMPBELL, A. 1997 'Ethical ethnicity: a critique', *Journal of Modern African Studies*, vol. 35, no. 1, pp. 35–79
CHAZAN, N., LEWIS, P., MORTIMER, R., ROTHCHILD, D. and STEDMAN, J. 1999 *Politics and Society in Contemporary Africa*, 3rd edn, Boulder, CO: Lynne Rienner
CROWDER, M. 1978 *The Story of Nigeria*, London: Faber
DUDLEY, B. J. 1973 *Instability and Political Order: Politics and Crisis in Nigeria*, Ibadan: University of Ibadan Press
EDIE, CARLENE J. 2003 *Politics in Africa: A New Beginning?*, Belmont, CA: Wadsworth/Thompson Learning
ENLOE, CYNTHIA 1980 *Ethnic Soldiers: State Security in a Divided Society*, London: Penguin

ERIKSEN, THOMAS H. 1996 'Ethnicity, race, class and nation', in Hutchinson John and Smith Anthony D. (eds), *Ethnicity*, London: Oxford University Press, pp. 28–31
ESMAN, MILTON 1994 *Ethnic Politics*, Ithaca, NY: Cornell University Press
FALOLA, T. and IHONVBERE, J. 1985 *The Rise and Fall of Nigeria's Second Republic 1979–1984*, London: Zed Books
GANGULY, RAJAT and TARAS, RAYMOND C. 1998 *Understanding Ethnic Conflict: The International Dimension*, New York: Longman
HENDRICKS, C. 1995 'The national question, ethnicity and the state: some reflections for South Africa', paper given at Biennial Conference, African Political Science Association, Ibadan, Nigeria
IBRAHIM, JIBRIL 1994 'Political exclusion, democratization, and dynamics of ethnicity in Niger', *Africa Today*, vol. 1, no. 3, pp. 15–39
IHONVBERE, J. O. 1992 'The military and political engineering under structural adjustment', *Journal of Political and Military Sociology*, vol. 20, pp. 107–31
IKPE, U. B. 1999 'Pragmatising participation and representation in grassroots democracy in Nigeria', *International Journal of Social Sciences*, vol. 1, no. 2, pp. 141–57
—— 2004 'Public culture and national integration in multi-cultural states: comparative observations from the United States and Nigeria', *Comparative American Studies*, vol. 2, no. 1, pp. 91–114
—— 2005 'Towards explaining the continuing dominance of patrimonial exchanges in state-society relation in Nigeria: the relevance of ethno-patrimonial incorporation model', *Unilag Journal of Politics*, vol. 2, no. 2, pp. 5–34
IRIN NEWS 2007 'Nigeria: focus on central region Tiv, Jukun clashes', UN Office for the Coordination of Humanitarian Affairs, http://www.irinnews.org.IRIN-Africa
JOSEPH, R. A. 1987 *Democracy and Prebendal Politics in Nigeria*, Cambridge: Cambridge University Press
KIRK-GREENE, A. H. M. 1967 'The peoples of Nigeria', *African Affairs*, vol. 66, no. 262, pp. 3–11
KURFI, AHMADU 1983 *The Nigerian General Elections, 1959 and 1979, and the Aftermath*, Lagos: Macmillan Nigerian Publishers
LEMARCHAND, RENE 1972 'Political clientelism and ethnicity in tropical Africa: competing solidarities in nation building', *American Political Science Review*, vol. 66, no. 1, pp. 68–90
—— 1988 'The state, the parallel economy and the changing structure of patronage system', in D. Rothchild and N. Chazan (eds), *The Precarious Balance*, Boulder, CO: Westview Press, pp. 149–70
LUCKHAM, R. 1971 *The Nigerian Military, 1960–67*, Cambridge: Cambridge University Press
MINERS, N. J. 1971 *The Nigerian Army, 1956–1966*, London: Methuen
NEWSWATCH 2004 'A ticking time bomb', 31 May, Lagos
NNOLI, O. 1978 *Ethnic Politics in Nigeria*, Enugu: Fourth Dimension
—— 1989 *Ethnic Politics in Africa*, AAPS Books Project Series, No. 1, Dakar: AAPS
ODION, LOUIS 2006 'Oyo: the end of politics', *Sunday Sun*, Lagos, 10 December
O'DONNELL, GUILLERMO 1996 'Illusions about consolidation', *Journal of Democracy*, vol. 7, no. 2, pp. 35–51
OJO, O. J. B. 1987 'Military rule, democracy and the post-military state', in S. E. Oyovbaire (ed.), *Democratic Experiments in Nigeria*, Benin City: Omega Publishers, pp. 149–72
OLZAK, S. and NAGEL, J. (eds) 1986 *Comparative Ethnic Relations*, New York: Academic Press
OSAGHAE, EGHOSA 1992 'Ethnicity and democracy', in Deji Fasoro, *et al.* (eds), *Understanding Democracy*, Ibadan: Centre for Democratic Information, pp. 40–52
—— 1994 'Ethnicity in Africa or African ethnicity?', in U. Himmelstrand, K. Kinyanjui and E. Mbrugu (eds), *African Perspectives on Development*, London: James Currey, pp. 137–51

OSUNTOKUN, JIDE 1979 'The historical background of Nigerian federalism', in A. B. Akinyemi, *et al.* (eds), *Readings on Federalism*, Lagos: Nigerian Institute of International Affairs, pp. 91–102

OYEWOLE, A. and IKPE, U. B. 1994 'Politics of regime stability and national instability in Nigeria', paper presented to the 20th Annual Conference of the Nigerian Political Science Association, Obafemi Awolowo University, lle-Ife, 28 February–2 March

PEIL, MARGARET 1976 *Nigerian Politics: The People's View*, London: Cassell

POST, K. and VICKERS, M. 1973 *Structure and Conflict in Nigeria, 1960–66*, London: Heinemann

ROTH, GUENTHER 1968 'Personal rulership patrimonialism and empire building in the new states', *World Politics*, vol. 20, no. 2, pp. 194–206

ROTHCHILD, D. 1986 'State and ethnicity in Africa: a policy perspective', in Neil Nevitte and Charles H. Kennedy (eds), *Ethnic Preference and Public Policy in Developing States*, Boulder, CO: Lyne Rienner, pp. 15–61

SAMATAR, ABDI S. 1997 'Leadership and ethnicity in the making of African state models: Botswana and Somalia', *Third World Quarterly*, vol. 18, no. 4, pp. 687–707

SCHRAEDER, PETER J. 2000 *African Politics and Society: A Mosaic in Transformation*, Boston, MA, and New York: Bedford/St. Martins

SUNDAY VANGUARD 1994 28 August, Lagos

TELL 1993 5 July, Lagos

—— 2003 6 October, Lagos

—— 2004 22 November, Lagos

THEOBAL, ROBIN 1982 'Patrimonialism', *World Politics*, vol. 34, no. 4, pp. 248–59

WEBER, MAX 1978 *Economy and Society*, Berkeley, CA: University of California Press

THE WEEK 2002 'Hausa–OPC war', 8 February, Lagos

WILLIAMS, GAVIN 1980 *State and Society in Nigeria*, Ondo: Afrografika

YOUNG, CRAWFORD 1976 *The Politics of Cultural Pluralism*, Madison, WI: University of Wisconsin Press

Basque-Atlantic shores: ethnicity, the nation-state and the diaspora in Europe and America (1808–98)

Fernando Molina and Pedro J. Oiarzabal

Abstract

Classical approaches to nationalism and ethnicity have traditionally understood ethnic groups as ethno-nationalist groups that were irrevocably predisposed to constitute political entities in order to preserve and promote their assumed unique socio-historical and cultural markers. However, we argue that the Basque case illustrates much the opposite. Basque ethnic identity was not only utilized by the Basque nationalist movement, but it helped to form diverse processes of national identifications such as the Spanish, French, or Venezuelan for that matter throughout the nineteenth century. In this sense, the debate on Basque ethnicity is not a marginal issue in the re-elaboration of Spanishness and identity politics on both sides of the Atlantic but a central and main one in the Spanish and Latin American national and state-building discourses.

Introduction

Ethnicity as a cultural tool may contribute to the formation of multiple processes of coexisting or opposing national identifications. Though not exclusively based on ethnicity, ethnic identities can help construct different types of nationalisms (Neils Conzen 1992; De Vos 1995). Ideologies and political cultures can also make use of certain elements of a given ethnic identity; although identity in relation to a group is something quite different from an ideology, which refers to a specific political project. Moreover, a given identity does not owe its existence to a particular ideology, and the association of an identity with a particular ideology is not always exclusive.

By examining the Basque-Spanish case in the nineteenth century, we will explore how ethnic nationalism, as well as other diverse and contradictory contemporaneous cultures and ideologies in states with multiple nations capitalized on ethnic identity. Our argument is that an ethnic identity did not always become a unique ethno-national identity, but rather helped to formulate diverse political expressions in a changing world, such as that of nineteenth-century Europe and America.

The Basque diaspora and transnational spaces, 1492–1898

As of June 2007, the Basque diaspora has engendered 198 associations in twenty-four countries,[1] each explicitly self-defined as Basque. Authors such as Douglass and Bilbao (1975) and Oiarzabal (2004, 2005, 2006) have reformulated contemporary and past Basque identities in a global, transnational, and diasporic context. Diaspora communities are formed by emigrants who shared a collective identity in their homeland, which socio-economic and/or political conditions forced them to leave, or who for other reasons chose to settle in another country. Collectively and associatively, some of them attempt to preserve or develop cultural, religious and even political expressions of their identity, reflecting different degrees of assimilation into their host societies. Diaspora associations create transnational networks that maintain varying degrees of personal, institutional, cultural, social, economic, political and business ties with the homeland and with other countries where there is a Basque presence: a globe-spanning network of attachments and allegiances.

Pagden and Canny consider the history of the formation of specific identities in colonial societies to be 'the history of the transformation of (cultural or social) values', which were 'initially imported from the metropolitan cultures'. They argue that this transformation was the result of 'self-perception', 'self-assertion' and 'the recognition of separateness' (1987, p. 269) from metropolitan values. Historical and socio-anthropological studies (Douglass and Bilbao 1975; Douglass 1989; Azcona 1992; Iriani 2000) showed that Basques were already a self-aware, distinctive ethnic group when they arrived in the New World in 1492. Douglass and Bilbao argued that 'this awareness was translated into collective actions, mutual assistance, [and] a common stance towards outsiders [such] that the Basques were set apart from other Iberian and Creole groups' (1975, p. 74). Additionally, claims to universal nobility and pure blood made by the inhabitants of the Basque Provinces secured their access to administrative, military and other high positions throughout the Hispanic Empire, 'since access to administrative posts and honorific positions was reserved for persons who could demonstrate "Old-Christian" [i.e. pre-Arab conquest] genealogical credentials, which is to say those with a demonstrable claim to *limpieza de sangre* or clean blood' (Douglass 2000, p. 142).

Several authors (García 1996; Gonzalbo 1996; Herzog 1996; Ortíz de la Tabla y Ducase 1996) have demonstrated how the Basques knit themselves into tight networks of powerful families who were the hegemonic, socio-economic and political elites throughout the Empire's colonial and post-colonial eras. Casaus (1996, p. 298) estimated that in the eighteenth century, 70 per cent of the hegemonic elite in Central America were of Basque ancestry. The traditional Basque merchant role during early modern times in northern Europe was exported and exponentially increased in the New World through the formation of trans-oceanic colonial trading and business networks that linked Basque communities throughout the Hispanic Empire to the homeland. Lynch (1964, p. 35) estimated that an average of 65 per cent of New World trade was controlled by Basques between the beginning of the sixteenth century and the beginning of the seventeenth century.

Bonds of solidarity among members of Basque communities, expressed through historical associationism, collective action and mutual support, illustrate the dynamics of diaspora identity formation and the maintenance of cross-border, trans-oceanic and ethnic collective networks. Basques established aid societies, confraternities and voluntary religious, cultural and ethnic solidarity organizations in the Hispanic territories as well as in the Peninsula, soliciting benefactors and creating business networks on both sides of the Atlantic (Bilbao 1992; Escobedo, De Zaballa and Álvarez 1996). According to Pescador those associations and networks illustrated the emergence of a 'pan-Basque colonial identity that emphasized common cultural traits over Old Country social markers, such as status, origin, and household membership' (2004, p. 21). He argued that these organizations, particularly the confraternities, united Basques from different provinces to common religious and linguistic purposes, creating a generic sense of Basque identity. Consequently, 'the differences among provinces and historic rivalries among neighboring jurisdictions withered' (ibid., p. 116).

By 1825, all the American colonies had achieved political independence after long, brutal civil wars against the Spaniards and their local allies, 'undergoing the process of transformation from societies of immigrants to societies of natives' (Elliott 1987, p. 12). Spanish control in *Las Americas* was reduced to the Antilles and the Philippines. Peninsular Spaniards were given the choice of either leaving the new American countries or renouncing their old world 'citizenship', with the option of retaining their national identities symbolically or sentimentally. Basque post-colonial emigration continued to America, particularly to Río de la Plata (today's Argentina and Uruguay) during the 1830s. A rough estimate of around 200,000 Basques immigrated legally into the New World from the 1830s to the early 1900s (Azcona 1992; Iriani 2000). Douglass and Bilbao commented that 'there was no discontinuity in the awareness of a former migratory tradition' (1975, p. 135); emigration had been etched into the collective memory of families and villages over the previous 400 years. Moreover, the Napoleonic military campaigns on the Basque territories of Spain, followed by civil wars (1833–9 and 1872–6) between liberals and traditionalists (called *Carlists* because their candidate to the Spanish throne was Carlos/Charles of Bourbon), and the famine of 1846–7, forced many Basques into exile or emigration (Douglass 1989). The rise of capitalism and the demand for wage labourers pulled many Basques out of their homeland and into countries such as Argentina, Australia, Canada or the United States, constituting a Basque labour diaspora.

In the 1850s, the newly independent countries of Argentina, Uruguay and Chile created positive discrimination immigration policies that specifically requested Basques, among other European groups, as new settlers and manual labourers in a 'civilizing' enterprise based on racial purity (whiteness) and Catholicism. Additionally, in 1853 a Spanish Royal Order lifted previous restrictions on emigration. Within an assumed 'anti-Spanish' post-colonial and post-war context, peninsular immigrants found it easy to detach themselves from the negative stereotyping associated with Spanish identity, which was seen not only as colonial, or imperial, but also as national and in clear competition with the host identity. To a certain degree, they could claim other dimensions of their multiple identities, such as Basqueness. At that particular time, being Spanish or Basque was not yet thought of as hierarchical – national vs. local – or in terms of mutually exclusive identities, which was intensely the case by the end of the nineteenth century. The rise of Basque nationalism and the reinvention of Spanish nationalism after the loss of Cuba and Puerto Rico to the United States fostered the polarization between Basque and Spanish identities in political terms (Álvarez Junco 1996).

Basque identities were shaped by Basques' own experiences of migration and its complex interrelation with nation-state building processes taking place throughout the American continent. The ethnic politics of Basque identity construction spread throughout the American continent by the establishment of immigrant associations and the work of ethnic leaders in diaspora communities. In the last quarter of the nineteenth century and the beginning of the twentieth century, waves of Basque post-colonial immigration established new ethno-cultural transnational organizations in every Latin American country (Douglass and Bilbao 1975, p. 170). Several periodicals by and for the diaspora communities began around this time, connecting

Basques across geographies and generations. They offered general news on local communities and helped construct a Basque diasporic consciousness among immigrant communities and their descendants. Diaspora media helped to promote a sense of a common transnational and transatlantic identity. This increased the sense of interconnectedness among Basques, who shared common experiences of migration and identity on both sides of the Atlantic (Molina 2005a). Diaspora media were instrumental in shaping and articulating their own particular sense and understanding of local culture, which was openly influenced by interaction with political and cultural identities and by cohabitation with other groups in their host societies, resulting in multiple interpretations of a generic sense of being Basque.

From the Hispanic Empire to the Spanish State: the origins of the Basque question, 1808–98

In a war with the United States of America in 1898, what was once one of the largest Western empires on earth lost its last colonies, Cuba, Puerto Rico and the Philippines (Balfour 1995, 1997; Portillo 2006a), and found itself reduced to an embryonic, modern European liberal state with a Castilian nucleus and barely more than its original lands in the Iberian Peninsula. Under the tutelage of conservative and liberal theorists, the once-hegemonic Spanish monarchy managed to retain a third-class seat in the Western concert of nations. Scholars such as Boyd (1997), de Pablo, Mees and Rodríguez (1999) and Mees (2001) argued that Spain as a modern nation was still far from 'complete' by the end of nineteenth century, because it lacked uniformity, alleged distinctiveness and uniqueness, which theoretically must be present in a 'classical nation' (Smith 1992). They argued that, due to its weak oligarchic state, inadequate mass schooling system, divided political class and the triumph of liberal-moderate positions, Spain was incapable of developing mechanisms for political, economic and cultural integration, exemplified by the late creation of national symbols, such as flag, anthem or historical myths of origin. In addition, autonomous political systems in the Basque Provinces and Navarre defied the formation of a unique and centralized judicial, fiscal and administrative system for the whole Spanish national territory.

Consequently, de Pablo, Mees and Rodríguez argued that 'the failure of Spanish nationalism in the nineteenth century, or the crisis of its social penetration' facilitated 'the political success of alternative nationalisms in *fin-de-siècle* Spain' (1999, p. 20). They contended that 'Basque nationalism offered a new identity, a new sentiment of community, with their own symbolic references, emotional communitarian ties, and relationships and mechanisms of socialization' (1999, pp. 56–7). Rubio (2003, pp. 28–9, 155–77) strongly supported this argument by stating that 'the weak penetration' of the Spanish State in the Basque Country allowed the development of a specified Basque national conscience. The loss of the Basque autonomous system in 1876 provoked an identity crisis, a sense of having lost the traditional values of the collective imaginary of society. These scholars were strongly influenced by theories of nationalism such as Hroch's (1985) stages for 'national awakening' and presupposed that increased social communication and weakened local and regional identities were necessary 'preconditions' for a nation-building process. This perspective has permeated historical research on Spanish nation-state building, asserting that the survival and strong maintenance of identities, such as those of the Basques, Catalans or Galicians in the nineteenth century, should be seen as a sure symptom of weak nation-building, especially in those historical regions, and a forerunner to state-seeking nationalisms (de Riquer 1994, 2001). However, authors such as Sahlins (1991), Núñez Seixas (2001a), Archilés and Martí (2001) and Molina (2005b) give evidence of more complex and shifting loyalties in nineteenth-century Spain. They argue that state nationalism and even the states that carried out nation-building policies during that century also supported local and regionally based ethnic identities in order to reinforce the roots of national identity among the population.

The nineteenth-century Basque Country shows potential for a new reading on the changing frontiers of loyalties and allegiances in Western culture. We propose that nation-building also implied region- and ethnicity-building, to the point that the former may have been very dependent on the latter. Collective identity should be seen as a set of concentric (emotional) spheres that complement each other while acknowledging that all forms of social identity result from historical processes that can be modified by political and social change. In modern political terms, the idea of the Spanish nation began with the birth of liberalism during the 'War of Independence' against Napoleon (1808–14), and experienced quick and intense social diffusion in the heat of the conflict unleashed by the long struggle between liberals and traditionalists. The 1812 Constitution of Cádiz was the first liberal attempt to transform a monarchical empire into a national community of 'Spanish people in both hemispheres'. Spain was imagined as a nation of citizens, though plagued by history and religion, which was allegedly the necessary precondition for the emergence of the Spanish political *body*. Similarly, the need to come to terms with the claims of representatives from the colonies forced Spanish liberals towards a more organic concept of the nation. Anxious for Spain to continue as a multi-continental political community, they proclaimed the American territories to be part of the nation, and the rights of their citizens equal to those living in Europe. Spain was to become a nation extended within the Empire and moulded to its shape (Portillo 2006a).

At the beginning of this revolutionary period, peninsular liberals found themselves caught in contradictory situations regarding the American colonies and the Basque Provinces. Following the principles of liberalism, representatives of the American Creoles proposed to the Parliament of Cádiz political autonomy and self-government for their diverse territories within a supra-transoceanic imperial parliament to be established for the equal representation of all 'Spanish citizens' – meaning those with Hispanic European ancestry (Anna 1998). Nonetheless, the Constitution of 1812 decided to exclude the Creole elite from full and equal participation in the new project of the Hispanic liberal state. The euro-centric position of the peninsular liberals ultimately forced the colonies to seek independence as the only viable solution for achieving the ideals espoused by those same liberals. However, in a contrary move the peninsular liberal governments opted for a singular solution in relation to the quasi-autonomous territories of the Basque Provinces and Navarre, which were ruled by the old provincial laws (*fueros*): one of the last surviving remnants of the *ancien régime*, which promoted an extensive system of fiscal, legal and administrative self-government (see Monreal 2005). These provinces were included in the liberal project and their local laws recognized, granting them political autonomy. In some ways, this tolerance towards the Basque privileges was a lesson learned from the recent crisis with the American Empire and was linked to the necessity of having to cope with what remained of it.

Toward the end of the First Carlist War (1833–9), the Law of 25 October 1839 was enacted to regulate relations between the Basque Provinces and the central power of Madrid. The result was the survival of the ancient Basque territorial privileges under a new liberal form (Portillo 2006b). Modifications to the Basque autonomous system after 1839 safeguarded most of its predominant elements, such as the financial autonomy of the region, exclusion from compulsory military service and the control of regional politics by local elites. It was the Spanish national identity, brought about by the liberal revolutionary process that inspired the Basque elite to join forces in order to construct a modern national culture. Spanish liberalism appealed to a strong historicism and regionalism by presenting new political thought as a revival of medieval local parliamentary institutions, thus defending itself against conservative accusations of moving too far away from national tradition. Along these lines, Basque local laws were presented as an outcome of the liberal character of the Spanish nation. They were broadcast in the public sphere as something purely Spanish, an idealized relic of 'pre-Liberal constitutionalism'.

Consequently, Basque liberals and most Spanish liberals identified with the Basque tradition (Molina 2005b).

This identification process clashed head on with the roots of Basque ethnic singularity, which was based on their own autonomous history, the local home-rule tradition and the Basque language, *Euskara*. These elements were connected to the iconographic history and culture of the Spanish nation. The medieval wars against Arab invaders (the *Reconquista*), the American and Asian Empire and the 'national' war against Napoleon were the three main myths that demonstrated the essential link between Basques and Spaniards. *Fuerismo*, the discourse of the collective identity associated with local traditional laws or *fueros*, played the role of an ethnic regionalism, encouraging a strong and primordial local ethnic tie to the Spanish national sphere, defined by Castilian ethnic parameters. With its local commemorations and symbolic mobilizations presented as a kind of multiple patriotism – local, regional and national – it became a widespread elite movement including all Basque liberal factions as well as neo-absolutist groups such as the Carlists. *Fuerismo* defined Basque identity as an ethnicity based on an orthodox religion (Catholicism), the *Euskara* language, a sense of historical continuity given by the *foral* (adjective of *fueros*) tradition and a sense of common ancestry. This was fed by a secular mythology related to the supposed first inhabitant of the Iberian Peninsula, called Tubal – the grandson of the biblical Noah. There was also a sense of an unbroken biological continuity related to the assumed aristocratic origin of the Basque people, defended by one of the most important local myths – that of universal nobility. This secular myth imagined all Basques to be common descendants of one original family, distinct from the rest of Spanish peoples, and provided some sense of genetically inherited differences associated with enduring rural traditions and a local political system embedded in traditional laws (Molina 2005a, following Barth 1969; Horowitz 1985; De Vos 1995; Hutchinson and Smith 1996).

Within the framework of the liberal revolution, Basque regionalism was a movement of ethnic leaders who attempted to create a dual identity: ethnic-Basque and civic-Spanish. The relation between regional and national identities was not immutable; they tended to clash in times of civil wars and revolutions. In fact, the linking of Basque local laws to the traditionalist insurrection during the Second Carlist War (1872–6) brought about the vehement abolition of the Basque autonomous system. The Spanish nationalist elites considered Basque identity an intrinsic element of the peripheral traditionalist revolt that had firmly rejected the democratic State founded by the Revolution of 1868, which ended with the proclamation of the Spanish Republic in 1873. As a result of the liberal military victory over the traditionalists, the old Basque laws were abolished by the Law of

21 July 1876. However, in 1878 the President of the Spanish Government, Cánovas del Castillo, designed a special autonomous fiscal and administrative status for the Basque Provinces in the form of economic agreements, which were a pragmatic transition between the traditional local system and the liberal regime. Thus the Basque tradition was reinserted into the unitary idea of the Spanish nation (Castells 2003; Oiarzabal 2004; Molina 2005b).

After 1876, the *'foral* question' became not only a question of defending historical legal rights within the Spanish nation-state, but also a question of preserving collective values bound to an ethnic identity, which had lost its most important political reference – the local laws. The *'foral* question' became the 'Basque question'. Basque regionalism maintained its dual patriotism, but strongly mythologized the old political way of life embodied in the lost laws. The historical context was changing. Industrial modernization and mass society brought thousands of immigrants and new socio-cultural and political movements, such as socialism, anti-clericalism and new local economic and political elites allied with the Madrid elite (Glas 1998). Sabino Arana (1865–1903), a son of defeated traditionalism, proposed a new conception of the Basque Country as an ethnic nation, heavily influenced by ethnic local culture. By mythologizing its history and culture, Basque nationalism imagined a pre-existing Basque identity and culture. Basque authenticity was believed to be based on a remote past that justified the present existence of the Basque nation. Nationalist discourse and its *raison d'être* was projected into the past, asserting certain direct links to what were considered common Basque myths of ancestry, origin and election: direct descent from the first inhabitants of Europe, with mysterious pre-Indo-European origins evidenced by linguistic, racial and biological distinctiveness (see Smith 1992, p. 21). According to Douglass, Lyman and Zulaika (1994, pp. 90–3) those ancient myths recreated a culture of continuity, purity, isolation and resistance, which ended the historical cohabitation of Spanish and Basque identities (see also Conversi 1997).

Arana's nationalist discourse also meant an abrupt split with Basque regionalism. He reinterpreted local laws as national and constitutional Basque laws, the expression of independence and sovereignty. He stressed the incompatibility of these laws with the Spanish constitution, and by extension the nation-state, and called for the independence of the seven historical Basque Provinces – four in Spain and three in France – under the motto of *Jaun-Goikua eta Legi Zarra* (God and the Old Law). According to Conversi (1997), Corcuera (2002) and de la Granja (2002), Basque nationalism was born as a reactionary anti-Spanish and anti-liberal ideology, a doctrine perfectly reflected in its definition of who was considered Basque: those who had Basque ancestry, spoke Basque and were Catholic.

Sabino Arana believed that Basque identity was given by God and threatened by Spain, who sought to insert Spanishness into the Basque people. Conversi (1997) particularly argues that the Basque language also become a clear differentiating factor of great symbolic value for the national mission. Arana's political project was the creation of a Confederation of Basque States or *Euzkadi* for Basques of pure race and Catholic religion. In 1895, he founded the *Bizkai-Buru Batzar* – the embryonic Basque Nationalist Party. The general outcry over the end of the Spanish Empire was still being heard when on 11 September 1898, Arana was elected provincial council member for the district of Bilbao and proceeded to demand independence for *Euzkadi*.

Across the Atlantic: Basque diaspora and homeland discourses

The processes of reconstructing diverse identifications transcended the frame of the Basque Provinces and the Spanish State as they were transplanted in America. The Atlantic Ocean was not a border but a channel for communicating national cultures and collective representation and identification. Basque identity travelled across the ocean and was reinterpreted, adjusting for migration experiences and the different socio-historical, cultural and political contexts of the host societies. The independence of the Hispanic colonies did not sever the personal, economic, commercial, cultural or political-institutional ties on both sides of the Atlantic, but those links were modified by the emergence of the nation-state both in Spain and in post-colonial America. The trans-oceanic relationships between the peninsula and the newly independent nation-states fuelled a complex exchange and reconstruction of collective identities in the nineteenth century.

Particularly from 1870 on, Basque emigrants arrived in countries that were engaged in nation-state-building processes similar to those developing in Spain, and which actively focused on the cultural and national homogenization of their inhabitants, including immigrants. This national politicization process was not incompatible with the promotion of ethnic loyalties among the emigrant communities, who were in effect new communities of citizens. In general terms, host countries such as the United States, Argentina or Uruguay promoted the creation of multiple and complementary identities around the idea of the nation as a civic identity, through the use of positive stereotypes related to immigrants. These countries modelled a multi-ethnic national state characterized by varying degrees of national assimilation of successive waves of European migration, through public education programmes, mandatory military service, intense commemoration policies, symbolism and nationalist saturation of the public space with patriotic parades and national monuments (Moya 1998; Devoto and González 2001). In a sense, new civic loyalties to the new national host societies became part of the immigrant identity. Basques re-elaborated and reconstructed their own sense of identity to accommodate the diverse host-society identities, particularly the national identity. This illustrates the dialectical contradiction between becoming like those in their new countries while staying different, affirming their uniqueness and exclusiveness within the host societies, particularly in relation to other ethnic immigrant groups. This identitarian mechanism was not so different from what developed in European countries such as France, Germany, Italy or Spain in relation to identities described as ethnic, regional or local (Gjerde 1999, pp. 3–21).

American countries that lacked prestigious pre-Columbian civilizations as immediate patriotic ancestors upon which to build their new nation found the central racial/ethnic constituent for their nations in the massive waves of European immigrants, such as the Basques. As a significant example of this, Aristides Rojas (Professor at the Universidad de Caracas, Venezuela) (1874, pp. 3–6, 16–42) argued for the need to build a nation not only upon the heroes of the fight for independence against Spain, such as *el libertador* Simón Bolívar, but also on his Basque *etnia*. Basques thus became part of the essence of the new Venezuelan nationality, among others. Rojas contended that Venezuela as a nation existed prior to Columbus' arrival on the American continent but lay dormant, waiting for the Spanish people to 'awaken' it. Not just any Spaniard, but only the most biologically pure, a Basque, could accomplish this. Rojas went on to state that 'Bolívar, the genius of America, is also the genius (*genio*) of Spain.' The Basque element was the ethnic link between two worlds, and particularly between Venezuela and Spain. Rojas' argument closely resembled those of Basque regionalist leaders in Spain a few years earlier, such as Antonio de Trueba (1873), one of the most influential in the nineteenth century. All of them exalted the virtues of the Basque people as the '*Araucanos* of the Pyrenees', or as a 'unique and timeless people', a millenarian myth. The Basque *etnia*'s virtues, such as honesty, industriousness, stubbornness or patriotism, believed to be transmitted by blood, could be useful for stabilizing a nation – whether Venezuela or Spain – in periods of turmoil.

Basque ethnic leaders in America used local culture to create a new sense of Atlantic Basqueness, more symbolic than political, in order to accommodate the realities of the host country and avoid any potential clash between the two cultures and identities. Consequently, cultural elements of political origin, such as the *fueros*, capable of fostering strong internal cohesion in the homeland, had a more rhetorical content in America. Other elements, such as the Basque language, which was more symbolic in Europe, gained greater relevance in re-creating the Basque identity in the diaspora. The ethnic element of the

Basque identity allowed the immigrant community to manage its own identity in relation to specific circumstances and social and political contexts. In this regard, the nineteenth-century Basque diaspora associations were not far removed from Basque and Spanish politics. The first Basque diasporic organizations were created in Uruguay and Argentina as a response to the loss of political autonomy and the defeat of traditionalism in the Civil War of 1872–6. The *Laurac Bat* was established in 1876 in Montevideo (see Irigoyen 1998), and the following year *La Sociedad Vasco-Española Laurac Bat* – later known as *Laurak Bat* – was established in Buenos Aires as a political organization celebrating annual protests against the loss of Basque political autonomy in Spain in 1876. This act of remembrance for the lost *fueros* helped to amalgamate the diverse existing interpretations of regionalism. Both organizations sought to promote Basque culture, assisting *only* Basque immigrants from Spain. In 1895, the *Centre Basque-Français* and the *Centro Navarro*, both in Buenos Aires, were also established to attend to the needs of their respective compatriots: Basques from France and Navarrans from Spain (Cava, Contreras and Pérez 1992; Cava 1996; Márquez 1996).

The establishment of the *Asociación Cultural y de Beneficencia Euskal Echea de Buenos Aires y de Lavallol* (1901/1916), in Argentina, was the first successful diaspora venture to integrate *all* Basques, from both sides of the Pyrenees, into one common cultural project by softening the regional rivalries and particularities from back home. By the end of the nineteenth century, Basque diaspora associations such as the *Asociación Vasco-Navarra de Beneficencia* from La Habana and the *Laurac Bat* of Montevideo, which had previously embraced Basque regionalism and its *Laurak Bat* motto, began to promote a more inclusive approach towards French Basques. To reflect this new inclusive policy, the Basque club of Montevideo was renamed *Euskaldun Guztiak Bat* (All Basques are One) a decade after its creation and the Basque club from La Habana replaced the *Laurak Bat* motto with *Euskal-Erria Ari da* (The Basque Country in Motion), in order to include Basques from France. These associations exemplified an early pan-Basque (or *Zazpiak Bat* – Seven are One) identity, expressing a new Basque conscience and a new way of imagining themselves as a people united across homeland political divisions. This spread to other Basque diaspora associations the world over.

By the beginning of the new century, Basque identity was sometimes tied to Spanish identity, and sometimes not, due to the emergence of Basque nationalism as an identification-strengthening factor between Basque ethnic identity and the national identity of the host societies. Basque nationalism was exported to the diasporic communities in America under the motto of *Zazpiak Bat* – a nation-state-building project based on an imagined ancestral territory formed by seven historical provinces. However, it was not until the 1920s that a true Basque national politicization of diaspora associations began in Argentina, Chile, Cuba, Mexico, the Philippines, the United States and Uruguay (Álvarez Gila 1996, 2000, 2005). Once again, the symbolic national politicization of the Basque ethnic identity in the diaspora depended on the participation of ethnic leaders (see Núñez Seixas 2001b, 2002, 2003). Increasing and diverse nationalist and regionalist propagandistic literature enhanced the imagination of diaspora Basques as part of wider Spanish and/or Basque communities. This Spanish or Basque 'long-distance nationalism' was understood as the 'ideology of belonging that extends homeland politics into transnational social fields' and 'links together people living in various geographic locations and motivates them to action in relation to an ancestral territory and its government' (Anderson 1991, p. 327).

Conclusions

The nineteenth century was a period characterized by 'ethnic fever', expressed in a search for an ancestry resulting from political efforts to establish authenticity and antiquity as the foundations for the European and American models of the nation-state (Thiesse 1999). The value of the ethnic element increased in the cultural market of the nation-state: the French searched for the Franks, the Germans for the Germanic tribes and the Italians for the eternal Rome. It acquired added value, guaranteeing the nation-state by recreating the inherited authenticity of ethnic groups, whose assumed essence was linked to past golden eras.

The Basque case of 'ethnic fever' is paradigmatic. It became the guarantor of the authenticity, and thereby the right to existence, of various nations, such as Spain, Argentina or Venezuela, which were culturally linked across the ocean by this ethnicity. Basque identity in the nineteenth century was neither homogeneous nor static, as it was composed of multiple loyalties and consciousnesses within the political panorama of Spain and the independent American countries. It also ratified the development of a *status quo* – the national identity as the supreme identity – which overrode other identities and loyalties. We have seen how the ethnic component of the Basque identity was utilized by diverse national identities to satisfy the need for patriotic ancestors on both shores of the Atlantic. This identity was profoundly reinterpreted and reutilized by the different ideologies and political cultures involved in the Atlantic crises of the Hispanic monarchy, and in the subsequent development of the nation-state system in America and Spain.

To some extent, the different ideological postulates of the century – liberalism, regionalism, traditionalism and Spanish and Basque nationalisms – assumed Basque identity as the basis for their different conceptions of nations as territorial and somewhat homogeneous entities both in America and in Europe. Throughout the entire nineteenth century, these specific ideologies redefined the meaning of Basque ethnicity to fit their own political agendas: whether to regain power, build a state or impose an ideology. Every meaning given to the conceptualization of Basqueness is an historical construct tailored to its spatial and temporal context. Basques were bound by a multiplicity of institutional, economic and psychological ties to their localities, regions and metropolises. However, their attitudes and experiences of migration and settlement transcended the conventional identity boundaries of the country of origin. This helped them to reshape and bring out their own sense of identity as Basques, as Atlantic colonists and later as diverse American nationals.

During the nineteenth century Basque identity continued to reconstruct itself as a transnational, de-territorialized and diasporic identity that created a common identitarian space on both sides of the Atlantic and interlinked Basques from diverse nation-states and territories throughout the American continent. Consequently, Basque culture was a transatlantic network of multiple identifications, loyalties and consciousnesses that encouraged a multi-directional movement of ideas, materials and people, evidenced by the influence and the rapid dissemination of homeland political ideologies. This provides an Atlantic framework for analysis of American and peninsular identities, cultures and ideologies.

Acknowledgements

This paper draws on two previous works by the authors: 'Towards a diasporic and transnational reading of Basque identities in time, space, and history' by Pedro J. Oiarzabal, which was prepared for delivery at the 2004 Meeting of the Latin American Studies Association, Las Vegas, Nevada (USA) 7–9 October 2004, and 'La disputada cronología de la nacionalidad: fuerismo, identidad vasca y nación en el siglo XIX' by Fernando Molina, published in the journal *Historia Contemporánea* 16 (2005), pp. 219–45. The authors would like to thank Dr Xosé Manoel Núñez Seixas at the *Universidade de Santiago de Compostela* (Galicia, Spain) for reviewing previous drafts of this paper. This article stems from University of the Basque Country's research project 'Autonomía e Identidad en el País Vasco Contemporáneo' (Autonomy and Identity in Contemporary Basque Country), HUM2004-04956 (Principal Researcher: Dr Luis Castells).

Note

1. Andorra, Argentina, Australia, Brazil, Canada, Chile, China, Colombia, Cuba, Dominican Republic, El Salvador, France, Germany, Italy, Mexico, Paraguay, Peru, Puerto Rico, Spain, Switzerland, the United Kingdom, the United States, Uruguay and Venezuela.

References

ÁLVAREZ GILA, ÓSCAR 1996 '"Vascos y vascongados": luchas ideológicas entre carlistas y nacionalistas en los Centros vascos del Río de la Plata (1900–1930)', in Ronald Escobedo, Ana de Zaballa and Óscar Álvarez (eds), *Emigración y Redes Sociales de los Vascos en América*, Vitoria-Gasteiz: UPV
―――― 2000 'Los inicios del nacionalismo vasco en América: El Centro Zazpirak Bat de Rosario (Argentina)', *Sancho el Sabio*, vol. 12, pp. 153–76
―――― 2005 'Euskal Herrias americanas: los vascos y las emigraciones ultramarinas (1825–1950)', in Joseba Agirreazkuenaga (ed.), *La Crisis de la Civilización de los Vascos del Antiguo Régimen y Estrategias de Revolución Liberal e Industrial: 1789–1876*, Historia de Euskal Herria, Historia General de los Vascos, Vol. 4. Donostia-San Sebastián: Editorial Lur
ÁLVAREZ JUNCO, JOSÉ 1996 'The nation-building process in nineteenth-century Spain', in Clare Mar-Molinero and Angel Smith (eds), *Nationalism and the Nation in the Iberian Peninsula*, Oxford: Berg
ANDERSON, BENEDICT 1991 *Imagined Communities: Reflections on the Origin and Spread of Nationalism*, London: Verso
ANNA, TIMOTHY E. 1998 *Forging Mexico 1821–1835*, Lincoln, NB: University of Nebraska Press
ARCHILÉS, FERRAN and MARTÍ, MANUEL 2001 'Ethnicity, region and nation: Valencian identity and the Spanish nation-state', *Ethnic and Racial Studies*, vol. 24, no. 5, pp. 779–97
AZCONA, JOSÉ MANUEL 1992 *Los Paraísos Perdidos: Historia de la Emigración Vasca a Argentina y Uruguay en el Siglo XIX*, Bilbao: Universidad de Deusto
BALFOUR, SEBASTIAN 1995 'The loss of empire, regenerationism, and the forging of the myth of national identity', in Helen Graham and Jo Labanyi (eds), *Spanish Cultural Studies: An Introduction, the Struggle for Modernity*, Oxford: Oxford University Press
―――― 1997 *The End of the Spanish Empire 1898–1923*, Oxford: Clarendon Press
BARTH, FREDRIK 1969 'Introduction', in Fredrik Barth (ed.), *Ethic Groups and Boundaries: The Social Organisation of Cultural Difference*, London: Allen & Unwin, pp. 9–38
BILBAO, JON (ed.) 1992 *América y los Vascos*, Vitoria-Gasteiz: Gobierno Vasco
BOYD, CAROLYN P. 1997 *Historia Patria: Politics, History, and National Identity in Spain, 1875–1975*, Princeton, NJ: Princeton University Press
CASAUS, MARTA ELENA 1996 'La redes familiares vascas en la configuración de la elite de poder centro Americana', in Ronald Escobedo, Ana de Zaballa and Óscar Álvarez (eds), *Emigración y Redes Sociales de los Vascos en América,* Vitoria-Gasteiz: UPV
CASTELLS, LUIS 2003 'La abolición de los fueros vascos', *Ayer*, no. 52, pp. 117–49
CAVA, BEGOÑA 1996 'El asociacionismo vasco en Argentina: política cultural', in Ronald Escobedo, Ana de Zaballa and Óscar Álvarez (eds), *Emigración y Redes Sociales de los Vascos de América*, Vitoria-Gasteiz: UPV
CAVA, BEGOÑA, CONTRERAS, LUIS FERNANDO and PÉREZ, FRANCISCO JAVIER 1992 *La Sociedad Laurak Bat de Buenos Aires (1876–1992)*, Vitoria-Gasteiz: Gobierno Vasco
CONVERSI, DANIELE 1997 *The Basques, the Catalans and Spain*, Reno, NV: University of Nevada Press

CORCUERA, JAVIER 2002 *La Patria de los Vascos: Orígenes, Ideología, y Organización del Nacionalismo Vasco (1876–1903)*, Madrid: Taurus
DE LA GRANJA, JOSÉ LUIS 2002 *El Nacionalismo Vasco: Un Siglo de Historia*, 2nd edn, Madrid: Tecnos
DE PABLO, SANTIAGO, MEES, LUDGER and RODRÍGUEZ, JOSÉ ANTONIO 1999 *El Péndulo Patriótico: Historia del Partido Nacionalista Vasco*, 2 vols, Barcelona: Crítica.
DE RIQUER, BORJA 1994 'La débil nacionalización española del siglo XIX', *Historia Social*, vol. 20, pp. 97–114
―――― 2001 *Escolta Espanya: La Cuestión Catalana en la Época Liberal*, Madrid: Marcial Pons
DE TRUEBA, ANTONIO 1873 'Los vascongados: observaciones sugeridas por la lectura del libro que con este título ha publicado el Ilmo. Sr. D. Miguel Rodríguez Ferrer', *La Época*, vol. 18, no. 19
DE VOS, GEORGE A. 1995 'Ethnic pluralism: conflict and accommodation: the role of ethnicity in social history', in George A. De Vos and Lola Romanucci-Ross (eds), *Ethnic Identity: Creation, Conflict and Accomodation*, London: Altamira Press, pp. 1–36
DEVOTO, FERNANDO and GONZLEZ-BERNALDO, PILAR (eds) 2001 *Emigration Politique: Une Perspective Comparative: Italiens et Espagnols en Argentine et en France (XIXe–XXe siècles)*, Paris: L'Harmattan
DOUGLASS, WILLIAM A. 1989 'Factors in the formation of the New World, Basque emigrant diaspora', in William A. Douglass (ed.), *Papers in Basque Social Anthropology*, Reno, NV: Basque Studies Program
―――― 2000 'In search of Juan de Oñate: confessions of a crytoessentialist', *Journal of Anthropological Research*, vol. 56, no. 2, pp. 137–62
DOUGLASS, WILLIAM A. and BILBAO, JON 1975 *Amerikanuak: Basques in the New World*, Reno, NV: University of Nevada Press
DOUGLASS, WILLIAM A., LYMAN, STANFORD M. and ZULAIKA, JOSEBA 1994 *Migración, Etnicidad y Etnonacionalismo*, Bilbao: Universidad del País Vasco
ELLIOTT, JOHN H. 1987 'Introduction: colonial identity in the Atlantic World', in Nicholas Canny and Anthony Pagden (ed.), *Colonial Identity in the Atlantic World, 1500–1800*, Princeton, NJ: Princeton University Press
ESCOBEDO, RONALD, DE ZABALLA, ANA and ÁLVAREZ, ÓSCAR (eds) 1996 *Emigración y Redes Sociales de los Vascos en América*, Vitoria-Gasteiz: UPV
GARCÍA, TERESA 1996 'La formación de la redes familiares vascas en Centroamérica, 1750–1880', in Ronald Escobedo, Ana de Zaballa and Óscar Álvarez (eds), *Emigración y Redes Sociales de los Vascos de América*, Vitoria-Gasteiz: UPV
GJERDE, JON 1999 'Identidades múltiples y complementarias: inmigrantes, líderes étnicos y el Estado en los Estados Unidos', *Estudios Migratorios Latinoamericanos*, vol. 14, no. 42, pp. 3–21
GLAS, EDUARDO JORGE 1998 *Bilbao's Modern Business Elite*, Reno, NV: University of Nevada Press
GONZALBO, PILAR 1996 'Familias vasco-novohispanas', in Ronald Escobedo, Ana de Zaballa and Óscar Álvarez (eds), *Emigración y Redes Sociales de los Vascos de América*, Vitoria-Gasteiz: UPV
HERZOG, TAMAR 1996 'De la autoridad al poder: Quito, los Larrea y la herencia inmaterial (Siglos XVII y XVIII)', in Ronald Escobedo, Ana de Zaballa and Óscar Álvarez (eds), *Emigración y Redes Sociales de los Vascos de América*, Vitoria-Gasteiz: UPV
HOROWITZ, DONALD L. 1985 *Ethnic Groups in Conflict*, Berkeley, CA: University of California Press
HROCH, MIROSLAV 1985 *Social Preconditions of National Revival in Europe: a Comparative Analysis of the Social Composition of Patriotic Groups among the Smaller European Nations*, Cambridge: Cambridge University Press
HUTCHINSON, JOHN and MITH, ANTHONY 1996 'Introduction', in John Hutchinson and Anthony D. Smith (eds), *Ethnicity*, Oxford: Oxford University Press, pp. 3–14

IRIANI, MARCELINO 2000 *'Hacer América': Los Vascos en la Pampa Húmeda, Argentina (1840–1920)*, Vitoria-Gasteiz: UPV

IRIGOYEN, ALBERTO 1998 *Laurac Bat de Montevideo: Primera Euskal Etxea del mundo (1876–1898)*. Vitoria-Gasteiz: Gobierno Vasco

LYNCH, JOHN 1964 *Spain under the Habsburgs*, Vol. 1, *Empire and Absolutism 1516–1598*, Oxford: Blackwell

MÁRQUEZ, REYES 1996 'Colectividad vasca y asociacionismo en Argentina', in Ronald Escobedo, Ana de Zaballa and Óscar Álvarez (eds), *Emigración y Redes Sociales de los Vascos de América*, Vitoria-Gasteiz: UPV

MEES, LUDGER 2001 'Between votes and bullets: conflicting ethnic identities in the Basque Country', *Ethnic and Racial Studies*, vol. 24, no. 5, pp. 798–827

MOLINA, FERNANDO 2005a 'La disputada cronología de la nacionalidad: fuerismo, identidad vasca y nación en el siglo XIX', *Historia Contemporánea*, no. 30, pp. 219–45

—— 2005b *La Tierra del Martirio Español: El País Vasco y España en el Siglo del Nacionalismo*, Madrid: Centro de Estudios Políticos y Constitucionales

MONREAL, GREGORIO 2005 *The Old Law of Bizkaia (1452): A Critical Edition*, Reno, NV: Center for Basque Studies

MOYA, JOSÉ C. 1998 *Cousins and Strangers: Spanish Immigrants in Buenos Aires, 1850–1930*, Berkeley, CA: University of California Press

NEILS CONZEN, KATHLEEN 1992 'The invention of ethnicity: a perspective from the U.S.A.', *Journal of American Ethnic History*, no. 12, pp. 3–43

NÚÑEZ SEIXAS, XOSE-MANOEL 2001a 'The region as essence of the fatherland: regionalist variants of Spanish nationalism (1840–1936)', *European History Quarterly*, vol. 31 no. 4, pp. 483–518

—— 2001b 'Leadership ethnique, exil politique et ethnonationalisme chez les collectivités ibériques en Amerique Latine (1880–1960)', in Fernando Devoto and Pilar González-Bernaldo (eds), *Emigration Politique: Une Perspective Comparative: Italiens et Espagnols en Argentine et en France (XIXe-XXe siècles)*, Paris: L'Harmattan

—— 2002 *O emigrante imaxinario: estereotipos, representacións e identidades dos Galegos na Arxentina (1880–1949)*, Santiago de Compostela: Universidade de Santiago de Compostela

—— 2003 'Liderazgo étnico en comunidades emigrantes: algunas reflexiones', in Nicolás Sánchez-Albornoz and Moisés Llordén (eds), *Migraciones Iberoamericanas: Reflexiones sobre Economía, Política y Sociedad*, Columbres: Fundación Archivo de Indianos

OIARZABAL, PEDRO J. 2004 'Towards a diasporic and transnational reading of Basque identities in time, space, and history', paper presented at the 25th International Congress of Latin American Studies Association, Las Vegas, Nevada, 7–9 October

—— 2005 *La Identidad Vasca en el Mundo: Narrativas sobre Identidad más allá de Fronteras*, Bilbao: Erroteta

—— 2006 'The Basque Diaspora Webscape: Online Discourses of Basque Diaspora Identity, Nationhood, and Homeland', PhD dissertation, Center for Basque Studies, University of Nevada, Reno, NV

ORTÍZ DE LA TABLA Y DUCHASE, JAVIER 1996 'Presencia vasca en el Ecuador Colonial: linajes y redes de parentescos: S. XVI–XVII', in Ronald Escobedo, Ana de Zaballa and Óscar Álvarez (eds), *Emigración y Redes Sociales de los Vascos de América*, Vitoria-Gasteiz: UPV

PAGDEN, ANTHONY and CANNY, NICHOLAS 1987 'Afterword: from identity to independence', in Nicholas Canny and Anthony Pagden (eds), *Colonial Identity in the Atlantic World, 1500–1800*, Princeton, NJ: Princeton University Press

PESCADOR, JUAN JAVIER 2004 *The New World inside a Basque Village: The Oiartzun Valley and its Atlantic Emigrants 1550–1800*, Reno, NV: University of Nevada Press

PORTILLO, JOSÉ MARIA 2006a *Crisis Atlántica: Autonomía e Independencia en la Crisis de la Monarquía Hispana*, Madrid: Marcial Pons

———— 2006b *El Sueño Criollo: La Formación del Doble Constitucionalismo en el País Vasco y Navarra*, Madrid: Nerea

ROJAS, ARISTIDES 1874 *El Elemento Vasco en la Historia de Venezuel: Ofrenda Literaria de la Universidad de Caracas al Libertador en el Día de la Inauguración de su Estatua Ecuestre, 7 de Noviembre de 1874*, Caracas: Imprenta Federal

RUBIO, CORO 2003 *La Identidad Vasca en el Siglo XIX: Discurso y Agentes Sociales*, Madrid: Biblioteca Nueva

SAHLINS, PETER 1991 *Boundaries: The Making of France and Spain in the Pyrenees*, Berkeley, CA: University of California Press

SMITH, ANTHONY D. 1992 *National Identity*, Reno, NV: University of Nevada Press

THIESSE, ANNE-MARIE 1999 *La Creatión des Identités Nationales. Europe XVIIIe–XXe Siècle*, Paris: Éditions du Seuil

How master frames mislead: the division and eclipse of nationalist movements in Uzbekistan and Tajikistan

Lawrence P. Markowitz

Abstract
This article examines how a successful master frame in one location can promote mobilization failure in another by misleading movement entrepreneurs. It revisits two cases of low nationalist mobilization in Tajikistan and Uzbekistan to demonstrate that a fuller explanation should include the tactical choices – good and bad – of movement leaders. In both cases, a transnational anti-imperial master frame misled separatist nationalists, causing them to undervalue critical shifts in the political environments in their republics. In Uzbekistan, this frame left the *Birlik* nationalist movement open to division by the state in the aftermath of inter-ethnic violence, while it made Tajikistan's *Rastokhez* movement susceptible to eclipse by regionalist mobilization in Tajikistan.

This article revisits two cases of low nationalist mobilization in late Soviet Central Asia to demonstrate how the success of nationalist movements in one location can mislead movement entrepreneurs in another. From 1987 to 1992, a tide of nationalism swept across republics of the former Soviet Union. Yet nationalist movements within Central Asia were conspicuously weak in comparison to mobilization against the Soviet state in other republics. In fact, observers of Central Asia describe these years as a process of 'decolonisation by default' (Grant 1994) in which these countries found themselves belatedly 'discovering independence' amid the fragments of the Soviet Union (Gleason 1997).

Mobilization in Central Asia was not absent entirely, but the number of demonstrations and the number of participants among the titular groups in Soviet Central Asia (Kazakhs, Kyrgyz, Tajiks, Turkmens and Uzbeks) were much lower than those of nationalities in the Baltics and in the Caucasus, as well as in Moldova and Ukraine. Certainly, the cumulative effect of limited resources and constrained opportunities weighed against nationalist movements in Central Asia's republics. All five titular groups were creations of Soviet nationalities policies, impoverished and predominantly rural (with urban areas largely Russian dominated). Alongside these unfavourable background conditions, however, low nationalist mobilization was also a consequence of tactical choices made by movement entrepreneurs in applying a master frame diffused from other Soviet republics. As one study has shown, 'part of the explanation for the success or failure of separatist mobilization was the differential ability of movements to take advantage of the example of others' (Beissinger 2002, pp. 210–12, 242).[1] Through the examples of Tajikistan and Uzbekistan, this article examines why an anti-imperial nationalist master frame, which succeeded in promoting nationalist mobilization around secessionist claims in other republics, failed to produce an equivalent effect in these countries.[2]

I argue that, in deploying this master frame, nationalists in Tajikistan and Uzbekistan overlooked changing circumstances in their local environment that ultimately undermined their capacity to mobilize support. In particular, extending master frames in their republics left nationalist movements vulnerable to division in Uzbekistan and eclipse in Tajikistan. In the former, the state's effective use of the media depicted mobilization as a cause of inter-ethnic conflict. In line with the master frame it had acquired, however, the republic's *Birlik* (Unity) movement continued to press nationalist claims without effectively addressing the state's accusations; as a result, it lost public support, became divided and was quickly repressed. In Tajikistan, leaders of the republic's *Rastokhez* (Renaissance) movement failed to adapt their programme to shifting social cleavages. As a consequence, mobilization around nationalist goals was eclipsed by sub-national, regional assertions of political power in the republic. The fragmentation of the country along regional lines that followed – which has been portrayed at times as a failure of national identity itself (Akbarzadeh 1996) – was partly due to the failure of movement entrepreneurs who had been led astray by a transnational master frame that ceased to resonate in a regionally divided society. In each case, an anti-imperial master frame diffused from abroad inadvertently inhibited mobilization by hindering nationalists' ability to adapt to changing conditions on the ground.

The article is organized in five parts. First, I discuss tactical error as a contributing, though often overlooked, factor in ethnic and nationalist mobilization. Second, drawing on social movement literature, I propose several ways in which master frames may contribute to tactical error and to low mobilization within nationalist movements. Third, I examine the case of Uzbekistan, where reliance on a master frame from the Baltic republics exposed the *Birlik* movement to a government campaign that discredited it as a source of instability and inter-ethnic violence and cultivated divisions within it. Fourth, I analyse how that master frame also encouraged Tajikistan's *Rastokhez* movement to discount the regionalist social cleavages that emerged and overwhelmed its programme of national renewal and unity. Finally, I conclude with some general lessons drawn from this comparison for the study of framing and nationalist mobilization.

Nationalism and mobilization failures

The central argument in the article – that in extending a master-frame movement entrepreneurs may undermine nationalist mobilization by failing to adapt to changing local conditions – is not anticipated in the literature on nationalism. This is partly because scholars rarely explore theoretically the potential for nationalists to err in their attempts to promote mobilization. Instead, theories emphasizing the role of human agency within nationalist mobilization have generally focused on the *successful* activities of ethnic entrepreneurs (Hardin 1995; Snyder 2000), including elite manipulation of mobilization in large-scale violence in the former Yugoslavia (Oberschall 2000; Gagnon 2004) and central Africa (Des Forges 1999). Emphasis on the success of ethnic entrepreneurs has also underlined studies of nationalist mobilization involving master frames. Master frames are seen typically as a mechanism through which entrepreneurs can attach locally resonant issues to broader nationalist goals, such as a pan-Mayan identity among indigenous peoples (Warren 1998). Yet, while studies have uncovered the micropolitical mechanisms driving mobilization around identity (McAdam, Tarrow and Tilly 2001; King 2004), tactical error has not yet entered into the calculus of existing explanations.

Failed nationalist mobilization, on the other hand, tends to be attributed to the *absence* of political action – or its subordination to overwhelming structural impediments or institutional constraints. Traditionally, scholars have explained unsuccessful nationalisms by referring to groups' weak identity (Connor 1990), poor organizational capacity (Horowitz 1985), limited resource endowments (Tilly 1994) or the state's constriction of mobilization opportunities (Breuilly 1982). Empirical studies, however, suggest that failed mobilization may also reflect the capabilities of those within a movement. Separatist nationalists in late Soviet Kazakhstan, for instance, found themselves upstaged by movement entrepreneurs who established a link between eco-protests and a broad-based internationalism. As a result, anti-nuclear movements such as the Nevada-Semipalatinsk Movement emerged as major social forces instead of state-seeking eco-nationalist movements that flourished elsewhere in the former Soviet Union (Schatz 1999).

Likewise, several post-Soviet nationalist movements' early successes had led them to overstep the boundaries of acceptable political competition and to ostracize moderate groups. In Georgia, Zviadist nationalists misread the ethnic grievances of Abkhazian and South Ossetian minority populations, leading 'certain radical elements in the movement [to] capitalize on anti-minority sentiments, causing consternation in non-Georgian communities' (Hewitt 1993; Demetriou 2003, p. 114). In response to Zviadist exclusionary visions of Georgian nationhood, popular front organizations in Abkhazia and South Ossetia began to mobilize around alternative nationalist projects, promoting political fragmentation and civil war. In Belarus, 'radicalization' within the movement's ranks in the early 1990s led to a drop in its popular support and its demise in post-independence politics. As the movement's objectives became redefined, 'sharpening its demands rather than softening them', it broke with moderate nationalists in the republic. As Pal Kolsto explained, 'the nationalists of the popular front have not made maximum use of the possibilities that have emerged since independence. Several observers have pointed out how the movement underwent a major radicalization in 1992–1993 and how this sharper profile cost them many adherents' (2000, p. 165).

As these examples suggest, it is not unusual for nationalist entrepreneurs to make mistakes and, at times, such tactical errors can undermine mobilization. When considered alongside other explanatory factors, therefore, framing processes add valuable insight into the tactical choices that promote higher levels of mobilization in some nationalist movements but not in others. The next section examines these framing processes in greater depth.

Master frames and tactical choice

Within social movement literature, framing is usually seen as an enabling instrument that entrepreneurs within social movement organizations utilize to mobilize targeted groups (Snow *et al.*, 1986). Similarly, master frames are traditionally understood as facilitators of mobilization, promoting higher levels of turn-out when they are effectively coordinated with movement-specific frames, and causally absent from explanations when they do not resonate (Johnston 1991;

Noonan 1995; Snow 2004, pp. 390–1). There are, however, several ways that framing processes can inhibit mobilization.[3]

Crucial to the success of particular frames, however, is the stability of political alliances (Diani 1996). When the tactical choices behind framing are made in fluid environments, success often depends on movement leaders' capacity to adapt to shifting circumstances (Snow and Benford 1992). Changing cultural conditions can gradually erode previously resonant frames, and tactical choices that were initially successful may need to be amended over time (Wittner 1969). Alternatively, frames may be simply overtaken by events that suddenly eradicate the frame's credibility and real-world applicability (Beissinger 2002). Moreover, the potency and relevance of a frame may be undercut by the emergence of alternative, competing frames (Gamson 1992; Schwedler 2005; Romano 2006 pp. 99–270).

While bad framing choices inhibit mobilization, their effects can be exacerbated by master frames. Snow and Benford have noted how 'movements that emerge later in the cycle will typically find their framing efforts constrained by the previously elaborated master frame' (1988, p. 212). At times, master frames whose early resonance helped sustain a protest cycle may even contribute to the decline of that protest cycle (Tarrow 1998, pp. 106–22). But how exactly do master frames inhibit mobilization?

I contend that, in the course of linking movement-specific frames, master frames can direct the attention of movement entrepreneurs away from their own contextual conditions towards the successful examples of others. In the process of extending master frames, movement entrepreneurs can be swayed by the promise of success in other contexts, and undervalue the particular challenges of effecting mobilization in their own localities. This is particularly so when local conditions are in flux. Thus, movement-specific frames can be eroded over time, overtaken by events or sidelined by competing frames, but these developments may go on unappreciated when movement entrepreneurs remain focused on master frames that succeeded elsewhere.

The case studies of *Birlik* and *Rastokhez* that follow demonstrate how a master frame misled movement entrepreneurs in each republic. As early as 1989, both movements actively looked to the Balts as an example. Imitation of the Baltic Popular Fronts began in Uzbekistan with the formation of *Birlik* in November 1988 and in Tajikistan with the establishment of *Yaverani Bazsazi* (Helpers of Perestroika), a precursor of *Rastokhez* that was created in late 1988. One of the leaders of *Yaverani Bazsazi* had even travelled to the Baltic republics to learn how to form a Popular Front (Crow 1990, p. 20). Yet, conditions in Uzbekistan and Tajikistan were undergoing significant change, leading *Birlik*'s movement-specific frames to be overtaken by events and those of *Rastokhez* to be eroded by creeping regionalism. Both movements, focusing on the success of Baltic mobilization and linking their movement-specific frames to the master frame of secessionist nationalism, failed to appreciate the unique challenges posed by shifting political alignments in their republics. Misleading master frames played a critical role in their marginalization, making one movement vulnerable to division by the state and the other susceptible to eclipse by competing frames.

The division of *Birlik* in Uzbekistan

The case of Uzbekistan demonstrates how a master frame, effective elsewhere, can lead movement entrepreneurs astray and open them to division. Like Popular Fronts across the Soviet Union, intellectuals and scientists, who retained close ties to the republic's Union of Writers, established *Birlik* on 11 November 1988. *Birlik*'s early focus on language rights and environmental issues closely reflected popular concerns in the republic. As one of *Birlik*'s founders, Abdurahim Pulatov, explained, an environmental justice frame was not coincidental.

> The Aral had just begun to be a social and ecological issue. Many people were interested in this. Thus, we wanted to benefit from this in order to initiate our action. We discussed the matter with Pirmat Shirmukhammad, chairman of the Save the Aral Sea Committee and agreed to work together ... The Aral crisis was a matter related to the cotton monoculture. Therefore, through the Aral crisis it was possible to fight against the exploitation of our people. ... We thought that through this Aral question we could influence politics. So with such thoughts we initiated a popular movement. (Yuksel 1992)

A tangible issue that commanded public attention, the Aral Sea crisis was framed as state-perpetrated environmental degradation that resonated widely. The same focus on mobilization underscored *Birlik*'s promotion of Uzbek as the state language, which, Pulatov noted, 'wasn't only a popular matter for many at the time, but ... was also an easily understandable and necessary thing. And through this issue we were able to attract many to "*Birlik*"' (Yuksel 1992).

Indeed, among the eighteen 'main tasks' outlined in *Birlik*'s charter, several focused on language and environmental issues: 'the genuine establishment of the Uzbek language as the official state language of Uzbekistan', 'the elimination of cotton as the single crop of the republic', 'broad-scale care for the natural environment and, in particular, rescuing the Aral Sea' and 'releasing women and children from strenuous manual labour in all sectors of the national economy, primarily in agriculture' (*Programma narodnogo dvizheniia Uzbekistan 'Birlik'* 1991, pp. 12–15; Furtado and Chandler 1992, p. 518). Thus, *Birlik*'s tactical choices in its early days exploited locally salient issues to expand the movement's recruitment, though these movement-specific frames were loosely bridged with frames of eco-nationalism disseminated from abroad (Warren 1998).

In June 1989, however, inter-ethnic violence racked the Ferghana Valley in eastern Uzbekistan and fundamentally altered the context in which *Birlik* operated. In the new political environment following the violence, questions about the consequences and potential dangers of mass demonstrations emerged. *Birlik*, however, continued to promote its agenda – in line with frames and strategies acquired from their Baltic counterparts. *Birlik* increasingly advanced calls for Uzbek sovereignty, assuming a position that was readily portrayed as fostering inter-ethnic enmity. Yet, it failed to address the government's assertion that mass demonstrations were a step removed from outbreaks of violence and that the members of the *Birlik* had been involved in incidents of political violence in Ferghana and after. The more the government stressed law-and-order values, the weaker *Birlik*'s position became. In the wake of subsequent outbreaks of ethnic violence in the early 1990s, the movement never recovered.

Birlik's marginalization

Prior to the initial violence in Uzbekistan's Ferghana Valley, the state was making little headway in sidelining *Birlik*. The lines of confrontation between the two were vague, with the state simply charging *Birlik* with extremism and promoting social disorder. Quickly gathering support, *Birlik* was emerging as a force in the republic and on 28 May 1989, it held its founding congress. The outbreak of political violence in Ferghana Province a week later, however, dramatically altered Uzbekistan's political environment.

In early June 1989, inter-ethnic violence occurred between ethnic Uzbeks and Meskhetian Turks in the densely populated eastern provinces of the country's Ferghana Valley. Attacks on and massacres of Meskhetian Turks began in the cities of Marghilan, Ferghana and Kuvasai on 3 and 4 June 1989, spread to the city of Kokand on 7 June and on to the city of Namangan by 11 June. The violence led to a massive investigation involving over 200 law enforcement officials, resulting in 265 arrests and 120 cases brought to trial (*Pravda vostoka*, 1989a, 1989b, 1990a). These events brought major changes to Uzbekistan's political setting, to which *Birlik* failed to adjust.

Most immediately, the violence provided an opening for the state to promote speculations over who was behind the upheaval. Even in areas where the violence had occurred residents held vastly different theories of who was to blame.[4] Attributions of blame within the general public revealed more about impressions of ethnic 'others' than any consensus over the actors involved.[5] Most accounts, however, shared a conviction that the perpetrators were organized by forces larger than those involved. The government exploited this ambiguity over the identity of the perpetrators – as well as the widespread belief that they had not acted of their own volition – to reinforce its suggestions that *Birlik* was somehow involved in the violence.[6]

Birlik attempted to refute these accusations in the immediate aftermath of the violence through its newsletter. First published in June 1989, the editors hoped the newsletter was designed to counter state propaganda, proclaiming to readers, 'Now you have the means to give appropriate answers to the chauvinistically written articles in various newspapers that make baseless accusations against the popular front' (Kocaoglu 1989, p. 36). In a joint appeal with two other informal groups, leaders of *Birlik* charged that '[a]ttempts have been made to discredit innocent informal groups in Uzbekistan by accusing them of being behind the Ferghana tragedy' (Turan and Kocaoglu 1989). Despite efforts to extricate *Birlik* from associations with the violence, however, such claims of innocence did not bolster turn-out at public meetings or demonstrations in the months that followed.

More long term, however, the violence brought to power a new CPUz First Secretary, Islam Karimov, who 'proved much more sensitive to local Uzbek concerns, and especially to the underlying roots of social protest' (Critchlow 1991, p. 178). In the weeks and months that followed, the Karimov government focused on the violence as an example of how mass demonstrations, even those begun with the best of intentions, could lead to violent disruptions. Controlling the media, news reports sought to foster doubt among the public over demonstrations and protests as an appropriate means of change. Within a relatively short time, there arose anxieties among the public over the potential for violence to spread in the republic – anxieties that undermined the credibility of mass demonstrations generally and *Birlik* in particular.[7] Over the next two years, the violence in Ferghana became a frequent reference in the state's call to disband *Birlik* as well as a legitimization of its use of repression against subsequent demonstrations.

At the same time, the new leadership made several concessions that offered *Birlik* a chance to enter formal politics, forgo continued mobilization and cooperate with the Party on key issues (Critchlow 1990; Gleason 1990, p. 21). In the aftermath of the violence, these overtures planted a seed of division within the movement. During a meeting of the movement's leadership in September 1989, a group of activists within *Birlik* declared their opposition to the use of mass demonstrations and even threatened to break away from *Birlik* (Fane 1996, p. 283).[8] The remainder of the leadership of *Birlik*, however, remained unmoved by these concessions. Influenced by movements in Ukraine, Georgia, Armenia and Azerbaijan in the first half of 1989, *Birlik* initiated a series of demonstrations in the fall of 1989 around the capital, pressing for the use of Uzbek in public. When the regime responded with a mixture of concessions and coercion,[9] divisions within *Birlik* began to harden over questions of the movement's strategy. The government pressed ahead, intensifying an information war that portrayed *Birlik* as engaged in illegal activities and a threat to public order.[10]

The regime also raised questions about the credibility of *Birlik*'s leadership. Charges in the press suggested that members of *Birlik*'s leadership had misappropriated funds, enabled *Birlik*'s 'left wing' to be penetrated with Islamic extremism or represented regional, not Uzbek interests. In each of these charges, care was taken to distinguish between the programme of *Birlik* (which was rarely questioned by the state) and its degenerated leadership (which was often viewed as tarnishing the goals of the organization). Attacks on the credibility of the frame articulators, but not on the frame itself were effective given the popular belief that external forces had penetrated local organizations and societal groups to foster conflict in Ferghana.

Ultimately, the organization formally split into *Birlik* and *Erk* at the former's Congress on 11 November 1989 (Fane 1996, pp. 283–4). This was partly over questions of strategy, with *Erk* seeking to participate in elections and work within state institutions,[11] while *Birlik* advocated the use of mass demonstrations to effect change. But, more importantly, *Birlik* sought regime change by linking its claims to the master frame used by nationalist movements in other republics. As Pulatov later recalled, in refusing to compromise with the Uzbekistani leadership, 'he insisted on working with democratic forces wherever it be, in the other republics of the former Soviet empire in order to get rid of the relics of the communist empire' (Yuksel 1992 p. 39). This tactical choice, partly due to *Birlik*'s growing dependence on a master frame of secessionist nationalism, led the organization to step up its pursuit of ethnic nationalist claims.

On 3 March 1990, two demonstrations in regions outside the capital were organized by *Birlik* to protest electoral fraud in the parliamentary elections and the resettlement of Meskhetian Turks to the area (Gleason 1990). Police responded to these demonstrations by firing on demonstrators, killing four and injuring seventy people. More than fifty leaders of *Birlik* were taken into custody, and then later released. Having recently passed resolutions stipulating penalties for gatherings that threaten public order or 'spreading panic' among the populace (*Pravda vostoka* 1990b),[12] the regime blamed the violence on *Birlik* and its leaders for inciting the mass public to disregard government policies and resolutions by organs of the state (*Pravda vostoka*, 10 March 1990c; Fierman 1997, p. 372). This justification of state-perpetrated violence was possible only in the environment after the 1989 violence. Indeed, the fact that state coercion did not provoke a reaction among the mass public indicated the state's success in discrediting *Birlik* and undercutting public support for mass demonstrations as an opposition strategy.[13]

Rather than adjust tactics, or seek out an alternative frame, *Birlik* pressed ahead, failing to appreciate how much public opinion had shifted against mass demonstrations under the rubric of ethnic nationalism. On 18 March 1990, *Birlik* staged another demonstration openly calling for Uzbek sovereignty and in support of Baltic independence. Again, protesters (several *Birlik* leaders among them) were attacked by police and over fifty activists were arrested (Beissinger 2002, p. 260). *Birlik* had clearly miscalculated the government's success in undermining the credibility of the organization and its tactics of mass mobilization. In the wake of these demonstrations, state measures to counter *Birlik* became overtly reliant upon the use of coercion. Government repression steadily increased through 1993. By the mid-1990s, polls found significant popular support for the state's use of coercion as a means of maintaining inter-ethnic peace.[14]

Increasingly identified as a source of instability and conflict in the Uzbek SSR, therefore, a discredited *Birlik* was led astray by the false promise of the master frame's mobilization potential which was realized in other republics. But was the marginalization of *Birlik* inevitable? Were alternative framings not possible? In the following, I put forward a scenario of what *Birlik* could have done differently had it realized the mobilizational potential of another frame.

What Birlik *could have done differently*

Evidence on local politics during the late Soviet period suggests that *Birlik*'s use of a regionalist frame in the months following the violence would have resulted in higher mobilization.[15] In making this counterfactual proposition, I argue that, had *Birlik* deployed it, a regionalist frame emphasizing regions' economic inequality *vis-à-vis* the centre would have garnered mobilizational support from local and regional elites.[16] Three developments at the time suggest that elites were susceptible to cooption by the opposition. First, a significant portion of Uzbekistan's regional elite had been removed from their positions at the time, disconnected from the regime, resentful of 'Moscow's grip on elite recruitment' (Critchlow 1991; Collins 2006). *Perestroika* and anti-corruption reforms applied to Uzbekistan had led to widespread dismissals throughout the 1980s, generating grievances within the republic's elite against 'the centre' – a cleavage that persisted into the early 1990s (Luong 2002). By 1989, six years after the initiation of anti-corruption reforms in Uzbekistan, disaffected regional and local elites were open to an overture by *Birlik*.[17]

Second, grievance and disaffection were coupled with growing regional interests in loosened controls over local economies, direct access to markets for the sale of local products and an enhanced position for regional over national economic interests. In particular, many members of the republic's local elite chafed at the low price at which the state purchased cotton.[18] Yet, while a similar perception of economic inequality between Moscow and Russia's regions was a powerful source of support for regional autonomy movements in Russia (Herrera 2005), *Birlik* failed to tap into this reservoir of financial and symbolic resources through frames that linked their reformist agenda to regional grievances and interests.

Third, *Birlik* had an institutional presence in six of Uzbekistan's fourteen regions and its leaders claimed to have contacts in rural and urban areas of the Ferghana Valley (Collins 2006, p. 147). This organizational base would have facilitated *Birlik*'s efforts to create a coalition with local and regional elites had it sought to do so. Taken together, these three circumstances left open to cooption a set of actors whose informal networks and other mobilizing structures were crucially influential on the mobilizational outcome in Uzbekistan.[19]

Birlik's failure to recognize the potential of a regionalist frame and the possibility of a coalition with the republic's traditional elite was an opportunity lost. Although the window of opportunity was brief, a regionalist frame situating *Birlik*'s concerns in terms of increased autonomy from the centre would have garnered support from powerful yet disaffected regional and local elites in Uzbekistan. Ultimately, regional and local elites sided with the centre and followed the President's call for the repression of independent movements. Across Uzbekistan local and regional elites, reined in by the central government through renewed access to resources and positions, applied Karimov's stability-over-change approach to *Birlik* and other independent movements.[20]

The eclipse of *Rastokhez* in Tajikistan

The case of Tajikistan illustrates how a master frame can mislead movement entrepreneurs and facilitate the eclipse of nationalist claims by regionalist ones. In the early stages of *glasnost'*, *Rastokhez* reflected many Popular Fronts throughout the former Soviet Union. It was formed on 14 September 1989, in the wake of the informal groups' successful mobilization around language rights, which had led to the enactment of a new language law in July 1989. A constituent meeting approved *Rastokhez*'s regulations, programme, board and presidium and it was quickly joined by local informal groups such as *Vahdad* (Unity) and *Ehyeyi Khudzhand* (Renaissance of Khojand). At that meeting, the leaders of *Rastokhez* proclaimed the movement's objectives to be support for *perestroika* in Tajikistan and an end to the economic and political crisis in the republic. Its programme focused on ecological issues, language rights and a renaissance of Tajik culture: 'protection of our environmental surroundings and the health of our population' and 'revival of the national language, culture, and the best traditions and customs of [our] ancestors' (TsIMO 1990, pp. 116–17). As one of its leaders explained, the movement aimed to redress the republic's underdevelopment through national renewal:

> The fundamental goal of our association is to lead [us] out of the existing crisis situation of the republic, in which it finds itself. To assist in this, to raise the living level of the people of the republic, and to implement the law on social justice, Tajik language and national Tajik traditional culture has been renewed, and past traditions made even better. (*Kommunist Tadzhikistana 1990*)

Rastokhez's lofty goals, however, were grounded in strategies of mass mobilization. As several leaders explained, 'In order to attain the goals of *perestroika*, one needs to have a mass organization. That is why we organized our group along the lines of a Popular Front so as to mobilize mass efforts for a democratic society' (Helsinki Watch 1991 p. 17). In terms of its programme and organizational structure, and based on support from prominent figures within Tajikistan's leadership, *Rastokhez* seemed well poised to influence the republic's political trajectory.

Rastokhez's *marginalization*

Between 1987 and 1992, two shifts in Tajikistan's political environment enabled regionalist claims to predominate in the republic, ultimately undermining *Rastokhez*. First, amid opportunities for public expression during *glasnost'*, ideological divisions widened between political elites in the centre, juxtaposing those who sought to dismantle the political-administrative system and its ties to the republic's lucrative cotton economy against those elites who sought to preserve that system. Second, ideological divisions in the centre became increasingly tied to regional interests. This was primarily due to purges of conservative political elites throughout the republic, which threatened the entrenched interests of Tajikistan's powerful collective farm chairs and other 'rural grandees' (Dudoignon 1997, p. 70). In response, the latter attempted to retain their privileged access to state resources by making claims on the centre in regionalist terms. As a result, reformist and conservative positions in the centre became increasingly defined by regionally based claims to power. Amid the growing regionalization of Tajikistan's politics, however, *Rastokhez* continued to focus on drawing mobilized groups together under a frame of national renewal and separatist nationalism.

Primarily made up of intellectuals, with a social base among the republic's cultural elite (Olimova and Olimov 1991), the movement eschewed addressing the issue of regional divisions. As one observer has noted, 'The leaders of *Rastokhez* did not want to condemn any particular group openly for putting its own regional or clan interests first but to consolidate all Tajiks, irrespective of their clan or place of origin, under the banner of rebirth' (Juraeva 1996, p. 261). Instead, the movement focused on fostering mobilization based on the creation of 'a natural social structure of the Tajik nation' (Kosach 1995, p. 128). The movement's message of national rebirth, however, failed to address the divisive nature of redistributive politics in Tajikistan. Intense competition within Tajikistan's elite over the division of national spoils between regions (mostly over the allocation of political posts and economic resources) had become omnipresent in the republic. As a result, an impasse marked *Rastokhez*'s relationship to the practice of republican politics, which ultimately undermined its ability to adapt to the growing regionalization of Tajikistan's political environment.

Ideological divisions within the republican centre began in the spring of 1987, when Tajikistan's Communist Party First Secretary Kahhar Makhkamov introduced a number of reforms designed to limit and eventually eliminate the influence of the republic's old-regime elite. Makhkamov's attacks on the patronage networks within the Communist Party – particularly those in the provinces of Kuliab, Kurgan-Teppe and Leninabad – had removed many long-standing elites from political positions within the state apparatus. Many posts were filled with reformist politicians who came from the Karategin Valley and Gorno-Badakhshan Autonomous *Oblast'* [GBAO] in eastern Tajikistan.[21] These changes within the republic's economic and political apparatus, combined with legislation making Tajik the republic's national language in July 1989, had emboldened many of the informal groups that had emerged in 1989–90.[22] *Rastokhez* emerged as the most prominent among them. During this phase, reformist elements in Tajikistan – members of the intelligentsia, students and informal groups calling for greater national and cultural rights – had largely sided with Makhkamov. The conservative Communist Party elites, for their part, had not yet regrouped from the attacks on their patronage bases (though they still occupied a majority of the seats in the republican legislature, the Supreme Soviet).

Throughout 1990, however, there was a growing radicalization among reformist groups as they reacted to Makhkamov's repeated concessions to conservative forces in the republic. In particular, his decision to abandon reform in Kuliab, Kurgan-Teppe and Leninabad prompted some reformists to call for the full abolition of the structural underpinnings of Tajikistan's political economy.[23] At the same time, *Rastokhez* was allowed to promote reformist views in its own newsletter *Tun'o* (Peace), which had a circulation of 10 to 20 thousand by May 1990, and its independent journal *Sukhan* (Vorb'ev 1990, p. 3).

The outbreak of violent riots in February 1990 in Dushanbe, however, brought the growing disillusionment among reformist elements to a head. Initially a demonstration opposing the relocation of Armenians to Tajikistan, these protests also called for political reform and appeared to be led by several prominent reformist elites (many from the Karategin Valley). *Rastokhez* initially entered into negotiations with the authorities, but, failing to extract concessions, it broke with the moderates and joined the protests (Berkhovskii 1992, p. 41; Niazi 1993). The protests devolved into three days of rioting and twenty deaths and, in the months that followed, the government implicated *Rastokhez* in the events and portrayed the movement as a source of social conflict. A wave of news articles charged that *Rastokhez* leaders had misrepresented facts surrounding the violence, slandered prominent figures in the republic and based their assessments on conjecture not evidence (Vorb'ev 1990; Azimov 1990a, p. 3, 1990b, pp. 1–2; Mavlonazarov 1990, pp. 1–2). *Rastokhez* emerged from the February 1990 riots a target of pro-regime voices and significantly weakened. As Deputy Chairman Mirbobo Mirrakhimov lamented, 'the February events had a tragic effect on *Rastokhez*. [Although] it did not play any role in these events ... in the eyes of the people of Tadzhikistan, the *Rastokhez* reputation has been blackened' (Helsinki Watch 1991, p. 61).

At the same time, *Rastokhez* was becoming more aggressive in its criticism of the regime and demanded a ban on all activity of the Communist Party in the republic in July 1990 (Dudoignon 1997, p. 61). But the movement failed to exploit the regionalist politics underlying the leadership's weakening commitment to *perestroika*, even when Makhkamov dismissed a number of elites from the Karategin Valley and GBAO after the riots.[24] As a result, other groups forming were able to mobilize some of *Rastokhez*'s dissipating support.

By the end of 1990, *Rastokhez*'s influence in national politics was displaced by new political movements – including the Democratic Party of Tajikistan [DPT] and Islamic Renaissance Party [IRP] – which established themselves as the major opposition groups in the republic. *Rastokhez*, unable to command a significant following on its own, decided to ally with these groups. This unusual alliance with democrats and Islamists illustrates the effects of growing regionalization in Tajikistan. Facing a diminishing base, ideological differences among the movements were of 'secondary importance' and 'tactical matters took precedence over strategic issues' (Zviagelskaya 1997, pp. 8–9). The manoeuvre, however, backfired. Both DPT and IRP usurped much of *Rastokhez*'s programme, framing their agendas broadly in line with international norms of democracy and human rights.[25] As a result, support for *Rastokhez* continued to decline, reaching 6 per cent in 1991 and 3 per cent in 1992.[26]

What Rastokhez *could have done differently*

Could *Rastokhez* realistically have used a regionalist frame to exploit rising tensions between Tajikistan's regions? The republic's history of political power based among ruling elites from Leninabad Province – a region with high concentrations of ethnic Uzbeks – provided *Rastokhez* with a unique opportunity to link its nationalist claims to Tajikistan's regional inequalities. Several local political movements, including *Oshkoro* (*glasnost'*) and *Bokhtar* in southern Tajikistan (Khatlon Province), were already mobilizing other regions against Leninabad's control over political and economic affairs. Both movements characterized these elites as 'half-Uzbeks' who did not represent genuine Tajik interests but advanced parochial interests of their region (Khudonazar 2004, p. 17). Mobilizing against elites they perceived as 'Uzbekizing' Tajikistan, *Oshkoro* and *Bokhtar* were potentially valuable institutional support for *Rastokhez*.

Yet, *Rastokhez* leaders failed to take advantage of this opportunity. Despite the rise of regional tensions in 1990, and the growing claims for redress of Tajikistan's ethnic and regional inequalities by these movements, *Rastokhez* continued to promote its aims across all groups, eschewing 'vertical' segmentations in society (Helsinki Watch 1991, p. 61). The movement remained firmly tied to the master frame of national sovereignty, couching it as a universal goal of all nationalities 'to achieve the rights of all peoples, all nations' (Helsinki Watch 1991, p. 17). Even after Tajikistan declared independence, *Rastokhez* continued to formulate its mobilizational programme around the cultural and social renewal of the Tajik nation. Thus, *Rastokhez* failed to advance a regionalist frame to capture this layer of pro-Tajik sentiment, the exclusionary nature of which it viewed as an anathema and contrary to the spirit of its master frame of national sovereignty.

Throughout 1991, regionalist claims were exacerbated by elite manoeuvres in national politics. Gradually over the year, Makhkamov moved away from reformist groups.[27] The August 1991 coup to unseat

Gorbachev prompted massive daily demonstrations in front of the Supreme Soviet in Tadzhikistan (as elsewhere) lasting several weeks. When Makhkamov resigned, his interim replacement Kadriddin Aslonov openly favoured regional interests of the Opposition, provoking a reaction from conservative deputies in the Supreme Soviet.[28] The latter called an emergency session, and replaced Aslonov with conservative hard-liner Rahman Nabiev. Nabiev's efforts to revive the Soviet-era political and economic system generated demonstrations through September and October, organized by a coalition of opposition movements (*Rastokhez*, IRP and the Democratic Party of Tajikistan). These demonstrations went unchecked by repression from the state because the Minister of Internal Affairs, Mamadaez Navzhuvanov, refused to enforce the state of emergency that the Supreme Soviet imposed in September 1991 (Brown 1992).

In March 1992, Nabiev reversed Aslonov's decrees, restoring the CPSU and publicly dismissing and disgracing Navzhuvanov (Akbarzadeh 1996). These reversals, particularly the latter (which occurred on public television), sparked a series of protests led by residents from GBAO under the banner of *La'l-i Badakhshan* (Ruby of Badakhshan), who feared they would be excluded from power. Although initiated by an informal group from GBAO, mobilized under explicitly regionalist frames, these protests were quickly joined by the DPT and *Rastokhez*. By now, framing claims in regionalist terms had clearly displaced alternatives. As Olivier Roy notes of these groups in the crowd, 'All were officially demanding Kenjayev's resignation, but the real issue was the rising power of the excluded regionalist groups (Gharmis and Pamiris) against the Communist establishment ... localist conflicts were exported to the capital' (2000, pp. 139–40).

Whereas previous cycles of protest (in 1989 and early 1990) were mobilized around frames of national renewal, self-determination and democratization, this cycle in the spring of 1992 had become imbued with an explicitly regionalist and localist character. The master frame of national self-determination diffused to Tajikistan was taken up by *Rastokhez* and linked to ecological issues, democratization and national cultural renewal. However, through their repeated interactions with the state, opposition movements in the republic became increasingly focused on regional issues. As a result, *Rastokhez* had become completely incorporated with regionalist mobilization with its programme of separatist nationalism and national cultural renewal eclipsed by regionalist claims.

Conclusion

Why were the levels of nationalist mobilization so low in Central Asia compared with other parts of the former Soviet Union? The cases of Uzbekistan and Tajikistan suggest that a full explanation should include the tactical choices – good and bad – of movement leaders. The failure of movement entrepreneurs to appreciate shifts in their respective political environments was a major contributing factor undermining mobilization in each republic. In both case, moreover, these tactical missteps were facilitated by a master frame diffused from abroad.

In the wake of political violence in Uzbekistan's Ferghana Valley, *Birlik*'s continued use of a secessionist master frame paradoxically strengthened the state's ability to justify its use of repression and depict the movement as a source of inter-ethnic conflict. Amid growing regionalization of Tajikistan's political environment, *Rastokhez*'s continued dependence on that master frame failed to capture the growing inter-regional tensions around resource distribution and political power in the republic. In outlining how master frames misled nationalists in each of these cases, this article illustrates one way in which framing processes and tactical choice influence movement outcomes and nationalist mobilization.

Acknowledgements

The author wishes to acknowledge fellowship support from Fulbright-Hays and International Research & Exchanges Board, which enabled field research that contributed to material presented in this article.

Notes

1. In this paper, I define mobilizational failure as the movement's failure to achieve a level of mobilization that overcomes constraints imposed by the state. Alternatively, others have defined failure in terms of policy shift, altering the power relations between challengers and the state or bringing about more significant structural change (Giugni 2001, pp. xxii–xxiii).
2. Secessionist mobilization in the former USSR was predicated upon identifying the 'imperial persona' of the Soviet state and advancing claims of self-determination and sovereignty. The anti-imperial master frame diffused by Baltic Popular Fronts focused on both of these aspects, seeking to pull together multiple movement-specific frames (on environmental, language, cultural and other issues) under the master frame promoting separatist nationalism (Beissinger 2002, pp. 159–62).
3. In some cases, the content and nature of the frames themselves may be a source of low mobilization, even where tactical choice is not necessarily a contributing factor. Frames that are inflexible, for instance, may fail to resonate and thus limit the mobilization. In other cases, tactical choice and the potential for error arise in processes of frame alignment, in which attempts are made to establish links between the movement-specific frames and target population (Snow et al. 1986, p. 477).

4. The events themselves were marked by confusion and rumour at the time. Workers were mobilized by their bosses to protect local industries and *mahalla* (community and village) leaders mobilized members of the community to defend their locality. In both cases, the threat was understood as little more than the presence of 'hooligans' perpetrating destruction and disorder (author's discussions with residents in Marghilan city, Uzbekistan, July 2001 and April 2003).

5. One study found that some Uzbeks attributed the violence to the concentrated wealth of Meskhetian Turks, an Armenian claimed that Islamists were key influences and several Russian respondents noted the likely role of Uzbek nationalists (Abramson 1997).

6. Jack Snyder (2000, p. 56) notes that weak democratic institutions provide an opportunity for elites to 'hijack the media' and use them to control information flows and divide public opinion. But, while all post-Soviet movements were vulnerable to this form of 'elite persuasion', the missteps by *Birlik* made it particularly susceptible.

7. The state promoted fears of ethnic violence in Uzbekistan to justify its repression of opposition well into the early 1990s. Based on 200 interviews conducted in the summer and fall of 1992 in the region, Martha Brill Olcott found 'persistent fear of the consequences of ethnic disorder, amounting almost to a "cult of stability" at any price' (1997, p. 118) in response to televised accounts of the 1989 Ferghana riots and the 1990 Osh riots just across the border in Kyrgyzstan, as well as the civil war in Tajikistan.

8. Led by poets Mohammed Solih and Erkin Vohidov, these members would eventually form a separate informal group named *Erk* (Freedom).

9. Nearly 100 of *Birlik*'s leaders were held by police during the demonstrations (though they were quickly released), and a law was passed authorizing police to use any means necessary to prevent demonstrations. Simultaneously, however, the regime adopted a new language law making Uzbek the official state language (Fierman 1997, p. 370).

10. For a discussion of the regime's use of the media to declare that *Birlik* and other movements sought 'to paralyze the work of the government and to destabilize the situation', see Vyzhutovich (1991, p. 3).

11. The leader of *Erk*, Muhammed Solih would later run against Karimov for President in 1992, but was soundly defeated (though candidates were not given equal access to the media).

12. This law revised an earlier version passed on 19 August 1988, as described by Uzbekistan's Prosecutor General D. A. Usatov. See *Pravda vostoka* (1989a).

13. The lack of a public response in Uzbekistan contrasts sharply with the surge of nationalist mobilization that followed a similar government crackdown on demonstrators in the Georgian SSR in April 1989. The difference in these reactions illustrates the effect of the inter-ethnic violence on the public mood in Uzbekistan. On the Georgia case, see Beissinger (2002, pp. 178–86, 347–54).

14. A survey conducted in late 1996/early 1997 under the auspices of International Foundation of Election Systems found that 76 per cent of respondents (n = 1830) felt that 'strong presidential power is necessary for the maintenance of inter-ethnic stability' (Wagner 1997, p. 64).

15. Regionalism in this context refers to regions within Uzbekistan and not to relations among Central Asian republics.

16. On the use of counterfactual analysis, see Tetlock and Belkin (1996) and Fearon (1991).

17. For example, at Norin District's twenty-fifth Party Conference in March 1990, 'Pobeda' Kolkhoz Chair M. Mirzaboev (the district's former *Raikom* First Secretary) openly called for the dismissal of his boss – Norin *Raikom* First Secretary A. Haydarov – and the reinstatement of the local elite: 'Our district has been combined and split up twice. This has brought much material and spiritual harm. A number of cadres have been cut down [in their youth]. And nothing has been done to rectify these mistakes. They are not holding anyone responsible' (Jambulov 1990).

18. As one collective farm chair explained, 'The price of cotton on the world market runs 18 times more expensive [than state-purchased cotton]. ... The state is paying *us* two and a

half times less for our cotton. Therefore, *we* are earning an income of 4 trillion rubles instead of 10 trillion rubles from *our* cotton' (*Namangan haqiqati* 1990b, emphasis added).

19. Radnitz (2005) has discussed the power of localist mobilization in post-Soviet Kyrgyzstan, its mechanisms and their integration into a national-level opposition.

20. On Namangan, see *Namangan haqiqati* (1989, 1990a); on Kashkadarya Province, see Ochilov (1992); on Navoii Province, see Habibov (2000).

21. Autonomous Oblast' [AO] was a unit within many republics of the Soviet Union designated to regions that possessed cultural attributes distinct from the broader population in the republic. Although AOs possessed a certain status, institutionally it was not a significant basis of nationalist mobilization (Guiliano 2006).

22. On the concept of emboldening in mobilization, see Beissinger (2002, pp. 153–9).

23. Based on his analysis of public writings by members of the Opposition, Stephane Dudoignon describes their goals at the time as 'the dismantlement of structures of the administration of agricultural and industrial enterprises [was] to be accompanied, in the political domain, by the abolition of administrative regions of Tajikistan, the explicit goal of which was to bring down the social foundations of the [power] of the Communist leaders, and to bring an end to the political "localism" that arose from it' (1994, p. 98).

24. Following the riots several top officials, blamed for being linked to the violence, were dismissed: Supreme Soviet Chair Goibnazar Pallaev (often viewed as a representative of GBAO), Gosplan Head Buri Karimov (from Garm) and Minister of Culture Tabarov (from Garm). Despite these dismissals, the Chair of the Supreme Soviet was passed to Kadriddin Aslonov (from Garm), the Soviet of Ministers Chair was kept by Leninabadi loyalist Izatullo Hayoyev and Kuliab's traditional representation in the top levels of the MVD continued to be displaced by elites from GBAO. Analysis based on Niiazi (1997), Roy (2000) and author's collection of biographies. These biographies were drawn from national, regional and district newspapers as well as published (and unpublished) histories of individual regions – research yielding over 400 biographies of central and regional officials and large databases of elite turnovers at all government levels covering Tajikistan and Uzbekistan from 1960 to 2003.

25. On DPT, see *Adolat (1992)*; on IRP, see Nuri and Turadjonzoda (1993).

26. In contrast, Communists received 36 per cent in 1991 and 40 per cent in 1992; Democratic Party of Tajikistan received 21 per cent (1991) and 10 per cent (1992); Islamic Renaissance Party 6 per cent (1991 and 1992). Data drawn from Kosach (1995, p. 134).

27. In a sign of his growing wariness of reformists, Makhkamov appointed Safarali Kenzhaev as Adviser on the Surveillance of Implementing Laws and Decisions of the President and Soviet of Ministers. Kenzhaev, an orphan who began his career as a local prosecutor in Lenin District and viewed Leninabad Province as his adopted region of origin, was later seen as a hardliner generally opposed to reform. In the heady days surrounding the August 1991 failed putsch, however, even he was not above suspicion. In his autobiographical account, Kenzhaev claims that he was privately accused by Makhkamov at one point of having ties to the Opposition – which points to the shifting allegiances within the political elite (Kenzhaev 1996, pp. 1–15).

28. Aslonov issued decrees banning the CPSU and appointing Mamadaez Navzhuvanov as Minister of Internal Affairs (which replaced Kuliab's influence over that ministry since 1980 with someone from GBAO). In banning the Communist Party, Aslonov was removing the institution through which patronage was distributed by Leninabad's political and economic elites to other regions in the republic. Second, removing Kuliab's elite from the prominent posts within the republic's internal security organs threatened to remove the elite's ability to influence directly law enforcement agencies' capacity to enforce rules in the republic. Author's collection of biographies.

References

ABRAMSON, DAVID M. 1997 'Remembering the present: the meaning today of the 1989 violence in Kokand', *Central Asia Monitor*, no. 3, pp. 18–21
ADOLAT 1992 'Oinnomai Hizbidemokrati Tojikiston', vol. 6, no. 18, p. 4.
AKBARZADEH, SHAHRAM 1996 'Why did nationalism fail in Tajikistan?', *Europe-Asia Studies*, vol. 48, no. 7, pp. 1105–29
AZIMOV, AMIRKUL 1990a 'Temnye mysli', *Kommunist Tadzhikistanao*, 26 June, p. 3
—— 1990b 'Vmesto argumentov – domysly: Takaya pozitsiia udobna dlia neformalov', *Kommunist Tadzhikistana*, 10 August, pp. 1–2
BEISSINGER, MARK R. 2002 *Nationalist Mobilisation and the Collapse of the Soviet State*, Cambridge: Cambridge University Press
BERKHOVSKII, ALEKSANDR 1992 *Sredniia Azia i Kazakhstan*, Politicheskii spektr, Moscow
BREUILLY, JOHN 1982 *Nationalism and the State*, New York: St. Martin's Press
BROWN, BESS 1992 'Whither Tajikistan?', *Report on the USSR*, vol. 6, 12 June, pp. 1–6
COLLINS, KATHLEEN 2006 *Clan Politics and the Transformation of Regimes in Central Asia*, Cambridge: Cambridge University Press
CONNOR, WALKER, 1990 'When is a nation?', *Ethnic and Racial Studies*, vol. 13, no. 1, pp. 92–103
CRITCHLOW, JAMES 1990 'Party leaders in Ferghana Oblast soften attitude towards "Birlik"', *Report on the USSR*, vol. 4, 25 March, pp. 19–20
—— 1991 *Nationalism in Uzbekistan: A Soviet Republic's Road to Sovereignty*, Boulder, CO: Westview Press
CROW, SUZANNE 1990 'Informal groups in Tajikistan – will they have a role?', *Report on the USSR*, vol. 4, 23 February, pp. 20–1
DEMETRIOU, SPYROS 2003 'Rising from the ashes? The difficult (re)birth of the Georgian state', in Jennifer Milliken (ed.), *State Failure, Collapse & Reconstruction*, Oxford: Blackwell, pp. 105–30
DES FORGES, ALISON 1999 *Leave None to Tell the Story: Genocide in Rwanda*, New York: Human Rights Watch
DIANI, MARIO 1996 'Linking mobilisation frames and political opportunities: insights from regional populism in Italy', *American Sociological Review*, vol. 61, no. 6, pp. 1053–69
DUDOIGNON, STEPHANE A. 1994. 'Une segmentation peut en cacher une autre: regionalisms et clivages politico-economiques au Tadjikistan', in Stephane A. Dudoignon and G. Jahangiri (eds), *Le Tadjikistan existe-t-il? Destins politiques d'une 'nation imparfaite'*, special edition of *Cahiers d'Etudes sur la Méditerranée Orientale et le Monde Turco-Iranien* (CEMOTI), vol. 18 (July–December), pp. 73–129
—— 1997 'Political parties and forces in Tajikistan, 1989–1993', in Mohammad-Reza Djalili, Frederic Grare and Shirin Akiner (eds), *Tajikistan: The Trials of Independence*, New York: St. Martin's Press, pp. 52–85
FANE, DARIA 1996 'Ethnicity and regionalism in Uzbekistan: maintaining stability through authoritarian control', in Leokadia Drobizheva, Rose Gottemoeller, Catherine McArdle Kelleher and Lee Walker (eds), *Ethnic Conflict in the Post-Soviet World*, Armonk, NY: M. E. Sharpe, pp. 271–302
FEARON, JAMES D. 1991 'Counterfactuals and hypothesis testing in political science', *World Politics*, vol. 43, no. 2, pp. 169–95
FIERMAN, WILLIAM 1997 'Political development in Uzbekistan: democratisation?', in Karen Dawisha and Bruce Parrott (eds), *Conflict, Cleavage and Change in Central Asia and the Caucasus*, Cambridge: Cambridge University Press, pp. 360–408
FURTADO, CHARLES F., JR. and Chandler, Andrea (eds) 1992 *Perestroika in the Soviet Republics: Documents on the National Question*, Boulder, CO: Westview Press
GAGNON, V. P. 2004 *The Myth of Ethnic War: Serbia and Croatia in the 1990s*, Ithaca, NY: Cornell University Press

GAMSON, WILLIAM A. 1992 *Talking Politics*, New York: Cambridge University Press
GIUGNI, MARCO 2001 'How social movements matter: past research, present problems, future developments', in Marco Giugni, Doug McAdam and Charles Tilly (eds), *How Social Movements Matter*, Minneapolis, MN: University of Minnesota Press, pp. xiii–xxxiii
GLEASON, GREGORY 1990 '"BIRLIK" AND THE COTTON QUESTION', *REPORT ON THE USSR*, vol. 4, 15 June, pp. 19–22
—— 1997 *Central Asian States, Discovering Independence*, Boulder, CO: Westview Press
GRANT, JONATHAN 1994 'Decolonisation by default: independence in Soviet Central Asia', *Central Asian Survey*, vol. 13, no. 1, pp. 51–8
GUILIANO, ELISE 2006 'Secessionism from the bottom up: democratization, nationalism, and local accountability in the Russian transition', *World Politics*, vol. 58, no. 1, pp. 276–310
HABIBOV, SHAROF 2000 'Inqirozdan chiqish: Yoki so'ngan shuhratning qayta tiklanishi', *Dostliq bayrog'i* 21 January
HARDIN, RUSSELL 1995 *One for All: The Logic of Group Conflict*, Princeton, NJ: Princeton University Press
HELSINKI WATCH 1991 *Conflict in the Soviet Union: Tadzhikistan*, New York: Human Rights Watch
HERRERA, YOSHIKO M. 2005 *Imagined Economies: The Sources of Russian Regionalism*, Cambridge: Cambridge University Press
HEWITT, G. 1993 'Abkhazia: a problem of identity and ownership', *Central Asian Survey*, vol. 12, no. 3, pp. 267–323
HOROWITZ, DONALD 1985 *Ethnic Groups in Conflict*, Berkeley, CA: University of California Press
JAMBULOV, J. 1990 'Siyosiy jangchi bo'lish qiyin', *Namangan haqiqati*, 7 April
JOHNSTON, HANK 1991 'Antecedents of coalition: frame alignment and utilitarian unity in the Catalan anti-Francoist opposition', *Research in Social Movements, Conflicts and Change*, vol. 13, pp. 241–59
JURAEVA, GAVHAR 1996 'Ethnic conflict in Tajikistan', in Leokadia Drobizheva, Rose Gottemoeller, Catherine McArdle Kelleher and Lee Walker (eds), *Ethnic Conflict in the Post-Soviet World*, Armonk, NY: M.E. Sharpe, pp. 255–70
KENZHAEV, SAFARALI 1996 *PEREvOT v TADZHIKISTAN*, DUSHANBE.
KHUDONAZAR, ANAITA 2004 'The other', *Berkeley Program in Soviet and Post-Soviet Studies*, Berkeley, CA: University of California
KING, CHARLES 2004 'The micropolitics of social violence', *World Politics*, vol. 56, no. 3, pp. 431–55
KOCAOGLU, TIMUR 1989 'Uzbek popular front "Birlik" publishes monthly newsletter', *Report on the USSR*, vol. 4, 8 September, pp. 36–7
KOLSTO, PAL 2000 *Political Construction Sites: Nation-Building in Russia and the Post-Soviet States*, Boulder, CO: Westview Press
Kommunist Tadzhikistana 1990 'Chto oboznachaet slovo "Rastokhez"?', 25 January, p. 1
KOSACH, GRIGORII G. 1995 'Tajikistan: political parties in an inchoate national space', in Yaacov Ro'i (ed.), *Muslim Eurasia: Conflicting Legacies*, London: Frank Cass, pp. 123–42
LUONG, PAULINE JONES 2002 *Institutional Change and Political Continuity in Post-Soviet Central Asia*, Cambridge: Cambridge University Press.
MAVLONAZAROV, M. 1990 'Pluralizm ili vandalism?', *Kommunist Tadzhikistana*, 29 June, pp. 1–2
MCADAM, DOUG, TARROW, SIDNEY and TILLY, CHARLES 2001 *Dynamics of Contention*, New York: Cambridge University Press
Namangan Haqiqati 1989 'Dolzarb vazifalar mas'uliyati', 31 October
—— 1990a 'So'z qadri', 28 February
—— 1990b 'Dadil harakat amalii natijasi', 10 April
NIAZI, AZIZ 1993 'The year of tumult: Tajikistan after February 1990', in Vitaly Naumkin (ed.), *State, Religion and Society in Central Asia: A Post-Soviet Critique*, Reading: Ithaca Press, pp. 262–89

NIIAZI, A.SH. 1997 'Tadzhikistan: konflikt regionov', *Vostok*, no. 2, pp. 94–107

NOONAN, RITA K. 1995 'women against the state: political opportunities and collective action frames in Chile's transition to democracy', *Sociological Forum*, vol. 10, no. 1, pp. 81–111

NURI, SAID ABDULLO and Turadjonzoda, Hodji Akbar 1993 '"My upolnomocheny zayavit'..." Slovo – lideram Tadzhiksoi oppozitsii', *Charoghi ruz*, vol. 2, no. 71

OBERSCHALL, ANTHONY 2000 'The manipulation of ethnicity: from ethnic cooperation to violence and war in Yugoslavia', *Ethnic and Racial Studies*, vol. 23, no. 6, pp. 982–1001

OCHILOV, I. 1992 'Novye veyaniia vremeni: Beseda s zamestitelem khokim oblasti R. R. Rakhmanovym', *Kashkadarinskaia pravda*, 19 December

OLCOTT, MARTHA BRILL 1997 'Ethnic violence in Central Asia: perceptions and misperceptions', in Roald Z. Sagdeev and Susan Eisenhower (eds), *Central Asia: Conflict, Resolution, and Change*, Chevy Chase, MD: CPSS Press, pp. 115–26

OLIMOVA, S. and OLIMOV, M. 1991 'Obrazovannyi klass Tadzhikistana v peripetiiah XX veka', *Vostok: Afro-azziatskie obshchestva: istoriia i sovremennost'*, no. 5, pp. 95–6

Pravda Vostoka 1989a 'Pomoch' narodu v bede', 16 June

—— 1989b 'KGB informiruyet', 18 June

—— 1989c 'Strogo i nekosnitel'no soblyudat' zakon', 26 October

—— 1990a 'Ekho Ferghanskikh sobytiy. Nakazanie neotvratimo!', 4 January

—— 1990b 'Ukaz Presidiuma Verkhovnogo Soveta Uzbekskoi SSR: Ob usilenii otvetstvennosti za deistviia, napavlennye protiv obshchestvennogo poryadka i bezopasnosti grazhdan', 11 February

—— 1990c 'K chemu prizyvayut lidery "Birlika"', 10 March

PROGRAMMA NARODNOGO DvIZHENIIA UZBEKISTANA "BIRLIK" 1991, in Etnopoliticheskaia programma Uzbekistana, Moscow: Panorama

RADNITZ, SCOTT 2005 'Networks, localism, and mobilisation in Aksy, Kyrgyzstan', *Central Asian Survey*, vol. 24, no. 4

RO'I, YAACOV 1992 'Nationalism in Central Asia in the context of glasnost and perestroika', in Zvi Gitelman (ed.), *The Politics of Nationality and the Erosion of the USSR: Selected Papers from the Fourth World Congress for Soviet and East European Studies*, New York: St. Martin's Press

ROMANO, DAVID 2006 *The Kurkish Nationalist Movement: Opportunity, Mobilisation, and Identity*, Cambridge: Cambridge University Press

ROY, OLIVIER 2000 *The New Central Asia: The Creation of Nations*, New York: New York University Press

SCHATZ, EDWARD A. D. 2000 'Notes on the 'dog that didn't bark': eco-internationalism in late Soviet Kazakhstan', *Ethnic and Racial Studies*, vol. 22, no. 1, pp. 136–61

SCHWEDLER, JILLIAN 2005 'Cop rock: protest, identity, and dancing riot police in Jordan', *Social Movement Studies*, vol. 4, no. 2, pp. 155–75

SNOW, DAVID A. 2004 'Framing processes, ideology, and discursive fields', in David A. Snow, Sarah A. Soule and Hanspeter Kriesi (eds), *The Blackwell Companion to Social Movements*, Oxford: Blackwell, pp. 380–412

SNOW, DAVID A. and Benford, Robert D. 1988 'Ideology, frame resonance, and participant-mobilisation', in Bert Klandermans, Hanspeter Kriesi and Sidney Tarrow (eds), *From Structure to Action: Comparing Social Movement Research across Cultures*, Greenwich, CT: JAI Press, pp. 197–217

—— 1992 'Master frames and cycles of protest', in Aldon D. Morris and Carol McClurg Mueller (eds), *Frontiers in Social Movement Theory*, New Haven, CT, and London: Yale University Press, pp. 133–55

SNOW, DAVID et al. 1986 'Frame alignment processes, micromobilization, and movement participation', *American Sociological Review*, vol. 51, no. 4, pp. 464–81

SNYDER, JACK 2000 *From Voting to Violence: Democratisation and Nationalist Conflict*, New York: Norton

TARROW, SIDNEY 1998 *Power in Movement: Social Movements, Collective Action and Politics*, 2nd edn, Cambridge: Cambridge University Press

TETLOCK, PHILIP E. and BELKIN, AARON (eds) 1996 *Counterfactual Thought Experiments in World Politics: Logical, Methodological, and Psychological Perspectives*, Princeton, NJ: Princeton University Press

TILLY, CHARLES 1994 'States and nationalism in Europe, 1492–1992', *Theory and Society*, no. 23, pp. 131–46

TSENTR PO IZUCHENIYU MEZHNATSIONAL'NYX OTNOSHENII 1990 *Grazhdanskie dvizheniia v Tadzhikistane*, Moscow: TsIMO

TURAN, YAQUB and KOCAOGLU, TIMUR 1989 'Appeal to the people of Ferghana', *Report on the USSR*, vol. 4, 16 June, pp. 26–7

VORB'EV, V. 1990 'Pogonia za populayar'nost'yu? O nekotorykh publikatsiiakh gazety "Sukhan"', *Kommunist Tadzhikistana*, 10 June, p. 3

VYZHUTOVICH, VALERY 1991 'Uzbekistan posle ob'yavlenii nezavisimosti', *Izvestiia*, 13 September, p. 3

WAGNER, STEVEN 1997 *Public Opinion in Uzbekistan 1996*, Washington, DC: International Foundation for Election Systems

WARREN, KAY B. 1998 *Indigenous Movements and Their Critics: Pan-Maya Activism in Guatemala*, Princeton, NJ: Princeton University Press

WITTNER, LAWRENCE S. 1969 *Rebels against War: The American Peace Movement, 1941–1960*, New York: Columbia University Press

YUKSEL, IBRAHIM 1992 'Abdurahim Pulatov', *Umid/Hope*, vol. 1, no. 2, pp. 37–41

ZVIAGELSKAYA, IRINA 1997 *The Tajik Conflict*, Moscow: Russian Center for Strategic Research and International Studies/Reading: Ithaca Press

Index

Page numbers in *Italics* represent tables.
Page numbers in **Bold** represent figures.

Abacha, General 103, 104
Abiola, M.K.O. 103, 107
Abkhazia: ethnic grievances 132
acculturation 10
Adedibu, Lamidi 105
Africa: central 131; class struggle 94; colonialism 98; ethnic situation 97
Aguilar, Paloma 81, 82
Akwa Ibom State: Eket-Ibeno crisis 97
All Nigeria People's Party (ANPP) 104
Alliance for Democracy: Nigeria 104
American colonies: independence from Spain 113
American Creoles 117
American Declaration of Independence 75
American nationals: Basques 124
American War of Independence 78
Anambra state 105
Anatolia: Kurdifying 62
Anderson, Benedict 85
Arana, Sabino 82, 84, 119, 120
ARBiH (Bosnian government army) 13
Aretxaga, Begoña 88
Argentina 114, 120, 122, 123
Armenia 137
Armenians 57, 68; relocation 142
Aslonov, Kadriddin 144
assimilationism 54
Atlantic Basqueness 121
Atlantic colonists 124
Atsiz, Nihal 58
Atyaps 106
Audiencia Nacional 86
authoritarianism: Turkey 57
Azerbaijan 137

Babangida, General 103, 107
Balearic Islands 49–50
Baltic Popular Fronts 133
Barongo, Yolamu 94
Barzani, Massoud 69, 70
Basque communities: bonds of solidarity 113
Basque Country 37, 46, 47; states of exception 81
Basque diaspora: homeland discourses 120–3; transnational spaces (1492–1898) 112
Basque ethnicity 3142
Basque identity: Spanish identity 122
Basque laws: abolishment (1876) 118–19
Basque Movement of National Liberation (MLNV) 74, 86
Basque nationalism 119
Basque nationalism (radical) 2, 34, 89–90; fallen soldiers 84–9; introduction 73–4; memory and the nation 74–7; war memory 79–84; warfare and nation 77–9
Basque nationalist memory: Spanish Civil War (1936–9) 79
Basque Nationalist Party (PNV) 81, 120
Basque prisoners: posters 86
Basque Provinces 117; 1878 agreements 119
Basque question: origins (1808–98) 115
Basque States: Confederation of 120
Basqueness 114; character of 82
Basques: attitude to Spain 50; immigration to New World 114; nobility 112–13
Bastille Day 75
Batasuna, Herri 74, 82
Belarus 132
Beñaran, Miguel 87

INDEX

Benford, Robert D. 133
Beslan 15, 24, 25
Bilbao, Jon 112, 114
Billig, Michael: banal nationalism 31
Birlik: establishment of 134; marginalization 135–8; Uzbekistan 130, 134–9; what could have been done differently 138–9
Biscay: traitor province 81
Bizkai-Buru Batzar 120
Bokhtar 143
Bolívar, Simón 121
Bollen, Kenneth 35
Bora, Tanil 55
Bosnia-Herzegovina 1; and North Caucasus survey 12–25; preference for ethnic separatism **14**
Bosniac nationalism 13
Bosnian Federation 13
Bosnian War 13
Boyd, Carolyn P. 115
Britain: militarism 78
British coronation ceremony 75
Buenos Aires: Laurak Bat 122

Caballero, Largo 81
Cádiz: Constitution of (1812) 116
Calhoun, Craig 3
Canary Islands 46
Canny, Nicholas 112
Carlist War: First (1833–9) 117; Second (1872–6) 118
Carlist Wars 82, 83
carlistas 84
Casaus, Marta Elena 113
Castilian Spain 34
Catalan nationalists 34
Catalonia 37, 46; attitude to Spain 50
categoric politics: Nigeria 94
Catholic Church 19
Catholicism 39, 41, 114; impact 42; Spain 34
Central Asia: mobilization 130
Centre Basque-Français 122
Centro Navarro 122
Chaho, Joseph-Augustin: *Voyage en Navarre* 84
Chazan, N. 98
Chechen conflict 13
Chechen war zone 23
Chechnya 21, 25
Chile 114, 123
clientelism 95; definition 95
collective identity 116

colonial societies: identity 112
colonialism: Africa 98; internal 9
conflict: ethnicity 2, 93
constitutional patriotism: (Sternberger and Habermas) 32
Converi, Danielle 119, 120
Corcuera, Javier 119
corruption 94
Criméan War (1853–6) 78
Croatia 8; post-war survey 10
Croatian identity 19
Cuba 114, 115, 123
cultural distinctiveness: Spain 39
cultural genocide 81

Dagestan 15, 21, 22; Muslims 17; Nogay 15
Danjuma, T.Y. 101
Dargins 18
de la Granja, J.L. 119
De Pablo, Santiago 115
decentralization: Spain 36
del Castillo, Cánovas 119
Delat State: Ijaw-Itsekiri crisis 97
Demitras Mahallesi: Mersi 65
democracy 143; transition to 33–5
democratic facade 95
Democratic Party of Tajikistan (DPT) 142
democratization 55; Turkish Republic 69
Douglass, W.A. 112, 114
Dowley, K.M. 10
Dunant, Jean Henri 78
Durango: bombing of 81
Dushanbe: violent riots 142

Eastern Anatolia 2
eco-nationalism 135
eco-protests 131
economic inequality 139
economics 9
Edie, Carlene 97
Edles, Laura Desfor 82
Ehyeyi Khudhand 140
Eket-Ibeno crisis: Akwa Ibom State 97
elites: mobilizing against 143
elitism: power preservation 10
environmental justice 134
environmentalism 74
Erdogan, Tayyip 58
Erk 137
Esman, Milton 94
Español, B.V. 87

INDEX

ETA 2, 74, 82; arrest 86; creation 82; emergence of 79; martyrdom 85; prisoners 86, 87; schisms 83
etarra 85
ethnic boundaries 77
ethnic chauvinism 94
ethnic cleansing 6
ethnic distance 12
ethnic entrepreneurs 131
ethnic fever 123
ethnic identities 111
ethnic intolerance: religiosity 8
ethnic origins: indifference 56
ethnic particularism 8
ethnic separatism: ethnic group **16**; ethnic group and material wealth **18**; geographic distribution **14**; preference by ethnic group and ethnic pride **21**; preferences by ethnic group and experience of violence **24**; preferences by ethnic group and trust **22**; rejection of 13
ethnic soldiers 101
ethnic/national pride: ethno-territorial separatism 7–8
ethnicity: class 93; conflict 2, 93; cultural tool 111; epicentre 8; patrimonialism 95–8; systemic chaos 92; theory 93–5
ethno-patrimonialism 101
ethno-political problem: Kurds 54
ethno-territorial separatism: ethnic/national pride and suspicion 7–8; geographic variations 13–15; geographical locations 10–11; preference by nationality 15–17; preference by nationality and ethnic pride 20–1; preference by nationality and religious observance 18–20; preference by nationality and trust/suspicion 21–3; preference by nationality and wealth 17–18; preference by war experiences 23–5; relative impoverishment 9–10; religiosity 8–9; solution to conflict 6; wartime experiences with violence 10
ethno-territorial separatist attitudes: hypotheses 7–11
ethno-territorialism 5–6; rejection of 13
Etxebarrieta, Txabi 87
European integration: Turkey 54
European Union: Helsinki Summit (1999) 57
European Values Survey 37, 40
Euskaldum Guztiak Bat 122

Euskara 82, 88, 118
Euzkadi 82, 120
Euzko Gudarostea 81
exclusive recognition: Kurds 56; social sources 59–70; sources 57

feminism 74
Ferghana Valley 135, 136, 139, 145
First World War 75, 78
food shortages 21
France 78, 120; *banlieues* riots (2005) 32; Franks 123; *La Marseillaise* 75; PKK 68; Third Republic 75
Franco, General F.: death 37
Franco regime 2, 33; end of 35; ETA 79; monopolization of patriotism 34
Francoism 82
Fuerismo 118
Fulani 99

Gagnon, V.P. 10
GAL 87
Galicia 49–50
genealogy 82
genocide 6
geographical locations: ethno-territorial separatism 10–11
Georgia 132, 137; Zviadist nationalists 132
Georgians 56
German nationhood: post-war 32
Germany 78, 120; Germanic tribes 123
Gernika: bombing of 81
Gipuzkoa: traitor province 81
glasnost 139, 140
González Catarain, Dolores 83
Gordy, Eric 10
Gorenburg, D. 10
Gorni Vakuf 13
Gorno-Badakhshan Autonomous *Oblast* (GBAO) 141, 144
Gowon, Yakubu 101, 102
Great War (1914–1918) 75, 78
Greece 57; PKK 68
Gudari Eguna 87
Gunther, R. 39

Habermas, Jurgen 32
Hacettepe University 61
Halbwachs, Maurice 73
Hausa 99, 106
Hausa-Yoruba conflict (Feb 2002) 106
Hechter, Michael 9
Helsinki Summit (1999 EU) 57

INDEX

hero: terrorist 89
Herri Batasuna 87
Hirschman, A.O. 33
hispanophile evolution 84
histories: official 77
Hobsbawm, Eric 75, 76, 83, 89
Hodson, Randy 8, 10
Hroch, Miroslav 116
human rights 143
HVO (Croatian Defence Council) 13

identity: colonial societies 112
identity strengthening 77
ideology: identity 111; national pride 49
Ife-Modakeke crisis: Osun state 97, 106
Igbo: elites 104
Ijaw-Itsekiri crisis: Delat State 97
Ikpe, Ukana 2
impressionable years: hypothesis 37
indigenous people: pan-Mayan identity 131
Ingle, David W. 85
Ingushetia 25
internal colonialism 9
internationalism 36, 74, 132
The Invention of Tradition (Hobsbawm and Ranger) 75
Iraq: Kurdish nationalist parties 69; Kurdistan 69; Middle East political balances after US occupation 67–70
Iraqi War: Turkish government 69
Ironsi, General Aguiyi 101
Islamic observation: war 19
Islamic Renaissance Party (IRP) 142
Islamists 143
Istanbul 56
Italy 120; eternal Rome 123; PKK 68
Izmir 65; field study 56; Jews and Greeks 59; Kadifekale 65; transformation 62
Izmir Mersin 56

Japan 78; kamikaze pilots 79
Jos conflict 106
Joseph, Richard 102

Kabardins 18, 23, 24, 25
Kadifekale: Izmir 65
Kaduna State 106; Zangon-Kartaf crisis 97
Kano: reprisal attacks 107
Karimov, Islam 136, 139
Katsina, Hassan 101
Kazakhstan: separatism 132

Kolsto, Pal 132
Kumyks 20, 23
Kunovich, Robert 8, 10
Kurdish identity 2
Kurdish invasion 55
Kurdish labels 60
Kurdish mafia 66
Kurdish migration: exodus from Eastern Anatolia (1980s-) 61–3
Kurdish nationalism 62
Kurdishness 65
Kurdistan: free 62; Iraq 69
Kurdistan Democratic Party (KDP) 69
Kurdistan Workers Party (PKK) 54, 61, 63, 67–70
Kurds: assimilation 57; cultural capital 60; employment opportunities 61; ethnicization of crime 67; ethnopolitical problem 54; exclusive recognition 56; *ignorant* 59–60; legal recognition 58; mainstream nationalist discourses 57–9; PKK 68; racism 58; security 61; stereotyping 56; unemployment 64; USA 70

LAB (Basque trade union) 74
Ladoja, Governor 105
Lagos International Trade Fair 103
Laks 18, 24
Land Use Decree: Nigeria 100
Laurac Bat: Montevideo 122
Laurak Bat: Buenos Aires 122
Lemarchand, Rene 95, 96
Leninabad 141, 143
Levi, Margaret 9
liberalism 123
Little, Alan 10
locality 1
loyalty 33
Lyman, S.A. 119
Lynch, John 113

MacClancy, Jeremy 82
Macpherson Constitution 98
Madrid 117
Madueke, Rear Admiral Allison 104
Makhkamov, Kahhar 141, 143
Markowitz, Lawrence 3
marriage: mixed 12
martyrdom 79; memory of 80
martyrs 79, 85
Marvin, Carolyn 85
Marxism 8, 93
Massey, Garth 8

INDEX

material status: separatism 17
Medrano, J.D. 35
Mees, Ludger 115
memories: common 75; legacy of 75
memory: and the nation 74–7
Meskhetian Turks 135
Mexico 123
migration: security-based 70
militarism: Britain 78
military: politicization 101
military cemeteries 78
military rule 101–4
minorities 36
minority oppression 6
mixed marriage 12
mobilization failures: nationalism 131–2
modernization 6
Mola, General 81
Moldova 130
monopolization of patriotism: Franco regime 34
Montero, J.R. 39
Monzón, Telesforo 89
Mosse, George L.: *Myth of the War Experience* 88
Mostar 13
Mostar West 16
Muguruza, Josu 87
Muhammed, Murtala 101, 102
multiculturalism 58
multiple identity 120; transatlantic 124
Muñoz, Jordi 2
Muro, Diego 2

Nabiev, Rahman 144
Nal'chik 23, 24, 25
Napoleonic Wars 77, 116
nation: and memory 74–7; and warfare 77–9
nation-building: alternative 37, 50; literature 31; sacrifice 77
national awakening 116
national exclusivism 12
national identities: local governance 6; shift in 31–3
national memories 89
National Party of Nigeria (NPN) 100
national pride: ideology 49
national renewal: separatist nationalism 140
national socialization 31
nationalism: long-distance 123; mobilization failures 131–2; unsuccessful 131

Nationalist Action Party (MHP): Turkey 58
nationalist history 75
nationalist ideologies: post-Communist societies 7
nationalist mobilization: failed 131
nationalist subjectivity: performance 7
nationalists: radical 80
nationalizing policies 33
nationalizing state 36
nationhood: official version of 32
nationhood reconstruction 31–3
Navarre 115, 117
Navzhuvanov, Mamadaez 144
neo-patrimonialism 95, 99
nepotism 94, 95
Nevada-Semipalatinsk Movement 132
Newroz: festivities (2007) 62, 69, 70
Ngige, Chris 105
Niger State 103
Nigeria 2; 1979 election 100; All Nigeria People's Party (ANPP) 104; Alliance for Democracy 104; bourgeoisie 96; British rule 98; coup (January 1966) 101, 102; coup (July 1966) 101, 102; ethnic conflict 92; ethnic situation 97; ethnicity and the socio-political environment 93–5; Festival of Black and African Arts 102–3; Indigenization Policy 100, 102; Land Use Decree 100, 102; military quotas 101; military rule, patrimonialism and inter-ethnic relations 101–4; North-South dichotomy 98; oil 100; Operation Feed the Nation 103; patrimonial politics and the Fourth Republic 104–5; patrimonial rule and ethnicity 98; patrimonial state and ethnic-communal conflicts 105–7; patrimonial state in First and Second Republics 99–100; People's Democratic Party (PDP) 104; political competition 92; political elites 96; presidential election (June 1993) 107; Provisional Ruling Council 104; separatism 98; summary and conclusion 107–8; three-region structure 99; universal primary education 102
Nightingale, Florence 78
Nnoli, O. 94
Nogay: Dagestan 15
Nogays 16, 23
Nora, Pierre 84; *Les lieux de mémoire* 73

INDEX

North Caucasus 1, 8, 25; preference for ethnic separatism **14**; religion 19
North Caucasus survey: Bosnia-Herzegovina survey comparison 12–25
North Ossetia 15, 22
Novi Grad 13
Novi Travnik 13

Ó Tuathail, Gearóid 1
Obsanjo, Olusegun 102, 104, 105
Öcalan, Abdullah 68
O'dua People's Congress 107
Oiarzabal, Pedro J. 3, 112
oil: Nigeria 100
O'Loughlin, John 1
Onur Mahallesi: Mersin 65
Osaghae, E. 94
Ossetia 24; religious 20
Ossetians 16, 18
Osun state: Ife-Modakeke crisis 97
Otaegi, Angel 87
Other: experienced 56; imagined 56; primary 55
Oyo state 105

Pagden, Anthony 112
pan-Mayan identity: indigenous people 131
Paredes, Jon 87
patrimonial system: characteristics 95–6
patrimonialism: ethnicity 95–8
Patriotic Union of Kurdistan (PUK) 69
patriotism 90; monopolization of 32; reconstructing 32
patronage 95
Peil, Margaret 94
People's Democratic Party (PDP): Nigeria 104
Perestroika 138, 140, 142
performance: nationalist subjectivity 7
Petersen, Roger 8
Philippines 115, 123
PKK *see* Kurdistan Workers Party
place: power of 25–6
Plateau State 106; state of emergency 106
political entrepreneurs 10
political mobilization 3
political parties: ethnic-based 97
political rituals 76
political violence 2
politicization: ethnicity 93; military 101
politics of war memory 84

Popular Fronts 139
popular zoning system 100
post-Communist societies: nationalist ideologies 7
power preservation: elitism 10
prebendalism 95, 99, 102
pride: difference by age 37
primordialism 7
prisoners of war 85
Puerto Rico 114, 115
Pulatov, Abdurahim 134, 137

racial purity 82, 114
racism: Kurds 58
radical theory: ethnicity 93, 94
radicalization: Belarus 132
radicalizing events 10
Ranger, Terrence 75, 76
Rastokhez: goals 140; marginalization 140; Tajikistan 130, 139–44; what could have done differently 143–4
rational choice theory: ethnicity 93
Red Cross 78
regime change 31–3
regional frames 1139
regionalism 123
religiosity: ethno-territorial separatism 8–9
remembrance 78
Renan, Ernest 74–5, 77, 89
resources: competition for 93–4
Rincón, Luciano 83
Rodriguez, José Antonio 115
Rojas, Aristedes 121
Roy, Olivier 144
Royal Christmas Broadcast 75
Royal March: Spain 75
Rubio, Coro 116
Russian Federation 13
Russians 17

sacrifice 90
sainthood 88
salience hypothesis 8
Santi Brouard 87
Santoña: Pact of 81
Saracoglu, Cenk 2
Sarajevo: rejection of ethnic separatism 13
Save the Aral Sea Committee 134
Scotland: Highland tradition 75
secularism 9
Seixas, N. 35
Sekulić, Duško 8

INDEX

self-assertion 112
self-perception 112
separateness: recognition of 112
separatism 7; Kurds 68; material improvement 10; material status 17
separatist nationalism: national renewal 140
Serb nationalism: Serb Orthodox Church 19
Serb Orthodox Church: Serb nationalism 19
settlement: politics of 103
Shaw, Martin 78
Shirmukhammad, Pirmat 134
Silber, Laura 10
Siroki Brijeg 16
Snow, David A. 133
social constructivism 7
social intolerance 8
social networks 21
social spatialization 11
socialization: warfare 77
South Ossetia 132
Soviet Central Asia 129–30, 130
Soviet nationalism 8
Spain 2, 120, 123; Catholicism 34; cohort analysis 37; cultural distinctiveness 39; decentralization 36; dynamic model of pride 35–7; EEC 33; glorious statues 76; the *national question* 33; Popular Party 49; Royal March 75; transition to democracy and redefinition of nationhood 33–5
Spanish Catholic church 49
Spanish Civil War (1936–9) 2, 33, 73; Basque nationalist memory 79
Spanish Constitution (1978) 33, 38
Spanish identity: Basque identity 122
Spanish national pride: analysis 40–7; data, variables and measurement 37–40; de-ideologization 42; dependent variable 38; discussion and conclusions 48–51; evolution by cohort **48**; frequencies *40*; independent variable 39–40; ordinal logit regression models *41*, *43–4*; predictions by left-right self-placement *46*; predictions by region *47*; predictions by religion *45*; progressive secularization 48; secularization 42
Spanish nationalism: unfulfilled renovation 35

Spanish Republic: proclamation (1873) 118
spatial socialization 10
spatial uneven development 9
Stars and Stripes 85
state largesse 95
Stavropol 22
Stavropol *krai* 15
stereotypes: polarization 77
stereotyping: Kurds 56
Sternberger, Dolf 32
Sukhan 142
suspicion: ethno-territorial separatism 7–8

Tajik culture 140
Tajikistan 3; *Rastokhez* 130, 139–44; redistributive politics 141
Tajikistan Communist Party 141
Talabani, Jalal 69, 70
Taraba State: Tiv-Jukun conflict 105
terrorism 83
terrorist hero 89
Titoist nationalism 8
Tiv 106
Tiv-Jukun conflict: Taraba State 105
Tomb of the Unknown Soldier 78
Torcal, M. 39
traditionalism 123
traitor provinces 81
transnational spaces (1492–1898): Basque diaspora 112
trauma: war 10
Treisman, Daniel S. 10
Trueba, Antonio de 121
trust 1, 10
Tubal 118
Tun'o 142
Turkey 2; anti-Kurdish discourse 55; authoritarianism 57; employment 64; European integration 54; insecurity 66; minorities 57; Nationalist Action Party (MHP) 58; political and economic reforms 63; slums 65
Turkish cities: neo-liberal transformation 63–7
Turkish government: Iraqi War 69
Turkish nation: official 57
Turkish nationalism 57
Turkish Republic: democratization 69
Tuzla: rejection of ethnic separatism 13

Uba, Chris 105
Ukraine 130, 137

unemployment: Kurds 61
Union of Writers 134
United States of America (USA) 123; flag 85; Kurds 70; multiple identities 120
unnaturalness 6
urbanization 6
Uruguay 114, 120, 122, 123
Uzbek language 134
Uzbek SSR 138
Uzbekistan 3; *Birlik* 130, 134–9

Valencia 49–50
Venezuela 121, 123
voice 33
Voyage en Navarre (Chaho) 84
VRS (Army of Republika Srpska) 13

war: Islamic observation 19; trauma 10
war crimes: Bosniac residents 13
war memorials 78
war memory 2; Basque nationalism 79–84; politics of 84
warfare: and nation 77–9; socialization 77

Weber, Max 95
whiteness 114
Wieland, Carsten 8
Woodward, Susan 9, 21
World Values Survey 37, 40, 41
World Wars 73
Wukari Local Government Council 105

Yegen, Mesut 55
Yoruba 99, 107
YOYES 83
Yugoslavia 131; breakup 8, 10

Zana, Leyla 69
Zangon-Kartaf crisis: Kaduna State 97, 106
Zazpiak Bat 122
Zenica: rejection of ethnic separatism 13
Zerubavel, Eviatar 82
Zulaika, Joseba 119
Zviadist nationalists: Georgia 132